Morningside Library

Date out	Returned

AIN'T NO TOMORROW

AIN'T NO TOMORROW

Kobe, Shaq, and the Making of a Lakers Dynasty

ELIZABETH KAYE

Contemporary Books

Chicago   New York   San Francisco   Lisbon   London   Madrid   Mexico City
Milan   New Delhi   San Juan   Seoul   Singapore   Sydney   Toronto

Library of Congress Cataloging-in-Publication Data

Kaye, Elizabeth.
    Ain't no tomorrow : Kobe, Shaq, and the making of a Lakers dynasty /
Elizabeth Kaye.
        p.   cm.
    ISBN 0-07-138736-6
     1. Los Angeles Lakers (Basketball team).   2. Bryant, Kobe, 1978–
3. O'Neal, Shaquille.   I. Title.

GV885.52.L67 K39   2002
796.32'364'0979494—dc21   2002017519

Contemporary Books

A Division of The McGraw·Hill Companies

1 2 3 4 5 6 7 8 9 0   AGM/AGM   1 0 9 8 7 6 5 4 3 2

ISBN 0-07-138736-6

This book was set in Sabon by Ellen Kollmon
Printed and bound by Quebecor Martinsburg

Interior design by Nick Panos

McGraw-Hill books are available at special quantity discounts to use as premiums and
sales promotions, or for use in corporate training programs. For more information, please
write to the Director of Special Sales, Professional Publishing, McGraw-Hill, Two Penn
Plaza, New York, NY 10121-2298. Or contact your local bookstore.

This book is printed on acid-free paper.

For Stephen

CONTENTS

ACKNOWLEDGMENTS

I am indebted to many people. Above all to Stephen Keber, without whose enthusiasm, faith, and patience this book would not exist. Nor would it exist without the prescience of Matthew Carnicelli at Contemporary Books, or without the extraordinary agenting and editorial insight of Susan Reed at IMG Literary. A special thanks to Ellen Vinz at Contemporary Books, whose high standards and intelligence were invaluable. I am also indebted to Kit Rachlis, a writer's best friend and editor-in-chief of *Los Angeles* magazine. John Black, public relations director of the Los Angeles Lakers, extended every possible courtesy and made reporting this work possible.

This book could not have been written without drawing on the knowledge of the beat reporters who know far more, and work harder, than anyone. Howard Beck of the *Los Angeles Daily News* and Tim Brown of the *Los Angeles Times* were especially generous with their insights, knowledge, and time. The varying approaches of Broderick Turner and Kevin Ding were also immensely informative. Ric Bucher of *ESPN the Magazine* and Paul Sunderland of NBC and Fox Sports were unfailingly generous, as was the sports columnist Karen Crouse.

I also benefited from the insights and articles of Charley Steiner, Mark Starr, Allison Samuels, Bob Greene, Ian Thomsen, Gary Smith, Mike Wise, Suzy Shuster, Kevin Modesti, Sheron Bellio, Jim Hill, Mark Heisler, Bill Plaschke, Greg Christensen, Charley Rosen, Diane K. Shah, Joe Resnick, Phil Taylor, Lewis MacAdams, Jeff Miller, Janis

Carr, Rishi Agrawal, and James Bender. NBA.com TV was a great resource and a joy to watch, as were the wonderfully produced documentaries of ESPN. Larry Burnett's Laker Line on KLAC is an enlightening source of analysis and information. Stu Lantz, the Lakers' color commentator, and Chick Hearn, the NBA's greatest play-by-play announcer, are a gift to anyone covering the team.

Several books were invaluable: *Playing for Keeps* by David Halberstam, *Shaq Talks Back* by Shaquille O'Neal, *Sole Influence* by Dan Wetzel and Don Yaeger, *Sacred Hoops* by Phil Jackson and Hugh Delehanty, and *More Than a Game* by Phil Jackson and Charley Rosen. Among other enlightening books were *The Golden Game* by Roland Lazenby and Billy Packer, *The City Game* by Pete Axthelm, *Values of the Game* by Bill Bradley, and *A Sense of Where You Are* by John McPhee.

Michael Keber and Robert Schuster contributed guiding insights. David Caplan made helpful comments on portions of the manuscript. The friendship and support of Lynn Lane and Peggy Kaye are a constant gift.

I am especially grateful to Mike Uhlenkamp of the Lakers, to Alison Bogli, Josh Rupprecht, and Matthew Fleer. Thanks are also due the exceptional interns in the public relations department during the Lakers' 2000–2001 season: Matt Brown, Kim Gimbel, Jennifer Cohen, Alex Karpman, and Poornima Swaminathan. Thanks to Will Blythe and David Hirshey for early faith.

Finally, I am indebted to the men of the Los Angeles Lakers who gave time and consideration to this project: Phil Jackson, Kurt Rambis, Jim Cleamons, Tex Winter, Shaquille O'Neal, Kobe Bryant, Derek Fisher, Brian Shaw, Mark Madsen, Robert Horry, Ron Harper, Greg Foster, Mike Penberthy, Horace Grant, Tyronn Lue, and especially Rick Fox.

1

THE ONLY THING HARDER THAN LOSING IS WINNING

In the year 2000, on the 19th of June, at ten o'clock at night, the Los Angeles Lakers broke out of a huddle, took their places on the floor of the Staples Center, and proceeded to do what no one thought they could do. In the next minutes they would defeat the Indiana Pacers and seize the championship of the National Basketball Association, a standing that would establish their primacy and free them of the deadening burden of being almost good enough.

As the clock ran down, they fired off a barrage of slam dunks and layups. Then the buzzer sounded, the crowd roared, and Kobe Bryant took a running leap into Shaquille O'Neal's arms. Glen Rice hurled the ball into the air. It soared upward through a hailstorm of purple and gold confetti, spinning, gathering force, becoming what the Lakers' game had become: an emblem of possibility, of exultation.

Young players like Devean George and Tyronn Lue were ecstatic, hugging everyone in sight and jumping up and down. But older, seasoned players like Rick Fox and Brian Shaw, who had fought hard and long on losing teams, felt a sense of wonder, for they had come to believe that there is a mystical aspect to winning, that the fugitive mix of sweat, unity, and magic it requires cannot simply be willed into being.

These men were veterans of countless weeks of training, of the athlete's requisite self-absorption, of the missed family occasions that turn an NBA player's life into a case of haven't-been-there, haven't-done-that. Winning was a form of absolution. When you won, everything that once appeared obsessive and selfish suddenly seemed brave, sacrificial, necessary.

Rick Fox had spent thirteen years on losing teams, first the Tar Heels of the University of North Carolina, then the Boston Celtics. These were fabled teams, and he was thrilled at the prospect of joining them, but he arrived too late for their eras of greatness. Each season hope had faded, teaching him the bitter lesson learned eventually by every player: that losing is a trauma that cannot be assuaged or overestimated.

As Fox knew, you end each season on a high note or you don't. Either way, the last games you play are the ones you carry with you till the next ones. So, in a way, you were there on the court battling for a sense of achievement and pride to take with you through the summer. You got your pride or you spent your summers as Fox had, locked in misery, haunted by the losses. No wonder his young son was always asking, "Daddy, when are you gonna stop playing basketball?"

But as much as you hated to lose, victory had a primal power that you could not anticipate. For it to wash away fifteen years of pain—that's pretty powerful, Fox thought. All the years that basketball broke my heart, I'm falling in love with it again.

And that June night, as the locker-room carpet grew damp with champagne and the players leaned back in their chairs, put their feet up, and lit cigars, Rick Fox's son perched in his lap, beaming at him. "Daddy," he said, "you won the trophy!"

The victory parade was held three days later. An hour before it began, Phil Jackson called the players into the locker room. Some coaches had a hard time getting their team's attention. But in a world that measures credibility in championship rings, players usually listened to Phil Jackson. As he guided the Chicago Bulls to six championships in the 1990s he earned first a reputation and then a legend. And that tenure convinced him that the only thing more debilitating than failure is success.

This meant that Jackson tended to downplay any given victory, to favor the phrase of his assistant coach Tex Winter: you are successful only at the moment that you perform the successful act. This was not exactly what players wanted to hear after struggling through an eighty-two-game regular season and four rounds of play-offs. But it was a coach's job to distinguish between what players wanted and what they needed.

The first casualty of victory is hunger. And Jackson knew that players with brand-new gold-and-diamond championship rings had to guard against this all the time, had to battle to maintain the winning stance spelled out in white lights in the Boston Garden during the winning reign of the Celtics: WE WILL NOT BE DENIED. Now, in the locker room, Jackson delivered a warning for the coming season. "Once you win," he told the players, "the goal to repeat may not be as strong as the original goal to win."

They nodded politely, but they didn't believe him. They had just been through it. They knew how to win. They had the trophy to prove it. The coach has to give you the worst-case scenario, they told each other, so Jackson was doing his job and that was fine. But clearly, winning the next one could only be easier.

In any case, a double-decker bus was waiting to convey them through a city gone mad, a city that last saw a Lakers' victory parade in 1988, during that storied era that was Magic Johnson's Showtime.

The bus proceeded slowly through streets choked with people numbering in the thousands, men, women, and children chanting, cheering, shouting their names. The months of effort and bruising work had led to this, to a city receiving them as conquering heroes, as deities.

Later, looking back on this day, they would remember the cheering and forget the warning that Jackson gave them.

2

TWO MEN, DIFFERENT FROM EACH OTHER

When a season ends, the sounds of victory end with it. In the summer following their championship season, the Lakers' practice facility was silent. The court was empty. The six baskets spaced around it, with their orange rims and white nets, seemed a daunting distance from the ground. At the far end of the court a metal rack held a dozen balls. Nearby, a refrigerator case was half filled with bottles of Gatorade. Time was suspended. There was only what had gone before and what would come after.

High up, in the wall that edges the court, there was a window about 8 feet long. On the other side of this window, visible from the basketball floor, were the six gold NBA championship trophies displayed in the office of Jerry Buss, the Lakers' principal owner.

That summer of 2000, had Jerry Buss looked down from his window, he might have seen a lone individual traversing the court. From the man's particular length, speed, and intensity, he would have known at once that it was Kobe Bryant.

No player worked harder, and this was especially telling when you considered that few players were graced with such talent. Kobe worked no matter what. He worked through injury, through adversity, through those difficult first seasons when it was not certain that he would measure up to the off-the-charts hype that greeted his early entry into the league. His first season had ended when he shot an air ball to seal the Lakers' loss to Utah in the 1997 Western Conference semifinals. Early the next morning he let himself into the Pacific Palisades High School gym, picked up a ball, and began to raise his game a few notches.

Now he was twenty-two and viewed by many as the "Air Apparent" to Michael Jordan, though their games were very different, as Kobe kept saying with ever-mounting exasperation. He was an off-the-dribble player, handling the ball, creating—while at the same age Jordan got the ball more often than not when he was in a position to shoot it. In any case, he did not want to be the second Michael Jordan. He wanted to be the first Kobe Bryant, the greatest ever to play the game.

In this, his first summer as a world champion, he never rested. He made two thousand shots a day, literally two thousand makes, not attempts, shooting jumpers from 15, 18, and 20 feet. He charged toward the basket, then past it, and launched into the air to throw down two-handed reverse dunks. All summer, the silence of the court was punctuated by the squeak of his shoes on the polished maple floorboards, by his every breath, by the ball whooshing through the net, then bouncing with an echo that extended to the next bounce. Each shot brought him that much closer to the perfect release, the ideal arc, to encoding his technique into his hands and body, to achieving that elusive state that Phil Jackson describes as "not thinking, just doing."

The idea was to program yourself, to focus so intently on everything you need to work on during practice that in a game you would just find yourself doing spectacular things. This gave his playing a certain spiritual component, of which he was aware. At times, if you asked how he'd gotten his game, he would break into his slightly abashed, crooked grin, raise an index finger, and point upward.

Shaquille O'Neal, the Lakers' premier player, did not practice that summer. He had exhausted himself during the season, walking off with the MVP for the regular season and for the finals. He had also been MVP of the All-Star game, though to his annoyance he'd had to share that particular honor with Tim Duncan of the San Antonio Spurs.

Shaq had played in the NBA for seven years, and this would be his first summer free of regret, anger, or sorrow, the first summer that he would not hear people saying, "Sure, Shaq's a great player, but he can't lead a team to a championship."

"There's always that 'but' factor," he had said since coming into the league. "I just want to eliminate that 'but.'" Now that he had, he was happy to follow Jackson's instructions to take the summer off and return in September to prepare for the next season. He joked about eating Krispy Kreme doughnuts by the dozen and coming back weighing 400 pounds.

While Kobe shot jumpers, Shaq feasted on the fried shrimp, mayonnaise, ketchup, and cheese concoctions he called Shaq Daddy sandwiches. He took his posse to Las Vegas, gave them each $10,000 for the gambling tables, and kept hours that gave him headaches.

Shaq liked to quote philosophers. When he accepted the MVP trophy, he invoked Aristotle's observation that you are what you repeatedly do. That summer, as Shaq sightings occurred at what he called gentlemen's clubs and at Fatburger at three in the morning, that notion—you are what you repeatedly do—still had application.

To the considerable degree that the Lakers' fate rested with Shaq and Kobe, it rested with two men who differed from each other in ways both blatant and subtle. Shaq, the self-styled big brother, was gregarious, generous, impulsive; Kobe was introspective, disciplined, measured: neither wanting a big brother nor perceiving a need for one. For each hour that Kobe was sequestered in his room, playing video games and writing poetry, Shaq was out with his friend and bodyguard, Jerome Crawford, cruising around town in his silver Mercedes sedan with the Superman logo etched into the glass of the headlights. For Shaq, success meant that he would never have to be alone; for Kobe, it meant that he would never have to be bothered. Shaq craved attention as fervently as Kobe craved privacy.

For reporters covering the Lakers, the First Cliché was that Shaq had never become an adult while Kobe had never been a child, and prior to each game a moment occurred that lent credence to this supposition. Players gathered in a circle, arms around each other, as Shaq led them in jumping up and down while Kobe stood off to the side, amused perhaps, enjoying the spectacle, but not part of it.

But then, Kobe had never sought to join their world. Basketball had given him a world of his own. It was a world he returned to before each game, when he came out on the court to practice and engaged in the solo game he'd played as a child for untold hours, a game of shadow ball complete with feinting this way, that way, with faking out imagined defenders, overwhelming imagined opponents. "Man," he would say later, "it's just so much joy."

Kobe learned basketball from his father, Joe Bryant, who became known as JellyBean Bryant during the seven years he was an NBA player. One of the first players to declare early, Joe Bryant came out of LaSalle as a junior, joining the Philadelphia 76ers in 1975, the year after Moses Malone became the first player in nearly thirty years to enter the pro leagues from high school.

In many respects it was a heady, lucrative time to be a Sixer. Their franchise player Julius Erving, known as Dr. J, was in his prime, and management was upholding the team's recently achieved reputation as the best that money could buy.

Yet Joe Bryant could never be wholly satisfied there. His ball-handling skills were not utilized to advantage in the Eastern Conference, and he moved on, first to the Clippers in San Diego and then to the Houston Rockets, where he played under Del Harris, his last NBA coach and the man who would become his son's first NBA coach fourteen years later.

Most observers would say that Joe Bryant's career was not what it might have been. JellyBean was a great guy, they said, but maybe *too* great a guy, too happy-go-lucky and not aggressive enough. Bryant saw it differently, taking the view that a career's quality is in the eye of the beholder. Look at Magic Johnson, he would say. Magic was a guard the same height as he was, and possibly his favorite player. When Magic did these great things people called it Showtime, Bryant would say, adding that he did many of the same things himself and they called it schoolyard.

Kobe was born in 1979, the year that Magic and Larry Bird entered the league and one year after Dr. J's Sixers were routed in the play-off finals by Bill Walton's Portland Trail Blazers. He was the youngest of three children, the only son, an adored, active infant racing around in the Lakers jersey his father bought him, tossing a little ball into a tiny hoop, watching the Sixers on television, imitating their moves during games, and sitting down during halftime to gulp a glass of water.

When Joe Bryant went off to finish his career in the Italian league, his family went with him. They had always been close, and when they became the only black family in Rieti, Italy, they drew closer. Years later, seeing _The Godfather_, Kobe thought of his own family. Like the Corleones, he would say, they "pulled for each other no matter what." Within that safe, warm, and insular realm, Kobe was the central figure, inheritor of the gift, keeper of the flame, a child whose stunning gifts would dictate his family's course, mood, and fortunes.

Joe Bryant introduced his son to a number of sports. "But there was something about basketball," Kobe said later, "that I just loved so much."

With his first touch of a basketball, he found a sense of autonomy and transcendence that answered his most profound and urgent cravings, the cravings of an imaginative and self-contained child who was black in a white country, American in an Italian culture, and, as such, fated for a singular existence. The other sports, he thought, you have to rely on somebody to come with you. The thing about basketball is you just pick up a ball and go dribble.

Kobe Bryant knew he wanted to be an NBA player when he was about five years old. His grandparents would send him boxes of video-taped NBA games, and whole afternoons and evenings passed while he sat transfixed, taking in every nuance of every move made by Dr. J, Michael Jordan, Magic, and Bird. He watched them soar through the air, launch 3-pointers from the perimeter, stuff reverse dunks and right-hand jams, and he knew instinctively how they did it. No matter how difficult the move, he would tell himself, "I can do that." And it wasn't arrogance; it was an accurate assessment of his abilities. He was like a music prodigy who hears a concerto once and reproduces it. His favorite Italian phrases became *tira la bomba* and *bellísimo tira*—"shoot the three" and "beautiful shot."

He looked at the great players and saw qualities that he wanted. He wanted Bird's fadeaway, Magic's pass, everything Jordan had, Isiah Thomas's hands, Hakeem Olajuwon's fallaway jumper. OK, he thought, I'm going to try to combine those qualities.

Soon he was less interested in what these players did than in why they did it, why they spun to the left or moved to the right, and why it worked. He watched individual plays over and over until he had dissected them. Then he'd get a game going, often with players on his father's team, setting up his man to utilize the same movement. If it didn't work, he'd figure out why it didn't. These puzzles were like doors that he had to get through. Let me just crack this door open, he'd think. Once he cracked it, there'd be another door, then another.

"I was like a computer," he told *Sports Illustrated*'s Ian Thomsen early on. "I retrieved information to benefit my game." He didn't play on a team or learn street moves like the crossover dribble until he came back to the States for high school. This meant that his path to the NBA was devoid of the usual gyms and playgrounds—even, for the most part, of teammates. Thomsen came to think of Kobe as the NBA's first test-tube player.

That he grew up in circumstances made comfortable by the NBA's bounty was another sweeping difference between him and most players. As a rule, basketball players come from the inner city or poor rural areas where they play basketball twelve hours a day because they have nothing else to do with their time. This was the story of every player from Oscar Robertson to Larry Bird to Allen Iverson. But Kobe had access to the multiple perks of an affluent suburban life, with its imperatives to play a variety of sports, take up hobbies, and be "well rounded." He might distract himself briefly with video games or by taking a drive in his dad's BMW, but he soon returned to the court, where he played twelve hours a day because he wanted to.

You had to be very hungry to be a basketball player, to subject yourself to the rigors of training, the physical pummeling. That kind of hunger was understandable in a poor kid for whom basketball was his one chance to remake his life. But the origins of Kobe's hunger were mysterious. Unbridled, insatiable hunger like his is not generally found in young men who can go driving in their father's BMW.

Michael Jordan had that kind of hunger and was also a son of the middle class, if not in as exalted a berth as Kobe. The particular origins of Jordan's hunger, as explicated by the man himself, had become one of basketball's most repeated tales, so that kids shooting hoops on any American playground knew that the unexpected setback of being left off his school team in tenth grade had ignited in Jordan a fire that proved inextinguishable. Kobe had suffered no setbacks. His life was a wondrous journey, all forward motion and no turning back. But his great gift—on court and off—was the ability to use whatever was available to him, as he did on the court by working with whatever the defense gave him. The ease of his life did not make him soft. Rather, it gave him a deep and special hatred of losing, because losing disrupted his life's graceful flow, its sense of order, its insistently upward trajectory.

Hunger is isolating. Kobe was bound to be isolated in Italy, and when he returned to the States he remained isolated, his attentions fixed on the last game, the next game, on his progress, his future. Basketball's a game, he told himself, but it's not a game. It's nothing funny. His interest in what he called "the long picture" separated him from other young men, who tended to live for the moment. When he came to the NBA, he saw that the long picture wasn't occupying anyone's thoughts there either. This was another difference between him and his teammates, who were already uneasy about his youth, his talents, his instant celebrity, and his seriousness about basketball.

The rewards for that seriousness were great, but they did not overwhelm him. The clamoring for autographs, the accolades, the sight of his image on the cover of _Sports Illustrated_, the last-minute heroics and masterful moves that set the crowds roaring—when these things occurred, they were comfortingly familiar; they were scenes from his dreams.

As much as anyone could, he maintained his balance, held on to a sense of self that was both well developed and well defended. People often asked him how he dealt with success so gracefully. "I envisioned this happening," he would say.

Shaquille O'Neal was also introduced to basketball by his father. Not, he always noted, his biological father, a college basketball player whose involvement with him was such that Shaq's mother dismissed him as a sperm donor. The man who taught him the game was his stepfather, Phillip Harrison, who came into his life when Shaq was two years old. Shaq called him Sarge, and Sarge was one tough customer, a marine staff sergeant who adopted his attitude toward child rearing from the attitude General Patton took toward soldiers: you don't have to love me; you have to respect me, though you'll love me eventually when you realize all the good I've done for you.

Sarge rode Shaq hard on everything. In the mornings he'd toss a coin onto Shaq's bed. If the coin didn't bounce, Shaq had to make the bed again. When it came to basketball, he was even tougher. "If you don't play well, you don't eat," Sarge would say, and he meant it. Despite this, or because of it, nothing mattered more to Shaq than the approval and respect of the man who became his father.

Shaq was born weighing less than eight pounds but grew so quickly that his mother carried his birth certificate when she took him on train rides to prove that he qualified for the half-fare tickets extended to young children.

Being big was a terrible burden for a boy who was easily hurt and wanted only to be liked and to fit in. People stared at him. Children laughed at him and called him names like "Shaquilla the Gorilla." Years later, in his autobiography, *Shaq Talks Back*, he recounted that he had to stop trick-or-treating when he was eleven because by then he was 6'4" and no one believed there was a young boy beneath his disguises. When he walked or sat in class he took to hunching over. His classmates made fun of him or ignored him. He sought their attention by being a bully and sought their favor by playing the clown.

The more he grew, the more he became engulfed in shame and embarrassment, feelings that became basic and permanent and remained even after he had become one of basketball's most lauded players. Near the end of one game that the Lakers were winning, he fouled out and left the court to the strains of the *Star Wars* theme and the assorted boos and cheers of fans. Asked about it later, he muttered an embarrassed, "I ain't got shit to say." It was a situation that other players would have treated cavalierly or with anger, as the Lakers forward Robert Horry did when, having been ejected from a game, he strode out of the Staples Center referring audibly to the referee as "that asshole." Kobe, evicted from another winning game, had dismissed it. "I didn't really care, man," he said. But then Kobe was not a player to wallow in anything, least of all in shame.

The day that Shaquille O'Neal celebrated his thirteenth birthday he was 6′5″. He had become something of a juvenile delinquent, stealing gold chains, hanging with a rough crowd. An army doctor predicted he'd grow to 7 feet, a size that would reduce his life choices to being a misfit or being an athlete.

Of the many sports Sarge taught him, Shaq liked football best because he was lean and mean and loved to hit. But Sarge and his mother steered him toward basketball. It would open a lot more doors for him, they kept saying, and later Shaq often said that they must be seers, a curious comment given that it didn't take a seer to discern that Shaq was made to excel in basketball. Maybe what he found so astonishing was simply that they believed he could excel at *something*.

Even in a big man's game, Shaq did all he could to divorce himself from his size, honing the running, driving, passing, and footwork that he called "small-guy things." Sarge taught him key assets of the great players: Bill Russell's blocked shot, Wes Unseld's outside pass, Jerry West's jump shot.

At fifteen, living with his family in San Antonio, Texas, he was the shining star of the Cole High School team, "a child superstar," as he put it, the subject of countless action shots in local papers. When he played basketball, he was no longer ignored or laughed at. Girls waved and giggled. Boys crowded the sidelines, jumping up and down, their fingers held in Vs for victory. For Shaquille O'Neal, being a basketball player was transformative. The sport had alchemized a cumbersome liability into a marketable, enviable asset. He no longer hunched over. At times he was able to perceive himself as special rather than different. If it wasn't for basketball, he would think at those times, this would never have happened.

After high school he went on to Louisiana State University. He left after his junior year for the Orlando Magic, his entry into the league greeted by speculation that with his small-man's game and hulking body, he might become the game's greatest big man.

He entered the NBA with two burning desires: to dominate and to be loved. In pursuit of the first goal, he played hard. In pursuit of the second, he studied what made certain players popular. He'd watch Magic Johnson and think, He smiles a lot; they like that. He'd watch surly players who cursed and scowled at fans. I ain't crazy, he'd tell himself. I'll stay away from that. So he smiled a great deal and didn't curse, at least not in public.

Shaq was his own creation, presenting to the world the happy-go-lucky big brother he wanted to be. He loved giving himself names—the Big Aristotle, the Big Shakespeare, the Big Homage—a series of monikers so long that his Lakers teammate Ron Harper would later describe him as "The Big Whatever-He-Calls-Himself-Today."

Shaq's own feelings of being different prompted him to look out for others who didn't quite fit in. When one of the Lakers' ball boys, a 5-foot-tall Hispanic man who'd been deaf from birth, didn't show up at practice, Shaq asked, "Where's the little deaf guy?" When he found out that the young man had been fired as part of an economy measure, he said, "Well, I'll pay his salary." It's not just a salary, he was told. There are payments for insurance, he needs a car to get around, it adds up to a lot of money. "I'll pay it," Shaq said. And he did, though when the story got around, as it did inevitably, what impressed people who knew basketball players wasn't so much that a guy with Shaq's kind of money offered to pay the kid's expenses. What was impressive, in the enclosed, self-referential world of sports, was that a big-time star like Shaq had noticed that the little deaf guy wasn't there.

Opportunities to step in, to be there, to be the big brother were as satisfying to Shaq's ego as to his heart. He was happiest offering advice, dispensing helpful wisdom to his posse, telling them that you can deduct 80 percent of your cell phone bill as a business expense, that being honest with a girl will make her love you even more, that when you talk to Bill Gates you don't say, "What's up, Dog?", you say, "Mr. Gates, hi, how are you doing?"

Yet for all the good impulses and works and uncommon talent, being Shaquille O'Neal would never be easy. He remained vulnerable to slights, real or imagined, and his size was always a nettlesome issue. To see him ease into his silver Bentley was to see an exercise that ESPN's Charlie Steiner likened to double parking. And when his head collided with exit signs and wall-mounted TVs, he pounded on them with a fury so great that observers feared he would break his hands; it was as if he was beating up on a world not made to incorporate him.

All this was a far cry from Kobe's experience. As a child Kobe had been so small that, in first grade, he looked around the classroom thinking, Is there anybody here I'm taller than?

When Kobe's growth spurt came in his early teens, he grew so quickly that his knees hurt. He was 6′7″ when he stopped growing, a height that would later allow him to slide comfortably into his black Ferrari, to have fifty Armani sweaters in his closet, to move through the world with apparent ease. Kobe had never tried to figure out what other people liked. He had a glamour and charisma that made people anxious to please _him_. If there was a single, critical divide between these two men, it was that Shaq was preoccupied with the feelings of others, while Kobe was preoccupied with his feelings about himself.

Even the commercials they made revealed their differences. Shaq was pictured in settings drenched with primary colors; he was portrayed as a charming clown—slightly manic, totally accessible, the camera tight on his smiling face. Kobe's commercials tended to use color so sparingly that they often seemed shot in black and white. Cameras tilted up at him or were positioned at a distance, investing him with a mythic quality. One Adidas commercial was created around a long shot of him in a formal, arcadian setting, reclining against the base of a marble column, Rodin's *Thinker* in a white running suit and the white, black, and silver kicks of his own design, ruminating on the importance of being true to oneself as the camera edged closer. It was a smart view of him, one that caught the distance he established instinctively.

That distance would frustrate the many people eager for a piece of him. But he simply was not available. His psyche had no gaping wounds for strangers to fill. For a person so young he was surprisingly self-contained and tough of mind. If he had a mantra, it could have been the words he uttered at seventeen when he announced his availability for early entry into the league. "If I fall off the cliff, so be it."

Shaq had a mantra too, which he expressed when leaving the Orlando Magic for the Lakers: "I just want to feel appreciated," he'd said, and that need had never been sated.

Beneath Kobe's confidence was more confidence, while beneath Shaq's swagger—for all his talk about feeding the big dog and the tattoos proclaiming "Against the Law" and "Man of Steel"—there was something tender, wounded.

Yet on the court they were similar, two outsiders with a fierce will to win, a rage to beat people, to post 40 points a night. Kobe loved outfoxing the opposition; Shaq loved punishing them. His game was brutal. During a post-up drill in the preseason he hit one of the rookies, Mark Madsen, sending him reeling to the ground and needing the services of the Lakers' trainer, Gary Vitti, for a sprained back that ached for a week. "This is the kind of stuff every trainer deals with," Vitti told Madsen, "when their team plays the Lakers."

But Shaq was not just a blunt instrument, one of those big men whose game consists of being 7 feet tall on a basketball court. There was in him an incredible athlete who could move and spin, and his game would alter the standard for big men. The pride he took in this game was the tremendous, touchy pride of a player who did not want to be dismissed as an accident of nature.

Kobe's game had a different aspect. It was a finesse game that drew inspiration from his favorite animal, the great white shark, which, he would say, was stealthy, focused, and couldn't be stopped. It was a game with a subtext that he revealed when some guys he knew from New York were messing with him from the sidelines, getting him more upset than he'd ever been. Wanting to give them something to carry back to New York, he nailed an alley-oop dunk. Then he turned to them, hands on his hips, feet apart, and shouted, "Don't fuck with me."

Teeth bared, nostrils flared, betraying unbridled desire, he was liberated by his game from an inborn reserve and refinement, forced back to something within himself that was raw and basic.

Kobe's game was a rite of release, of communion.

Shaq's game was a rite of redemption.

When those games were forged together under Phil Jackson's aegis, the Lakers became unstoppable. At the presentation of the championship trophy for the 1999–2000 season, Shaq broke down and wept. After the ceremony he collapsed onto a sofa, clutching the trophy, relieved and exhausted. "Finally I got one," he said.

Kobe, though just twenty-one, apprehended the full meaning of the event. "Give the credit to the big guy," he said that night. "He's been waiting for this moment his whole life."

3

A TEAM COMES TOGETHER

In the seasonal life of a basketball team, summer is the time of endings and beginnings, of players acquired, players waived, of offer sheets, signings, and contract extensions.

In the summer of 2000, the most pressing matter for the Los Angeles Lakers was replacing two starters from the championship team, A. C. Green and Glen Rice. After fifteen years in the league, Green, the only player still active from the Showtime era, was nearing the end of a fine if not brilliant career, his most valid claim to legend being his status as the NBA's only self-proclaimed virgin. Once renowned for quick-footedness, he was also known for dropping the ball at inopportune moments, and this remained a joke among his former teammates long after he had departed. Months after Green's retirement, when Kobe was speaking at a press conference, a technician dropped a light that went crashing to the floor. Kobe laughed. "A. C. Green hands," he said.

Glen Rice was an outside threat, third option after Shaq and Kobe. Though he averaged 15.9 points a game in his two seasons with the Lakers, they were the weakest seasons of his eleven-year career. Once a solid defensive player, he seemed to have lost interest in defending, which did little to commend him to Phil Jackson and made his demands for a raise to the tune of $10 million a year seem delusional or absurd.

Rice's wife compounded an increasingly tense situation by choosing the NBA finals as the time to complain to reporters that Jackson was not playing Glen enough. This prompted those players who knew that she was of Cuban descent to refer to her as Mrs. Crisis.

Kobe wanted to move from guard to Rice's position, small forward, and Jackson favored this shift, provided that someone could be found to take over in the backcourt for Kobe. With this in mind, in late August the Lakers signed Isaiah Rider, known as J.R.

In his seven years in the NBA, Rider had played for three teams, usually becoming their focal point and emotional leader. He had an 18-point scoring average and was among the league's most gifted shooting guards. These qualities could make him useful starting in the backcourt or coming off the bench as a scorer.

Rider was complicated, by turns diffident and aggressive. "I'm nasty on the court," he said in 1993, on the day he was drafted. "Other than that, I'm a perfect young man."

Since then the perfect young man had become renowned for numerous suspensions, for clashes with teammates and coaches, for the thousands of dollars he had paid in fines for skipped practices and late arrivals. He had spit at a fan, kicked a woman in the Mall of America, and been arrested on assault and drug-related charges. During his stint with the Portland Trail Blazers, he and his teammates Rasheed Wallace and Jermaine O'Neal became the subjects of a *Sports Illustrated* article titled "The Portland Jail Blazers."

Players marveled at his gift for self-sabotage, but they liked him. He was his own man, if not always in ways that were admirable or productive. When he was not kicking or spitting, he had a spacey charm. Few players, when pulled over by a policeman and asked if there was anyone they wanted to call, would answer, "Ghostbusters."

Coming to the Lakers was something of a last chance for J. R. Rider. He had signed for $636,000, a fraction of the salary he would have commanded had his career gone as planned. If he doubted his capacity for reformation, he was savvy enough to know that his interest lay in appearing positive. "I can tell I'm going to start having fun," he said, "smiling on the court, being my old self out there. I'm going to be like a little kid on the floor."

And perhaps even he did not know whether these statements were products of conviction or attempts at self-hypnosis.

Derek Fisher played guard, and in four years with the Lakers had developed a reputation that was the polar opposite of Rider's. In the view of everyone on the Lakers' staff, Fisher was special as a player and as a man. If your daughter were to marry a player, they said, you'd want him to be Derek Fisher.

He was 6'1", 6 inches below the average height for NBA players and, as such, proof of the conventional wisdom that the smallest players are the most committed. He was not much of a scorer, averaging just 5.8 for the regular season, 5.5 for the play-offs. But he worked the court tirelessly, setting the defensive pace. His toughness of body and mind powered his game and lifted the spirits and energy of his teammates.

Two weeks before the start of training camp, doctors discovered a stress fracture in Fisher's right foot that would require surgery. The recovery time would keep him out of the game for at least half the season, a substantial blow to a team that considered Fisher its sparkplug.

A week after Fisher's operation, Shaq returned from summer vacation. When Jackson told him to come back in September and start preparing for the new season, the date he had in mind was September 1. But Shaq showed up four weeks later, on the 28th, a week before training camp started.

He was still joking about Krispy Kremes. He had let his hair grow in. He sported a narrow beard. He couldn't shave it off, he said, because Halle Berry had told him that it felt good on her cheek.

The team with which the World Champion Los Angeles Lakers would defend their title came together for the first time at the start of October. The occasion was Media Day, an NBA-mandated event that was compulsory for players and useful to a press corps gearing up for a new season. This was the first Lakers' Media Day held at Health-South, the training center that had opened the previous February in El Segundo to house the Lakers, the Kings, and the WNBA's Sparks. HealthSouth had been built for $24 million. It featured a therapy pool, 10,000 pounds of weight-training equipment, a nineteen-seat theater where teams and coaches could watch game videos, and, in the Lakers' portion of the structure, a striking amount of gold tile and purple carpeting. By late morning, the players' section of HealthSouth's ample parking lot was packed with well-waxed Range Rovers, Cadillac Escalades, Phil Jackson's dark blue Porsche, J. R. Rider's emerald-black Bentley convertible. Inside, Shaq was camping for reporters, having outfitted himself for the occasion in a Rasta hat and dreadlocks.

Among the new players was Horace Grant, a 6′10″ power forward who had played for Phil Jackson on the Bulls in the early nineties and later with Shaq on the Orlando Magic. "Get me a Horace Grant," Shaq had told management, and now here was Grant himself, huge and imposing, a player who did not require a lot of attention or coddling.

Grant was one of many NBA players who grew up poor in the rural South. His teammate on the Bulls, Scottie Pippen, had the same background. During their rookie year, 1987, they had been inseparable, two young men from the country who bought the same clothes, lived within blocks of each other on the North Shore, drove Mercedes SELs—a white one for Grant, a black one for Pippen—and hit the town at home and on every road stop with more money in their pockets than they had ever imagined. The fast life soon made Grant uncomfortable, and he escaped from it by becoming a born-again Christian. Since then he had read the Bible three times from beginning to end and become a regular attendee at the religious services held before games in makeshift chapels near the locker rooms. Soft-spoken and somewhat shy, he displayed in his locker a framed photograph of his mother, who had recently died. He was known for giving money to the homeless folk he encountered and was one of those old-school veterans who would tell a rookie to carry his bags but would never let him pay for a meal.

Grant's first year in Chicago highlighted a curious aspect of basketball life, namely the frequency with which players changed teams and, by extension, changed allegiances. A prime example of this was the fate of Sedale Threatt, a Bulls veteran who often took Grant and Pippen out drinking and whose misfortune it was to have the Bulls' management perceive him as a bad influence on impressionable young talent. He was traded as swiftly and unceremoniously as possible, then traded again to the Lakers, where he remained until 1996 when he was traded again to clear salary-cap room for Shaq. If the reasons for his transfer from team to team were unusual, the movement itself was characteristic and meant that teammates who had enjoyed warm friendships became opponents, while players who had fiercely contested one another were forced to play together in harmony.

The goal of these trades was to acquire one or two particular players, and other players were often shifted with him, or because of him, willy-nilly. In some cases these beside-the-point players ended up with incredible power, as Matt Geiger of the Philadelphia 76ers did during the summer of 2000. It was Geiger's refusal to waive his 15 percent trade kicker that derailed what would have been a twenty-two-player, four-team deal: trading Allen Iverson to Detroit while obtaining for the Sixers Eddie Jones and Glen Rice, former Lakers whose journeys had previously intersected when the Lakers traded Jones to acquire Rice.

Robert Horry was among the players that the Houston Rockets traded to the Phoenix Suns in 1996 for Charles Barkley. Horry had loved playing for Houston, where he was an integral part of two championship teams. He was miserable in Phoenix. Three months into the season, his shooting average had sunk from 12 to 6.9, and his loathing of the coach, Danny Ainge, was so extreme that when Ainge pulled him out of an important game Horry threw a towel in his face. Four days after that incident, Horry was traded to the Lakers for Cedric Ceballos, who was, Horry would say, "a crazy cat they wanted to get rid of"—which is exactly how the Suns had come to think of Horry.

The trade that brought Grant to the Lakers in 1999 was the largest trade in NBA history, a twelve-player trade involving four teams. Along with Grant came Greg Foster, a player whom Shaq had characterized as a bum and a fake when Foster played with the Utah Jazz.

Shaq was known for having little good to say about most players, except for the unequivocally great Hakeem Olajuwon. In Shaq's lexicon, David Robinson was "girly"; Robert Horry was "that chump," though this, of course, was before Horry turned up on the Lakers. And Shaq harbored a special aversion to Foster that dated from a game the Lakers lost to the Jazz late in the 1998 regular season, a game rightly viewed, at the time, as a test run for the approaching play-offs. In the final minutes, with the Jazz in the lead, Foster threw down a dunk on a breakaway, thumped his chest to the crowd's cheers, then ran a forefinger across his neck as if to say to the Lakers, "You're dead." This was far from the worst thing a player had done to opposing players, but Shaq was incensed by it, no doubt in part because Foster's assessment was accurate. "Next time he goes up he better go up strong," Shaq had said, "because a couple guys might try to take his head off." Now here was Foster, suited up in purple and gold shorts and jersey, seated beside Shaq for the team picture.

Throughout Media Day, players revealed to the assembled reporters bits of themselves that would reemerge all season, gradually forming a picture of the way that play is affected by character.

Asked how he'd come to the Lakers, Grant replied, "When you hope and pray, good things happen."

Then came Rider. "I'll be playing with a chip on my shoulder," he said.

"Why a chip?" asked a reporter.

"Why not?" said Rider.

Two players were absent from Media Day. One was Robert Horry, now in his fourth full season with the Lakers. In a game where players were fixated on posting big numbers, Horry was something of an anomaly. His ideal game, he liked to say, was to not score at all, and this preference did little to dispel the reputation he had developed with the Rockets for being gifted but uninspired. Yet he had his moments, usually in a game's heated, final few seconds, or in overtime when he scored most of his points, stepping up with a hot hand and a cool head that few players could muster.

Horry was still at home in Houston, dealing with an emergency involving his seven-year-old daughter, who had a birth defect that left her confined to a wheelchair, unable to speak or feed herself. While he played with the Lakers, his wife, daughter, and two-year-old son remained in Houston, where the doctors and hospitals were familiar. He and his wife often talked about whether he should play for a team closer to home. "I would love for you to come back to Houston," she told him on several occasions, "but they're not going to be as good as you all are." So he stayed, never entirely sure that he was doing the right thing, though there was no doubt that his $5.3 million annual paycheck came in handy.

Brian Shaw missed Media Day because he did not yet have a contract for the coming season. Shaw was another of those "have game will travel" players. In twelve years in the league he had played on seven teams, including the Orlando Magic, where he and Shaq appropriated a move that David Robinson had perfected with the Spurs— a lob pass followed by a dunk. It was a play they executed so frequently that it became known as the ShawShaq Redemption and gave them the special bond that players forge when they communicate through a hurried half-glance from across the court.

Shaw was thirty-four. He had spent the 1998–1999 season on the injured list in Portland, where he played just once. He was on the verge of retirement when he got a call from the Lakers' management at the start of the 1999–2000 season, asking him to fill in for Kobe, who had a broken right hand and would be out for the first fifteen games.

Shaw was a big guard, the kind Phil Jackson liked, with those exceptional passing skills and a good outside shot, another player known for cool under fire and court wiles. He looked like such a nice guy, Robert Horry said, that he could kill you without your even noticing it.

With most players there was a trade-off—you got certain benefits that you hoped would not be outweighed by certain deficits. Shaw was rare in that his considerable upside did not come with a considerable downside. His game was steady and reliable but not predictable. He was composed and collected but neither disengaged nor weak of spirit.

Standing in for Kobe, he did so well that, when Kobe returned, the Lakers kept him on. Later, in the play-offs, he pulled off some saving 3-pointers and finished the season with optimism about the year to come. But he spent the summer waiting, his contract delayed while management investigated other options that might better suit their needs. Kendall Gill, a swingman for the New Jersey Nets, was the preferred choice, and in early August the Lakers' new general manager, Mitch Kupchak, suggested that Shaq give Gill a call, the purpose being to impart a human, star-drenched touch to an offer that—however heartfelt and hopeful—was nonetheless a few million shy of the deal Gill had been offered by the Nets. Gill stayed with the Nets, and on Media Day Shaw was still waiting, holding out for a salary-cap exception of $4.25 million for two years instead of the $1.2 million a year he had been offered.

"I want him back," Shaq told Kupchak. "And if he doesn't come back, I'll be highly pissed off."

The next day, October 5th, Brian Shaw drove down to Los Angeles from his home in Oakland, having been offered the money he wanted and a contract ready for signing. Shaw returned neither as enthusiastic nor as confident as he had been before. The deal had been too long in coming, especially when he'd played so well and knew, given the rarefied financial arrangements of the NBA, that he really wasn't asking for much.

And other players could appreciate that, in the circumstances, you'd wonder if you were wanted.

4

A CUTTHROAT ASPECT

Training camp is the NBA's version of boot camp. It is a three-week onslaught of drills; of honing the fundamentals of passing, dribbling, free throws; of shooting basics like keeping your eyes on the rim before you release. And it serves as a player's bridge from a summer without basketball to the grueling eighty-two-game regulation season that is life with it.

The ambience at camp is casual, though it has a distinctly cutthroat undertone because there are always five to seven guys invited to work out who won't end up making the team. These new men are segregated. They have their own locker room. Veterans hardly speak to them. Professional athletes are masters at safeguarding their emotions and time, and aren't about to invest in guys who may not be there in a few weeks.

Once you make the team, you become part of the players' community, albeit the part that carries the suitcases of other players and is sent on runs to In-N-Out Burger before the team plane leaves the airport. But veterans also look out for rookies and always have. Jim Cleamons, one of Jackson's assistant coaches, was a Lakers rookie during the team's great 1971–72 championship season. He had never forgotten the excitement he felt at traveling out to an exhibition game at Magic Mountain in a Cadillac driven by the Lakers' premier player, Jerry West, the mythic Mr. Clutch himself—or that West had told him, "If there's anything you need, feel free to come to me."

As it happens, that Lakers team would hold the record for most wins in a season until it was surpassed twenty-four years later by the 1996 Chicago Bulls, a team coached by Jackson and Cleamons.

The year before, at the start of his first camp with the Lakers, Jackson had begun by stating his essential credo: "You win championships by playing defense." That had been the opening lesson in a basketball tutorial that would continue all season. Now that they were champions, Jackson took a different tack. He would not dictate to them, he said. He would give them the respect due to champions and see if they could figure things out for themselves. And he would take it easy on them since they'd played so long into June and had a short summer.

One goal of training camp was to find a third option to replace Glen Rice. The obvious candidate was J. R. Rider. But there was also Mike Penberthy, a twenty-five-year-old born-again Christian who'd played some basketball in Europe and worked a forklift until he got on a team in the summer league and caught the eye of Tex Winter, dean of Jackson's assistant coaches.

Penberthy was a pure shooter. He reminded Winter of Steve Kerr, a compliment of the highest order since Kerr was the all-time 3-point shooter, the guy, as Charles Barkley once said, you wanted to get the ball to when the game rested on a single shot.

During the summer, Penberthy was working out at a gym that Kobe frequented. When Kobe showed up one afternoon, Penberthy hurried over to him, saying how cool it was to see him, that they'd be teammates soon 'cause he was about to try out for the Lakers.

Kobe had taken a good look at Mike Penberthy. What he saw was a 6'3" pale-skinned individual he would later describe as "a little white guy." "Sure, right," Kobe had said.

Now here was the little white guy, making 20-foot jumpers and calling to Kobe, "I told you I'd be here!" All that remained was to win a spot on the team against six other guys who wanted it as desperately as he did.

The outside threat was a glamorous, coveted piece of territory. Kobe was ready to do some serious 3-point shooting himself. He was looking to expand his game, and he hadn't spent the summer making thousands of jumpers from downtown for nothing.

Kobe had come into camp nearly popping with excitement. He had made more progress over the summer than he imagined possible. He couldn't wait to show it, couldn't wait to dazzle his teammates with moves he could not have finessed even three months earlier. He was primed to slide over to small forward. He loved the idea of being on the wing, of attacking from behind instead of being in the forefront of the offense going head-on against defenders. But his hopes for this move depended on the unanswered question that was J. R. Rider. And there was the fact that Rick Fox wanted to play small forward.

In his three years with the Lakers Fox's game had declined. The year before, he had been down to 6.5 points a game, though he still had flashes of offensive prowess. And he was so rabid on defense that during the 1999 San Antonio play-off series he'd been put on Tim Duncan, though Duncan, at 7 feet, was 5 inches taller. Yet for all his talent, Fox could lapse into a sloppy, unfocused game, getting foul calls for small things, making errors that were surprising from a player who had the intelligence and the will to match his talent.

He was thirty now, consumed with the game, very emotional about it and about his place in it, and painfully aware that he had become expendable. He was intent on proving himself, on showing his parents they'd done the right thing when they let him leave the Bahamas at age fifteen to play basketball in the United States, a decision they still agonized over fifteen years later.

Even more than most players, Fox loved victory, loved the praise, the attention, the validation. All summer he'd been thinking, Yeah, we can win it again. A decidedly team-oriented player, he was embarrassed to find himself entertaining decidedly non-team-oriented thoughts, like How can I play a bigger role this time and How can I get more of the glory?

Jackson remembered Fox as the tough 15-points-a-game player he had been on the Celtics. "We need you to get back to your days in Boston," he kept saying. Jackson had wanted him to lose ten pounds over the summer. Fox dropped ten, then fifteen more, putting in an hour a day on the StairMaster, lifting weights, shooting for an hour, dunking, hitting 3-pointers. He came to training camp lighter on his feet, a bruising defender remade into a fleet scorer, a transformation proving that the fear of never reaching your dreams is a potent motivator.

Within the team community, Fox was a swing figure—in neither the younger group of guys nor the older one. At thirty he seemed more mature than Shaq was at twenty-eight, and the reason for this, Fox was convinced, was that he'd had more failure than Shaq.

He was through with failing. He'd worked his butt off all summer, put in as much hard work as Kobe. You want to be able to look back someday and smile, he told himself, not because of the money you made or even the championships but because you got out there and played the way you dreamed of playing. At camp, determined to convince Jackson to trust him with the small forward position, Fox played with the fervor of a man who'd become his own reclamation project.

During practice Kobe kept challenging him from his position as point guard, questioning his moves: asking why he passed, why didn't he pass, why did he hold the ball so long, why did he shoot it. No matter what he did, it seemed that Kobe was snapping at him, coming at him to take his position.

"What do we have going on here?" Fox asked. "Got a problem? Got something on your mind you want to say to me?"

"I just want to win," said Kobe.

"If that's where you're coming from, I'm coming from the same place."

But they kept getting into it. "You can talk to me any way you want to talk to me," Fox told him. "I can take criticism. But just respect me."

But he could sense that he didn't have Kobe's respect. I understand that, he thought. I haven't shown him much. He decided to let Jackson sort it out. "If you have a problem with what I'm doing," he told Kobe, "you can go talk to him."

But Kobe had another frustration that compelled him even more. When he showed his new skills in practice, no one seemed interested. It seemed like everyone expected him to be the player he'd been last season, like they had some formula and were just going to stick to it. It's like saying I can't express what I really can do, thought Kobe. For me to do that would be like cutting off my hand.

As the days passed, the situation confounded and baffled him. I've improved tremendously, he thought, but for some reason they don't want me to show it on the floor. Is it me? Is it the situation I'm in? What the hell is going on?

The NBA has two kinds of players: the kind who go into action only when the camera, lights, and announcers' mikes are on and the kind who play hard in every game and practice. Kobe Bryant was a practice player, always pulling out the stops, talking some serious trash to his teammates, playing as if the practice really counted, because to him it did count. Everything counted—every possession, every minute, all of it.

Kobe was always seeking to improve, and he understood how crucial practice had been in the development of the game's great players. Working on his own defensive game, he studied Scottie Pippen's, which had evolved less from playing against other teams than from defending Michael Jordan every day in practice.

In Kobe's first seasons he was on the court every day, two hours before practice and two hours after. Watching him, Kurt Rambis, an assistant coach who had played for the Lakers on four championship teams, saw an abundance of the qualities a player needs most: the athleticism, the competitive edge, the work ethic, the will to improve, the burning desire to be the best. To be missing any of these ingredients, or deficient in them, really held you back, thought Rambis. But Kobe was in no danger of being held back. And now he was poised to go for it with more vengeance than ever before, which was saying something.

But as Kobe looked around, what he saw were players who were not in go-for-it condition, whose energy level was, to put it mildly, subpar. These were players afflicted with the proverbial championship hangover, just now coming off a summerlong party, three months of hearing how great they were, of adulation and recognition in quantities far beyond what they'd previously experienced.

A player's basic job requirements were to be team-oriented and to maintain an edge. And nothing imperiled those attributes more than getting fatheaded and complacent, as you inevitably did when you spent a summer thinking, Look at me . . . look at how I'm doing and how much attention I'm getting.

The NBA finals for the year 2000 drew a television audience of 750 million households in 205 countries, and this entrenched the Lakers as prime-time invaders of the world's living rooms and dens. Basketball players were uniquely positioned to capture the hearts and imaginations of viewers, who saw, in the course of a single game, every human emotion pass over their faces—hope, joy, regret, anger, despair—all in living color and extreme close-up. It was a great show, like watching Tom Hanks or Robert De Niro, with the critical difference that basketball players were not working from a script.

Shaquille O'Neal claimed that NBA stood for "Nothing But Actors," and indeed there was a fair amount of posing. Games were laden with heavy-handed production features—the theatrical lighting that accompanied the announcement of the starting lineup, the fireworks, the dancing girls, dancing coyotes, dancing bunnies. Yet, basketball also had what most people looked for in life, and rarely found. It had absolute rules, and it had a winner. Beyond that, the basketball audience was privy to a forty-eight-minute drama of genuine struggle. This was reality TV at its most vicious and vivid, a drama replete with the setbacks, complications, and the small and large gains that were staples of the real-life struggle waged daily by every individual in the audience. This made basketball players more than mere celebrities. It made them "one of us"—though of course much bigger and better and richer, and as such adored, recognized, and praised wherever they went.

All this was a huge amount of baggage for players to grapple with, especially given that they were already unsettled by the dislocations of NBA life—the travel, the pampering, and the general impossibility of reconciling their profligate wealth with the spartan style demanded of world-class athletes. It made for some complicated attitudes, in a game in which attitude is everything.

Your attitude permeated your play, and then it was visible and not just some private thing you were thinking. A championship attitude had an aura of its own, and Phil Jackson and the assistant coaches he brought with him from the Bulls knew exactly what it looked like. It looked the way Michael and Scottie had looked when they practiced with a fervor so intense that if you didn't know better you'd think they were two young guys trying out for the team.

The 2000 World Championship Los Angeles Lakers did not have that look. They looked complacent. And Jackson's continuing cautions that repeating is harder than winning did not seem to faze them.

Nor did they pay attention in training camp to the admonitions of the four assistant coaches who told them, "You guys have no idea how difficult this is going to be."

"We know we're ready to repeat," the players answered.

Well, thought the coaches, we know damn well you're not.

5

THE MEN HE BROUGHT WITH HIM

When Phil Jackson came to the Lakers in 1999, he found a team in disarray, a team choking on its own energy and internal struggles and refusing to be reined in by its young coach, Kurt Rambis, though it was clear that Rambis had a very good head for basketball.

Jackson brought three assistant coaches from the Bulls, all of whom had played the game at one level or another. None had been stars, a plus in itself since stars rarely did well as coaches. There were different talents involved in coaching than in playing, the most important of which were patience and the ability to handle frustration—qualities that star players for whom the game had come with relative ease did not necessarily possess. The great Jerry West got his fill of coaching in three seasons, though in 1976 he coached the Lakers to a regular-season record of 53–29, the best in the league. The next playing legend to coach the team, Magic Johnson, had a tenure briefer and less successful than West's, and he would later joke that coaching was even more difficult and terrible than being a talk-show host, a profession at which he had failed miserably.

West and Magic were among that scant number of players who had stepped up whenever stepping up was required. They could not comprehend that their experience simply did not apply. That other players failed to step up was incomprehensible to them, leading them to the embittering conclusion that the players *could* have stepped up but simply didn't want to.

However generous a star player might be, that generosity could evaporate as quickly as a rain puddle in the sun once you became a former star standing on the sidelines in a business suit, watching young men do what you no longer could do but had once done better than most of them could ever dream of doing it. Larry Bird was coaching the Indiana Pacers when Reggie Miller made the winning shot against the Bulls in Game 4 of the 1998 Eastern Conference finals. When Bird played with the Celtics, he was known to prance around the court if he sank a great shot during practice against his own second team. But as the jubilant Reggie Miller jumped up and down in circles, Bird looked on, nodding slightly, unsmiling, as if to say he'd been there and done that and it wasn't all that big a deal.

Jackson's assistants were different. Jim Cleamons, who worked with the younger guys, was consistently encouraging and patient, always mindful of his own rookie year on the Lakers. To have been on the bench while Jerry West and Elgin Baylor were on the floor was a connection with myth that had left Cleamons awestruck, for he was one of those players who had grown up steeped in basketball lore. Baylor was in his last year as a player but still had a thrilling game. Wow, Cleamons thought, watching him. This is like going to the movies.

In the 1977–78 season, Cleamons played on the Knicks with Phil Jackson. They were a lot alike, two off-the-bench players known as good teammates who enjoyed doing the little things that made the whole team better. Like Jackson, Cleamons believed that your life on the court was inseparable from your life in general, that on the court and off, players should be of good spirit, balanced and centered, prepared to share and accept challenges, even those they didn't want. When Jackson was putting a staff for the Bulls together, seeking like-minded people, the first person he thought of was Jim Cleamons.

Tex Winter was already an assistant coach for the Bulls when Jackson took leadership of the team. Jackson did not regard himself as a particularly strong offensive coach, and Winter was the architect of the revered triangle offense, a system that first attracted attention in the 1950s when Winter instituted it at Kansas State and turned a minor team into a major contender. The triangle was very appealing to Jackson. With its continual passing and quick cuts to the basket, it satisfied his sense of the game as a flowing dance. Its particular spacing and ball and player movement were a more evolved version of the offense Red Holzman ran with the Knicks. And its concept of unselfish team play gave him what he sought above all: the means to meld the physical and spiritual aspects of his players.

Winter had played at USC, where he was a teammate of Bill Sharman, who would become the Lakers' renowned coach during the West and Baylor years. Winter's own coaching career began at Marquette University in 1952, when he was twenty-eight and the youngest coach of a major college team. By the time he came to the Lakers nearly fifty years later, he was the oldest coach in the NBA and had seen his offensive system transform the Chicago Bulls into one of the most extraordinary teams in basketball history.

Winter was not like the men he coached on the Lakers, who were products of the 1980s with its fixations on money and matter. Winter was an old-fashioned man raised during the Great Depression. He took a dim view of the fame and riches that robbed the game of a certain purity, a certain innocence, and was irritated by unseemly comparisons between basketball teams and rock bands.

Winter was a product of his own time. Its deprivations and hardship left him with a fondness for thrift in general and free food in particular. The latter was a source of continual amusement to the press and the team's staff, who saw him piling his plate at the free meals served prior to games or loading up plastic containers with leftover cold cuts and fruit salad.

Tex Winter, child of the Depression, hated waste. It was no accident that the offensive system he devised made maximal use of every player.

The triangle provided an antidote to the self-centered power basketball that Jackson decried, a style born in playground basketball in the inner cities. This style had dominated the NBA since the late 1970s, when the thrilling, creative games of Julius Erving, Larry Bird, and Magic Johnson reinforced the sense of basketball as a game of individual stars rather than of teams. Both Winter and Jackson loved generous players, team-oriented men who sought to make their teammates better and passed the ball to the open man.

That was the right way to play: right for the game, right for the team, and right in the highest sense. When Winter and Jackson spoke of basketball as being more than a game, they meant that it was a microcosm of how we might live if we lived in a manner that was wholly generous and ethical. This concept resonated with Jackson's spiritual and moralist strains. But Jackson was also a pragmatist who knew that the right way to play was the only way to win.

A basketball team is as strong as its relationship with its coaches. And one reason that teams often lack solidarity is that coaches have the bad luck of being authority figures for men whose respect for authority tends to be minimal. These men are usually black, often raised in the absence of a strong male figure, at times in the harsh poverty that extends to cooking meals on hot plates and boiling water before you drink it. For men like this, a man with a whistle around his neck—particularly a white man—is a policeman.

It is a received truth of coaching that you can get a player's attention only if that player has some failure and some success. Failure alone makes a player unteachable and downhearted. Success alone makes him unteachable and arrogant. Even in the best cases, coaching is destined to be a battle of egos and wills that falls somewhere between group therapy and a shell game. You could correct players only so much because the willfulness and ego strength that made them athletes did not, as a rule, make them receptive to criticism. In the end, all you could do was improve their judgment and put them in a position to succeed.

You had to understand where these guys came from, understand what it means to grow up poor and have your game be the one thing you take pride in, the one thing that makes you feel like Someone. For young men like this, coming to the NBA was an ego boost and an ego deflation, a boost for all the obvious reasons and a deflation because suddenly after all those years of people telling you, *you da best, you da man*, you were chilling on the bench while someone else out there on the floor was being the man.

Players put everything they had on the line—their hopes, their pride, their honor, their peace of mind. This made them raw, more readily wounded than they admitted. They prided themselves on having that certain swagger, but in truth they often were cocky rather than confident, their toughness a stance rather than a state of mind. So a coach had to proceed with caution, guiding players without dampening their energy and fire, keeping the lines open.

This meant that you couldn't pile too much on them. And you had to have clearly defined principles so that, when you were critical, the players knew you were taking issue with their actions and not with them. Otherwise they turned off, and whatever gains you had made would be lost. They would take you for a player hater and take your so-called efforts to help them as a way of trying to keep them down.

Phil Jackson had remarkable instincts with players partly because, at heart, he was one of them, and because he was something of a chameleon when it came to fitting in. He would have been a great actor, thought Rick Fox, in that actors absorb everything around them and make use of it. If a guy was bored or angry or on the edge, Jackson sensed it immediately. He joked about having a feminine side but placed a premium on the gentleness that was femininity's most evident aspect. One problem for the Lakers, he said, was that so many players made their homes in other places, depriving the team of the centering influence of wives.

Among Jackson's strengths was his respect for subtleties of communication, those nuances of timing and tone that are not a known feature of alpha-male interaction. Before the seventh, deciding game of the 1999–2000 Western Conference finals, his tone was brusque and to the point. "You either win and keep going," he told the players, "or lose and go home."

His tone changed during the NBA finals. The Lakers had been poised to win in the fifth game, but Indiana came back and beat them by 30 points, leaving them still one win from the championship. "OK," he said before the sixth, potentially deciding game, "this is the dream we've been waiting for. Let's do it."

But it is not always possible to convey your meaning precisely, and at training camp a communication lapse occurred when Jackson recounted a brief history of the 1995 Houston Rockets. After winning the 1994 championship, they had taken just forty-seven games in the next regular season, ending up sixth in the Western Conference and lacking home-court advantage. The point, he said, was that after you win a championship, it can all fall apart. But in fact, Houston had gone on to win back-to-back championships. And what the players took from this cautionary tale was that after you win a championship it can all fall apart and you still can win.

6

WELLNESS

Phil Jackson often talked to the team about their collective state of being. He called this "team wellness," and wellness was a delicate thing that could never be greater at any given moment than the team's confidence and sense of comfort with one another.

You could not always say what fed that wellness and what diminished it. Did it matter that, in the second week of October, the Lakers lost two preseason games to the Washington Wizards and the Atlanta Hawks? The prevailing wisdom was that it didn't, that preseason games don't matter, even if you lose to the league's weakest teams.

Toward the end of that second week, Shaquille O'Neal signed a three-year, $88.4-million contract extension. He celebrated by taking one of the rookies, Mark Madsen, on a shopping excursion, during the course of which he bought twenty-two Rolex watches—one for every guy at training camp, including the five guys who would be waived before the season started.

Madsen and Shaq were becoming friends. Shaq liked to test people, so he'd mess with Madsen to see if he could get to him. He couldn't. Madsen might not look tough, with his pale white skin and Ivy League handsomeness, but he was remarkably strong of character and mind, and Shaq recognized this and appreciated it.

Madsen was among that decreasing number of white players in a sport that began as a white man's game but had changed so much since Bill Russell entered the league in 1956 that scouts who once anxiously sought out the occasional black player were now anxiously searching for the occasional white one. Among black players there was a conviction that white players lacked their speed and agility. When they found those qualities in a white player, that player became something of an honorary black—as did Jason Williams, the skinhead guard of the Sacramento Kings, who was given the nickname "White Chocolate." It was not, Shaq would say, that there was prejudice in the NBA. It was just that if you were a brother, you didn't want a white guy dunking on you.

If the black guys were aware of a cultural difference, the white guys were too, and never was that more apparent than on the early spring day that the Staples Center was cordoned off for the L.A. Marathon, with policemen and barricades blocking the players' entrance. As it happened, it was a game day for the Lakers. When Mike Penberthy neared the arena, where the team was gathering for the usual morning shootaround, he found himself a few cars back from the veteran player Ron Harper. From this vantage point, he watched Harper drive his Range Rover right through the police barricade with more bravado than Penberthy could conceive of mustering. So instead, he tried reason.

"Hey, I play for the Lakers, too," he told a police officer.

"Yeah, right," said the officer.

"No, I really do," said Penberthy.

Penberthy was not merely a white player. He was a "little white guy," as Kobe had put it. Even Penberthy's own family couldn't believe it was their son out there with all those big Lakers. Seeing Mike on the court with Shaq, his mother would say, was like something out of *Forrest Gump*.

The policeman had perhaps not seen *Forrest Gump* and did not believe Penberthy was a Laker. He told him to get out of there, leaving Penberthy to drive home, vowing to carry his rookie card with him and frustrated by the futility of trying to solve a problem with politeness. "Part of my wonderful heritage," he muttered.

Madsen shared that heritage. He was a 6'9" forward from Stanford, where he had majored in economics. He was a Mormon and at twenty-four was entering the league after spending two years as a missionary in Spain. He described himself as a blue-collar player, a reference to his dedicated work ethic. His actual life was far from blue collar. Like Bill Laimbeer before him, he was one of the few NBA players from the upper middle class, one of the few whose father made more money than he did, at least initially.

Around the Lakers organization, where Shaq was regarded as a big teenager, Madsen was coming to be viewed fondly as the world's biggest Boy Scout. He had a friendly, open face, an eagerness to do the right thing, a knack for seeing the best in people. He never swore and didn't drink alcohol or coffee, or go to R-rated movies.

During a preseason practice Shaq told him, "You're too nice."

"On the court I'm nice," joked Madsen. "Off the court I'm mean."

Yet he was an anomaly: patiently tutoring kids, living in an apartment near the church he regularly attended, but possessed, on the court, of a fire and intensity that justified the nickname he'd had since fifth grade: Mad Dog. And it was a dog, Shaq would say, who never got his rabies shots and didn't want them. Madsen had no letup. He was the kind of player Kurt Rambis had been for the Showtime Lakers in the 1980s, a do-or-die, damn-the-torpedoes guy, loaded with energy and heart. "My game and your attitude . . . ," Shaq once told him.

On their shopping trip, Shaq's priority was getting Madsen a good lease on a dark blue Chevy Tahoe to replace the Toyota minivan his mother had passed on to him a few years before. "Mad Dog, Mad Dog . . . ," Shaq chided, "you can't roll into the Staples Center in a minivan."

Shaq loved spending money as much as Madsen liked saving it. At Rochester's Big and Tall, Shaq found him an XXXL black suit to replace the one Madsen had bought himself at JCPenney during his freshman year at Stanford. When Madsen found a pair of jeans he liked, Shaq told the salesclerk to bring eight pairs in every color. Madsen talked him down to one pair in each color. "You can't really argue with Shaq," he would say.

There were deeper benefits to Shaq's friendship, as Madsen discovered when the Lakers lost their next exhibition game to the

Phoenix Suns. Madsen got some minutes and came away with a black eye, a slightly sprained wrist, and the terrible conviction that, as he told Shaq, "I made mental errors that cost us the game."

Shaq put his arm around him. "It's just one game," he said.

If there is one feeling that separates a team that prevails from a team that doesn't, it is a sense of invincibility. Winning teams feel invincible because they develop a deep and special confidence, which comes from the recognition that they can do together what none of them can do alone. From the start of each season, this feeling increases play by play, game by game. Or it doesn't.

The World Champion Los Angeles Lakers played their first game of the regulation season on October 31, 2000, against the Portland Trail Blazers, their old nemesis and the team they had dispatched, a season earlier, in the seventh game of the Western Conference finals. That had been a bitter contest. In the end, there were those who said that it came down to who wanted it more. But no one could have wanted that win more than the Blazers' Scottie Pippen.

No player had more grit and grace. Pippen was a natural athlete, a basketball whiz, Jackson would call him, with exceptional court intelligence and arms so long that, at 6'8", his wingspan exceeded that of players 5 inches taller. He made his legend with Jackson's Chicago Bulls as second option to Jordan, or as Jackson sometimes put it, the Tonto to Jordan's Lone Ranger. Pippen was a true team player. As he encouraged and coached younger players, Jackson came to take a parental kind of pride in his growing maturity. Now he was out of the improbably long shadow that Jordan had cast, and had become the Blazers' mind, soul, and heart. And he ached to show his former coach that he could win without him.

When Jackson first came to the Lakers, he had tried to get Pippen for the team. Pippen was about to end a brief stint with the Houston Rockets and was entertaining the possibility of going to Portland. He knew Jackson's offense inside out and, as Jackson argued to the Lakers' management, letting a player with that knowledge join the enemy was not simply dangerous but possibly the difference between winning a championship and not winning it. But management was not persuaded. Unlike the Blazers, the Lakers were not about to shell out extravagant fees for a player—however great—who was entering his thirteenth year in the league.

Money was a key issue for Pippen, who had, on the Bulls, the dubious and rare distinction of being an NBA player whose value exceeded what he was paid. He had been, arguably, the second-best player in the game. But his salary was the 122nd-highest in the league, the result of his having sought security early on for himself and his eleven brothers and sisters back in Arkansas by signing a long-term deal that precluded him from the big money that came when salaries went sky-high in the mid-1990s.

And so, at the 2000 Western Conference finals, Pippen and Jackson met as opponents, each hungering for a championship ring that would be their first without Jordan: Jackson's as a coach, Pippen's as a player. Possibly to guard against warmer feelings just beneath their respective surfaces, their interchanges were edgy and personal. The Blazers were jackals, said Jackson, and Scottie was the lead jackal. At one point their eyes locked and neither looked away for a long time. They were not sizing each other up, for that was something they'd done long ago. They were conveying refusal to yield ground.

The Lakers took three of the first four games. The Blazers took the two that followed. In the seventh, deciding game, with little more than ten minutes left, the Blazers had a 15-point lead and were poised to become the seventh team in NBA history to recover from a 1–3 start to capture a series. For the next six minutes they failed to score while the Lakers surged and Pippen fouled out. In the end, Scottie Pippen was consigned to watch from the sidelines as the Lakers took the game 89–84 and with it, the Western Conference title.

It was the most bitter, disappointing defeat in the Blazers' history, one of those terrible losses that a team goes to considerable lengths to keep from happening twice, especially a team owned by Paul Allen, who was prepared to pour into it some portion of the billions he had made after he and Bill Gates founded Microsoft.

For this new season the Blazers had been reconfigured to stop the Lakers and to nullify Shaq. They had added two big men, Shawn

Kemp and Dale Davis, pushing their payroll to $84 million—beyond that of any team in the NBA.

Confronting the new Blazers at the Rose Garden, the Lakers were ready to leave it on the court. Shaq was unstoppable, scoring 36 points. Rider came off the bench to play against his former team, posting 13 points, 5 rebounds, and 3 assists in twenty-six minutes. The Lakers lost control of the game in the third quarter, but they rallied, and the final score, 96–86, sent them out of the Rose Garden satisfied they had proven that their victory last season was not a matter of luck.

Within weeks, the Lakers would come to see this game as a lose-lose proposition. A loss would have cost them confidence at a critical time. The win lulled them into a sense of security that was even more dangerous, convincing them that, as champions, they knew precisely what they were doing and didn't have to work that hard.

Six weeks later, they would return to Portland to play the Blazers, and again the score would be 96–86, but this time Portland would be the winner. By then, the Lakers' thoughts of invincibility would have receded into memory.

Kobe Bryant did not have a great first game against the Blazers. He had been *too* ready, hampered in the first half by a surfeit of adrenaline and just finding his way in the second. Though he made only 4 of 11 shots, he gave a fair preview of the game he would be playing: a high-risk, high-flying game, defying double and triple teams, posting big numbers. It was a youthful game, the kind you play in that short and precious time when you can soar and land and soar again with no apparent consequences. This was not a game that Shaq had ever played. Shaq was more earthbound, for obvious reasons.

The Krispy Kremes had added more reasons. After the Portland game Jackson told the press that this would be an important time for Shaq because of his age, adding that Shaq had the player intelligence to handle this potential hindrance. It was a harsh comment to make about a player whose game was strictly about dominance and who was, in any case, just twenty-eight years old. But it was classic Phil

Jackson: imply that Shaq could no longer play an all-out physical game in order to goad him into proving that he could.

Shaq, too, knew how to send a message, and in Portland his message came in the shape of successive poison darts aimed directly at Kobe. Kobe had taken shots over double and triple teams, so Shaq said, "I'm a smart player, I don't have to shoot over two or three guys all the time." Kobe tried to post big numbers, so Shaq said, "I'm not going to break my neck to be the leading scorer in the league." This, in turn, was classic Shaq. When he saw something he didn't think he could do, he made a virtue of not doing it. The other thing these remarks revealed was that Shaq knew how to read an offense.

That offense was Kobe's offense, and it wasn't aimed at Shaq. It was strictly about Kobe's personal ambitions and trajectory, and a manifestation of it came quite literally into view as the Lakers' bus brought the team from the airport into Portland. The bus rounded a corner, and there it was, a 60-foot-high poster of Kobe's face. This was one of many ads for Adidas's Kobe Bryant shoe campaign and an instance of high-profile advertising in the truest sense.

To have your own shoe line was a sign of arrival, and the endorsement fees accompanying it could dwarf the most inflated salary. These fees were, potentially, the pot of gold at the end of the NBA rainbow, and they occasionally led to tricky loyalties—as they did in 1992 when Alonzo Mourning was drafted from Georgetown by the Charlotte Hornets. His negotiations with the team soon soured, a misfortune of little apparent concern to Mourning, whose shoe deal was rock-solid and would, over the next five years, bring him $16 million. After the Hornets withdrew, Mourning was asked for whom he would be working in the coming season. "I work for Nike," he said.

Shoe lines and big fees were two more things for which players could thank Michael Jordan. Before Jordan's own groundbreaking deal with Nike in his rookie year, 1984, Kareem Abdul-Jabbar had a shoe deal for $100,000. Larry Bird and Magic Johnson each had one for about $70,000, while the most lucrative was James Worthy's New Balance contract for $1.2 million over eight years. Nike paid $2.5 million for the privilege of naming a shoe after the still-untested Jordan, and the irony of this was that in college Jordan wore Adidas and didn't really think much of Nikes. But the Air Jordan made Jordan and Nike rich and put dollar signs in everyone's eyes. For a time there seemed to be as many shoe deals as NBA contracts.

On and off the court, Jordan altered everyone's sense of what was possible because he transcended every barrier—race, religion, class— and because he arrived on the scene at the perfect moment, a time of uncertainty throughout the nation when the movie *Rambo*, released the year he entered the league, revealed a hunger in the American psyche for superheroes. As basketball's first crossover artist, Jordan became an icon even for people who never saw him shoot a basketball unless it was in a Nike commercial, his value understood and appreciated equally by habitués of the dankest, sweatiest gyms and of Madison Avenue's chrome-and-glass inner sanctums.

Selling overpriced sneakers was one more complicated thing that looked easy when Michael Jordan did it. A few years later Reebok would offer Shaq up as the Next Big Thing on the basketball horizon, an assessment that would prove more literal than figurative. Shaq had great appeal. He had verve and panache. But Shaq was a cutup, not a leading man, and the young men of the world who bought these shoes were more intent on being cool than on being comedians. The image Kobe projected was utterly cool, regal. It was the image of a young prince.

If Adidas was seeking to create its own Jordan, it had banked wisely on a player with Jordan's romantic quality, his unshakable confidence, his unlikely mix of brashness and mystery. A star had been born, and this undeniable fact was another log to toss on the smoldering fire that was the NBA's most intriguing rivalry, a contest all the more interesting for being between two players on the same team.

And that day in Portland, as the team bus passed that 60-foot-high image of Kobe, players glanced back at Shaq, wondering if he'd seen it and what he made of it.

The World Champion Los Angeles Lakers received their rings in a ceremony at the Staples Center before their first home game on November 1, an event attended by 18,997 people that included fireworks, a tribute sung by Seal, and Phil Jackson reciting a poem of his own com-

position. The crowd broke into cheers as Jackson read the poem's clos-
ing lines:

"If they stay on track, we might win back to back."

That night the Lakers lost 97–92 to the Utah Jazz. They were not
the first championship team to lose on the night their rings were presented. Even the Showtime Lakers had lost on two such occasions.

What was notable was that this Lakers team was already breaking
records. Their point total of 31 in the first half was the fewest points
they'd scored in a half since Phil Jackson had been coaching them.
The next event for the record books came a few days later during their
first extended road trip, when they lost to Houston 84–74 and tied a
franchise record established five years earlier for fewest points scored
in a game.

They arrived in Houston the day before the game. Some guys liked
the freedom of being on the road, but Shaq wasn't one of them. He
preferred to be at home, where meals were cooked by his own chef
and where he slept in his own customized bed. One of the many differences between him and Kobe was that Shaq played better at home,
while Kobe played better on the road, where the crowd was hostile,
familiar comforts were absent, and you weren't expected to win.

Shaq had friends in Houston, and that night they went out; the evening ended late even by Shaq's night-owl standards. And the next
night, after the Lakers lost the game, when the players gathered for
their customary locker-room meeting, Jackson commented that maybe
they shouldn't have come into Houston early, that they would have
done better to come in the day of the game.

"Are you saying we lost," asked Shaq, "because I was partying?"

"I'm not singling you out," Jackson told him.

But Shaq left angry, and the team's veterans thought back to
another game against the Rockets when Shaq got into it with Charles
Barkley, and Barkley got so mad that he went at Shaq like he was the
one who was 9 inches taller. Things never went right, they thought,
when they played the Rockets on their home territory. Some cities you
never play well in, and they had never played well in Houston.

As Shaq strode out of the arena, a group of kids asked him for
autographs. Shaq loved kids, and he stopped and talked to them,
teased them, and took care to sign something personal for each one.

Signing autographs was a special point of honor with him because of an incident when he was in high school and asked for the autograph of his favorite player, the San Antonio Spurs' David Robinson, known as the Admiral—basketball's 7′1″, defiantly clean-cut, jazz saxophone-playing product of the U.S. Naval Academy—whose photographs and posters adorned his bedroom walls.

Robinson had complied but signed his name hurriedly, failing to evince the degree of interest and enthusiasm Shaq considered warranted. Each time he saw Robinson after that, it became an occasion for him to demonstrate the length of his memory, as when he dunked on Robinson in the '95 All-Star game, knocked him to the ground, and told him, "Stay down. Don't get up."

If that response was excessive, it was also true that Shaq would never treat a young player as Robinson had treated him. When he played on the Orlando Magic and his teammate Penny Hardaway was rude to a kid who asked for an autograph, Shaq stepped in, talked to the kid, asking: Where do you go to school? How old are you? What's your name? The kid's name was Kobe Bryant.

And after Kobe came to the NBA, whenever he played Penny Hardaway, he was out to destroy him.

7

THE RIGHT WAY TO PLAY

The Lakers went on to San Antonio and their first contest of the season against the Spurs. There were only a few very good teams in the NBA, and the Spurs were one of them. In the estimation of many, they were the best. They were also a particular sore spot for those Lakers who were on the team in 1999, when the Spurs swept them in the Western Conference finals and took an especially vicious pleasure in the win.

The Spurs had gone on to win the NBA championship. The next year, when the Lakers took it from them, the Spurs were not gracious and not shy about saying that it would never have happened had their forward, Tim Duncan, been in good shape. With this for history, each team met the other primed for revenge.

The bus taking the Lakers to the Alamodome from their hotel arrived at the stadium without J. R. Rider. Ten minutes later Rider turned up with a handwritten note to Phil Jackson from the hotel operator stating that she had neglected to wake him as ordered. "I've had notes from mothers . . . ," said Jackson.

Jackson let Rider play for seventeen minutes. During that time, he posted only 2 offensive rebounds, a performance affirming Jackson's belief that lateness signals unreadiness. And it was an early suggestion that a bargain-priced player is not necessarily a bargain.

When the final buzzer sounded, the Lakers had lost, 81–91. Kobe had racked up 37 points for his second consecutive 30-plus game, while Shaq scored 13 points and made 3 out of 10 free throws. The rest of the team did not bring their best game either. They'd made a big push at the end but didn't get there.

The year before, they'd be on the verge of losing but somehow find a way to win. This year they weren't finding the way, and while this was troubling, it was less troubling to experienced players than the way the team reacted to it. We're kind of taking it, thought Brian Shaw, and not getting mad and upset about it.

It's funny, Shaw thought, how you always think you can get back to where you got the year before. Most of the guys were figuring that they made it happen last time, so when the time came they could pull the switch and make it happen again. But it didn't always work like that.

When Shaw was with the Orlando Magic, they had gone up against the Houston Rockets in the 1994 finals. They just about blew them out of the building in the first game, but the Rockets made a run in the second half, took it in overtime, and three games later the Magic lost the series. Disappointing as it was, they all assumed they'd win their championship the next time.

That was the team, Shaw often thought, that should have been the dynasty, with Shaq and Penny Hardaway and Horace Grant. But the Bulls took them 4–0 in the 1995 Eastern Conference finals. And they never got back.

One of the Lakers' starters in the backcourt was Ron Harper, once a key player on the championship Chicago Bulls, where he got the ball to Michael and Scottie. Harper came to the game in 1986, playing with the Cleveland Cavaliers. He was lean and hungry then, with great athleticism, a strong defensive player who could dunk like Jordan. But his knees got bad early on, and he recast himself as a role player, drawing admiration for taking that job on with the same panache and enthusiasm he'd brought to being a star. He moved to the Clippers when they were coached by Larry Brown, for whom he had great regard. Harper was a star on that team, but the general level of play made him miserable, and he likened the experience to being in prison. From there he went to the Bulls and the years he would describe as the best of his life. He would rather be a cog on a winning team, he often said, than be a star on a team that can't win.

Harper styled himself as tough and crusty, but he had a warm heart. He truly loved being a member of a team. Whatever his team needed done, he would do, he often said. When a young player like Tyronn Lue made a mistake during a game, it was Harper who told him, "Keep your head up." He calmed and soothed the other players, and when he was on the court the team was settled and flowing.

Harper had grown up with a severe stutter, and this was a sensitive issue when he was a young player. But he'd conquered it enough to be willing to speak on camera, and now that the guys felt free to kid him about it they adapted the name of the player Damon Stoudamire and called him Damon Stuttermire.

Harper was something of a bridge between Jackson and the players, an on-the-floor guide through the intricacies of the triangle offense, a wily veteran trying to instill a team ethic in a group whose attitude struck him initially as adolescent. It was all "I get to shoot the ball. . . . You get to shoot the ball. . . . Why don't I get to shoot the ball more?" Older guys, he said, don't give a damn who's shooting the ball. They want to be on a winning team.

In the 1999–2000 season, Harper's and Jackson's first year with the Lakers, Jackson had been certain that they could take it all. And when the shiny new trophy was ensconced beside the other five in Jerry Buss's office, Harper, exhausted but satisfied, went to Jackson.

"Can I retire now?" he asked.

"Hang around," said Jackson, "for one more season."

Now, a few weeks into that season, Harper pulled Jackson aside. "You know," he said, "we don't have the intelligence we had last year, and I can't put my finger on why."

Jackson knew this was true, and the lack, he thought, was not so much in individuals as in that larger entity, the team itself. But then, it was a different year, a different team.

A major absence, thought Jackson, was that of John Salley, who had played on the championship Detroit Pistons in 1989 and 1990 and briefly with Jackson's Bulls. Salley was inclined to discourse about poverty in India or Christianity in the sixth century and was one of the few players in NBA history with a claim to being an intellectual. It was Salley who took joking issue with the arcane names given to the various offensive plays, like "Moment of Truth," which was, he once said, exactly what he used to get each morning when he opened the front door of his house in Brooklyn.

Salley was not at all intimidated by Jackson, and this made him extremely useful on a team working with Jackson for the first time and somewhat in awe of him. During one game, Jackson failed to get his players' attention when he called out to them on the court. Afterwards, he paraphrased the Bible, as he often did, saying that players needed to be attuned to their master's voice. "P.J.," Salley countered, "do you want to further explain that politically incorrect statement?"

That first year with Jackson the Lakers were focused as they sought to master the triangle offense, to absorb all they could from the coaches who had guided Michael Jordan and the team that most of them considered the most extraordinary team ever. It was a slow process. Early into it, Scottie Pippen, who knew the triangle as well as anyone, commented that the Lakers' triangle looked more like a square.

The Michael Factor gave Jackson a tremendous, potent piece of credibility to bring to the Lakers' table, especially after Jordan left the game in 1999, not because he was ready to retire, he noted later, but because Phil Jackson had left it. When you added that to Jackson's championship rings—two for playing on the Knicks, six for coaching the Bulls, rings that made him one of the nine men in NBA history with rings for coaching and for playing—you had an individual with more clout and more mystique than any other coach in NBA history, whose presence prompted even the most jaded Lakers to go on about "this legendary coach we now have."

In his first season with the Lakers, when Jackson suggested they practice yoga, or breathe together, or meditate as a group, the guys would give each other a look that said, "Is this cat serious?" But in the end they did it because Jackson had suggested the same things to Michael Jordan, and Jordan had done them. Jordan had also been dubious, but in winning him over Jackson gained the key to unlock any NBA player's heart and mind.

So the men of the Lakers sat on the floor, breathed deeply, and kept their awareness on their exhalations. They did, in other words, what Jackson told them to do, because Jordan had done this and because they believed that if they couldn't get it done with Phil Jackson, they couldn't get it done.

But this season they were not listening or getting it done. They had not found a replacement for Glen Rice, and in a game where you were as good as your ability to rattle your opponent, what they'd lost, thought the *Los Angeles Daily News*'s beat reporter Howard Beck, was not just Glen but the *threat* of Glen.

The void left by Salley's retirement was evident in the locker room, where Salley had not let his numbers—as in 1.5 points a game—deter him from his self-appointed rounds as team policeman. If Kobe wasn't passing, if Shaq wasn't concentrating on free throws, if guys were goofing during shootarounds or laughing during a film session, they'd be hearing about it from Salley. He had no lock on his tongue, players said. This guy, thought Brian Shaw as he watched Salley in action, would get in any player's face, from one to twelve, for the betterment of the team.

A lot of times, other players would dis him. "Oh, Salley, be quiet," they'd say, "you aren't playing." But that didn't mean they weren't listening.

8

THE SEASON OF KOBE'S DISCONTENT

After a practice during that first road trip in November, Phil Jackson took Kobe aside. Nothing had changed from the year before, he told him. The offense was to run through Shaq. For the sake of other players, Kobe needed to turn down his game.

"Turn it down?" said Kobe. "I haven't turned it up."

This was the opening salvo in what Kobe would later term a battle of wills. His answer to Jackson was to score over 30 points in each of the next three games, for a total of five consecutive over-30 games and a point total that made him the league's leading scorer. In the five games after that, he went from an average of 16 shots a game to 26. He played with a killer's edge, unwilling or unable to heed Jackson's Zen-inspired admonition to "let the game come to him." The phrase Kobe preferred was "We have to beat people, dominate people. The only purpose is winning."

He wanted, he told Jackson, to be the best player in the game. "Well," said Jackson, "you have fourteen years to be that."

He wasn't about to wait. In this, his fifth year in the league, the waiting was over. "You need to save yourself, not put your body in such jeopardy," Jim Cleamons told him. "What matters is having a career over time. It isn't about having one great season where you play so hard that your body never bounces back. A lot of players have one great season."

Kobe was not daunted by the fate of other players. His career had shown him that he was not subject to the strictures that hindered them. God blessed me with this particular talent, he told himself, and I'm gonna maximize it to my potential.

In mid-November the Lakers went to Sacramento to play the Kings. The Kings were the un-Lakers, a team that *Sports Illustrated*'s Phil Taylor would describe later in the season as "retro," "fraternal," and "innocent." Their internal battles, Taylor wrote, were confined to who would get to buy the others dinner. Few teams had a claim to being the Lakers' equal, but the Kings did—in great measure because of their power forward Chris Webber, the player Kobe was already expecting would be league MVP. The night the Kings played the Lakers, Webber was on the injured list with a sprained left ankle.

When the game began, Rick Fox was on the bench. In the first six games, he had started as small forward, but when Jackson opted for Brian Shaw's steadier hand on offense, Fox was relegated to watching Kobe take over his position. But Fox was a fighter, with a fighter's stubborn faith. He had worked too hard and gone too far with his game to stop improving now. And he was practicing feverishly to step up his outside shooting.

That night Kobe's game was so uneven and off-kilter that the coaches sent word to keep the ball out of his hands. Kobe needed to start making some choices, thought Jackson. He needed to decide between what was a good opportunity for him and what was good for his teammates.

Ron Harper was poised to go into the game, watching the action from a vantage point in front of the scorer's table where the Los Angeles beat reporters were seated. Kobe was playing a real kindergarten game, thought Harper. He turned to Brad Turner of the *Riverside Press-Enterprise*, who'd been a friend since Harper's days with the Clippers. "This is ugly," he whispered to Turner.

In the fourth quarter, with less than nine minutes left, the Lakers were down 91–78. "Just open the floor," Kobe told Jackson, "and give me the ball." This was the kind of challenge that Kobe loved, with the odds stacked against him in an opponent's arena.

He played brilliantly in that last quarter, bringing the Lakers back into the game. With 2.3 seconds left in regulation, he sank a top-of-the-arc 3-pointer to tie it, then made another 8 points to win in overtime. When the buzzer sounded, he'd scored 17 of the last 22 points.

That game, thought Howard Beck, was a prime case of Kobe's best and worst. And in the locker room, the other players' praise of Kobe was measured, to put it mildly.

Jackson made no secret of his feelings when he spoke to the press. "If we had a little better defensive speed," he said, "I'd probably bench him."

The next morning, stories on the sports pages of southern California newspapers focused on Kobe's deficient performance in the first three quarters and barely mentioned his stunning play in the last quarter and in overtime. The harshest account appeared in the *Orange County Register*, written by Kevin Ding, who included in it Harper's remark to Brad Turner. By the time the team plane landed in Denver, Kobe was steaming. "Who the fuck is Kevin Ding?" he said.

That day Kobe refused to talk to reporters. This was unusual, something he did once a year, maybe twice, not more. Unlike most players, he saw the value of press coverage. "You wish all the players were like me, don't you?" he once asked John Black, director of the Lakers' publicity department, when Black was reviewing press requests with him. Kobe would never say to a reporter, as Shaq once had, "I'm not going to answer that dumb-ass question." He was cooperative, even helpful, asking the beat guys, "Need me for anything?"

But in Denver he emerged from the locker room after practice and hurried past the reporters. Howard Beck walked after him. "Can you talk?" Beck asked.

"No, I'm pissed off," said Kobe. He stopped at the elevator and pushed the call button. "Man," he said, "you guys are all so fucking negative."

The door to the elevator opened. Kobe got in and Beck followed. Kobe glared at him. "Howard, get off the elevator," he said.

Beck had been covering the Lakers for four years and had an acute understanding of players. Kobe couldn't be this pissed off about one reporter, he thought, or about one story about one game. His anger had to have a larger meaning, and what it was, Beck realized, was that the entire incident was symbolic of Kobe's season. In previous seasons, criticism of Kobe was leavened with praise. But he's getting it from all sides now, thought Beck. Whatever he does, even the great stuff, is being perceived negatively.

"There is a game within a game," Jackson told Kobe. "That game is a game with your teammates, and you need to play it. The way you're playing now will create a disharmonic feeling on this team."

But Kobe was intent on playing his own game. It was a game about creating shots, about breaking down defenses, pushing limits. It was not the game Mark Madsen thought of when he described basketball as "a game that unites," or the game Rick Fox had in mind when he called basketball "a brotherhood thing." Nor was it the game that Robert Horry remembered from his childhood in Alabama, where kids asked each other after school, "What time we meetin' at the park?" These were kids who caught the team spirit, who bonded through the sheer fun of basketball and valued winning only for the bragging rights it got you when you beat a team of older kids.

Above all, Kobe was not playing Phil Jackson's game, a game played in accordance with the tenets of Tex Winter's triangle offense. Initially, Kobe had been fascinated by the triangle. When Winter was still with the Bulls, Kobe had called him in Chicago to learn more about it. The Lakers' offensive system wasn't working, he told Winter. It didn't allow guys to feed off each other. It was just Shaq in the post and the other four guys on the perimeter waiting to see what happens.

The year before, when the Lakers were learning the triangle, it had seemed to Jackson that Kobe could hardly wait to get to the spot on the floor where Michael Jordan had been. He wanted, Jackson thought, to be Michael. At the least, he wanted Jordan's place in Winter's storied system, for Jordan's game was the measure of standard, and Kobe had long been primed to test himself against it.

His first opportunity came as a rookie when the Lakers' coach Del Harris played him in the fourth quarter of a game that quickly turned from Lakers versus Bulls into Bryant versus Jordan, the most intense and personal contest since Jordan had confronted Magic in the 1991 finals. Jordan had come to kill him, Magic would say later. His game had been a forty-eight-minute declaration that his time had come.

So Kobe and Jordan faced off, men of unmatched gifts, one at his peak, the other on the ascent. Jordan led the scoring, 36–33, but Kobe was on fire, slamming down ferocious dunks, launching perfectly calibrated shots from the perimeter.

"Did we used to jump like that?" Jordan would later ask Scottie Pippen.

"I think we did," said Pippen, "but it's so long ago I can't remember it."

Jordan was the first option of the Bulls' offense, the player Winter called the triangle's apex. The apex would ideally be a powerful center, but the Bulls did not have one, so they ran the offense through their strongest player.

The Lakers could run the triangle differently because Shaq was the perfect apex: an apex who could score, not just pass out to other players. This meant that Kobe's role in the triangle was different from Jordan's, a difference compounded because the Lakers did not have a Scottie Pippen, the player who made it possible, Jackson said, for Michael to be Michael. And while Kobe had the utmost regard for Pippen's talent and made a study of his defensive game, his particular ambitions went beyond making it possible for Shaq to be Shaq.

As the season progressed, Kobe looked so downhearted at times that Jackson would ask him, "What's the problem?"

"The game's too boring for me," Kobe would say. "The offense is so simple it doesn't display my talent."

"I realize that," Jackson told him at one point, "but we're trying to win games with the least amount of things going wrong, the fewest injuries, the least fatigue."

"But it doesn't give me what I have to have for my game."

Kobe wanted to play a creative game, to "showcase my skills," as he put it, but the triangle was not meant to showcase any particular player. The triangle was inclusive—it was about sharing the ball and passing to the open man. This kept every player involved, something that appealed equally to a rookie like Mark Madsen, who wanted to be a vital part of the team, and to seasoned players like Horry and Fox and Shaw, who reduced the game to essentials like *the more touches you get the better you play.*

Running the offense through Shaq kept the game simple. It freed opportunities for the other players because Shaq was always getting double-teamed, which meant that another man was always open. On the Bulls, Jordan had been free to break out in the fourth quarter, and Kobe was free to do the same. But if he dominated the ball throughout the game and other players didn't get their shots, they wouldn't care who you were, you'd be turning them off.

Jordan had resisted the triangle, too. "An equal-opportunity offense," he had called it, a phrase not intended as a compliment. But Jackson sold it to him on the basis that it would take pressure off him, a very smart thing to say to a player as gifted and competitive as Jordan. Jackson did not in the least suggest that Jordan couldn't do it alone. What he suggested was that of course Michael Jordan could do it alone; it was just that he didn't have to. In the end, the triangle made Jordan that most cherished of sports figures: the brilliant player who makes everyone around him better, a player who had learned "what to give," as Jordan himself put it. Players still spoke about the seventh game of the 1997 finals, when the score was tied with seconds to go and Jordan turned to his teammate Steve Kerr. "This is your chance," he told him.

"Give me the ball," said Kerr. "I'll be ready." Jordan passed out of a double team, and, with five seconds left in the game, Kerr hit the winning shot and went home a hero.

The point was that, in fact, you couldn't get it done with one guy no matter who he was, and to imply that you could was to insult your teammates, each of whom had at some point been a star himself, scoring on two guys and taking 25, 30 shots a game. Nothing was more obnoxious to players than a guy who thought he could do it all alone, who had what they called *a very individual attitude.*

They found that attitude in Kobe off the court too, when he stayed in his hotel room on the road working with his trainer, studying videos, declining to go to the mall with Derek Fisher or to have a meal with the guys or join them for a movie, even after Jackson told him that it bothered them that he didn't. In the locker room he offered a curt "What's up?" and went about his business. But then Kobe learned from experience, and he had been scathed early on by remarks from his teammates, occasioned by jealousy and by the fact that he was as far from the 'hood as a young black man could be.

When Kobe returned to the United States to go to high school, hip-hop culture was on the rise, and he was confused and startled to hear black kids speaking a language that didn't seem to be English. Later, in the NBA, when he acted like a brother or talked trash, it was a nod in his teammates' direction. But to them it seemed fake. Even the rap album he recorded owed more to the poetry of a young romantic than to the staccato rhythms of the street. True, he was tough. But he was not tough in the way guys are when they grow up hard, and most players respected only their own kind of tough. When you combined all that with his innate reserve and his youth, you knew the guys weren't likely to see much of Kobe.

That was too bad, they thought. Hanging with his teammates would give him a better sense of how to deal with them on the court and off. Players spent more time together than did most families, and it made them a brotherhood apart, with their own brand of humor and shared references, their nicknames like "B Shaw" and "D Fish," their postgame beers and cigars and that freewheeling cool that comes easily to men who expend their aggression in the game.

The guys always said that if you laughed at a joke about another guy, you were open to getting cracked on yourself. They had a saying for it: if you grin, you're in. Kobe didn't grin. On the team plane he watched movies on his DVD or pretended to sleep while across the aisle guys kept two card games going at once, of Guts and In Between. "Hey," Brian Shaw kept telling him, "your money's good at this table." But Kobe didn't join in.

Even Jordan played cards with the guys, players said. Not a lot, but enough to give his teammates a sense of what he was about, enough to let them know that he was interested in them. And the guys on the Lakers couldn't help wondering, Does Kobe think he's better than me?

In some ways, perhaps he did. Early on, he had said privately that he wasn't like the other guys. This was a boast, not a lament. He was not your typical basketball player, at least not if you held to the stereo-type that cast the essential concerns of players as *play basketball, get laid, sleep in.* "I almost fell asleep," he said after one team meeting. "They were talking about club drugs, and I don't go to clubs."

From the time he entered the league he'd noticed that he could do things easily on the court that were difficult from a coach's point of view or from the viewpoint of his teammates. By now, he had put so much work into his game that he believed he could make any shot in any situation. And it had become clear to him that most players did not work as hard as he did.

He saw around him players with old legs and out-of-shape bodies. He couldn't believe how much stretching B Shaw had to do to get out on the court or the shape that Harper was in. Kobe was twenty-two years old. He was in prime condition and had yet to encounter a chal-lenge he couldn't meet, had yet to set a goal he couldn't reach.

He might not think this meant that he was better. But it meant that he was different.

On November 14, 2000, the Lakers played the Denver Nuggets. Shaq sat out the game, nursing a slight sprain in his left ankle. Any game that Shaq didn't play in was a game that Kobe especially wanted to win, and he had his own ideas about how to do it. When Jackson told him to take the ball to the basket, he shot three consecutive outside shots. When Jackson told him to kick the ball out, he drove to the basket.

He would get the ball and dribble in place as the shot clock ran down, seeking an opening to charge through, ignoring teammates who were open. Man, what is this? players would think. He'll spin, double-pump, be falling away over two or three people, and he doesn't pass the ball to guys standing there waving.

But Kobe did not want to relinquish the ball when he drew a triple team, a circumstance that presented the exact sort of challenge that improved his focus. You can bring all you want, he thought, as the opposition gathered in front of him.

"Pass the ball," Tex Winter would tell him.

"Why?" said Kobe. "No one can stop me."

In the fourth quarter the Lakers led, 82–69. With seven minutes remaining, Denver went on a 15-point run. After six minutes the Lakers were down by one. Kobe had scored 32 points, but after he missed a jumper Jackson gave the last shot to J. R. Rider. With seventeen seconds left in the game, Rider got the ball and held it, trying to get a good look at the basket as Kobe clamored for the ball, frustration mounting by the second. That was typical Kobe, they all thought later. In situations where most guys don't want anything to do with the ball, he couldn't wait to get his hands on it.

Rider was still holding the ball when the buzzer sounded. Kobe stormed over to Jackson, furious that he had not been given that last shot. They were still getting into it as Rider left the court, thinking that Jackson's decision was surprising. He really hadn't expected to get a chance to be the hero.

Yet if Jackson wanted Kobe reined in, he also knew there was little he could do about it. Of the many things he learned from Red Holzman, his coach when he played for the Knicks, perhaps the most enduring was the wisdom of taking a breath and a step back and letting problems right themselves. There were things a coach did not have to deal with, Holzman used to say. The press and the team are judge and jury, and a coach can let many things go by because they'll take care of them.

Jackson had seen this syndrome play out dozens of times. A problem becomes public, causes pressure to build on an errant player, and forces him into line.

That process had already started. "Write what you see," Shaq was telling the press, by way of casting attention on Kobe's playing style, which he and other players regarded as selfish and disruptive.

They understood that Kobe's talent was on a different level. Putting Kobe on the Lakers, thought Brian Shaw, is like putting me on a high school team. I could dominate the game, I could shoot the ball every time and do whatever I want on the floor, and maybe they'd devise a way to stop me or maybe I'd keep shooting over four or five people. In Kobe's position you either dominate or you play the right way. It was a choice you had to make.

And in Denver, possibly to hasten that choice, Jackson told the press that the fissure in the team ran wider and deeper than generally imagined. "The problem isn't Kobe and Shaq," he said. "The problem is Kobe and everybody."

This was becoming the season of Kobe Bryant's discontent. That was ironic in itself, since it was also the season when informed observers watched him and knew they were seeing one of those once-in-a-lifetime players they'd be telling their children and grandchildren about.

Kobe's game had evolved light-years beyond his amazingly improved game of the season before. At twenty-two, he was reaching the level everyone expected him to attain someday, but not yet.

Why, Kobe wondered, would his players resent him for stepping up? It was as if they thought he was trying to destroy the team when he was just working hard: trying to improve, trying to make them all win, to bring a game that could daunt the opposition, that could let them take the next championship series in four or five games instead of six or seven. Yes, sure, he was playing this game for himself, but he was also playing it for them.

This was supposed to be his best season. He had looked forward to it so much. But it's getting to where it's so hard, he thought. Not being able to showcase my skills, so much criticism coming from my players. I don't know if I can take it anymore.

I just don't know if I can take it.

In the days following the Denver game, Kobe kept his own counsel, as he always did, looking to himself for strength and sustenance. For all the criticism, he had no plans to change. The fact was, he was leading the team in assists, though it didn't seem that anybody wanted to acknowledge it. As you go through the process, he told himself, you have to be ready to take a lot of criticism. You could say, "I'm just gonna fold," and go with what the bunch is telling you to do. Or you could be persistent and go with what you envision.

To persist, to envision. It was the language of a dreamer, the language of Don Quixote and of a player who loved every aspect of basketball and found sensual pleasure in the sound of the bouncing ball, the sound of shoes squeaking on the floorboards. For Kobe Bryant it always came back to this, to an involvement in the game that had as much to do with romance as with athletics. No wonder that when he was asked what a young man should do about turning pro, or not, he answered, "Follow your heart." He, too, was following his heart, unmindful of efforts to derail him.

"Dammit," the Lakers' general manager Jerry West said to him, "you're so damn stubborn you remind me of me when I was a player."

"You have to be stubborn," said Kobe.

But he felt miserable, beleaguered. One day he looked up at the sky. "Just guide me," he said. It was the strangest thing, he thought later, because after that it was like the game just opened up. He went on a hot streak, continuing to lead the Lakers in scoring and assists, playing the kind of game he had fantasized about, a game with jumpers that sent the ball swishing into the basket from 22 feet, with reverse layups and 360s that set the crowd shouting, "Kobe! Kobe! Kobe!"

I haven't seen anything like this, thought Horace Grant, since Number 23 retired.

Until now, Kobe's scoring average had been 40 percent. The reason for that, Jackson told him, was that he was taking 40 percent shots. But his shot choice suddenly improved dramatically, and Jackson was telling him, "You might become as good as Michael Jordan."

By late November, Kobe was in the zone. He could hardly believe the feeling. He'd be tearing down the court, and it felt like he wasn't even running hard. It seemed like everything slowed down. And when he was shooting and couldn't miss the basket, things got really, really slow and the basket seemed huge as he approached it.

He'd been hearing about the zone since he was a child. It sounded so magical that he had tried to get there. OK, he'd tell himself, focus on every part of your body; just concentrate and get really, really light. Only when he was older did he realize that the zone is something that just happens. Now that he was there, in it, the sense of possibility he had always felt became a sense of having no limits. Everything was effortless. It's just so easy, he kept thinking: I can do anything I want.

This was the state of being that Tex Winter called "relaxed abandon," the state that Phil Jackson had in mind when he wrote that basketball players live for those moments when they can lose themselves completely. Having entered that state, Kobe tried to understand how it came to him and what it was about. Things just got to the point, he thought, where whatever the path He put me on, it just broke me down and I let go. It's like God broke me down to build me up.

For all the work he'd put in, what he was feeling had to do with something more than the game. No amount of practice in the world is going to get you to this point, he thought, because at this particular point in time what you're feeling is faith in your skills. Belief. It's like you become something higher.

You become the game.

9

SOMETHING WAS WRONG WITH SHAQ

Something was wrong with Shaq, and it wasn't just that his field goal percentage had dropped from 57 percent to 41 percent or that his right thumb was sprained so that the ball couldn't roll off his hand as it normally did.

Watching him play, Derek Fisher could just about feel his exhaustion. Shaq had been on vacation from late June to late September. For most players that would be a good, solid rest. But big people, thought Fisher, need more downtime than other players—especially a big man who had just won the NBA championship, led the league in scoring with an average of 29.7 points, averaged 13.6 rebounds a game, and been MVP in the regular season and the play-offs. He expended himself so much to accomplish all those things in one season, thought Fisher, that he doesn't have anything left physically to put into it now.

This was not the Shaq who went ballistic when other guys failed to share his determination. Fisher still remembered an incident during the '98 Western Conference play-off series against Utah, when the Lakers were down 0–2 in the series. At the end of a practice huddle, when it was customary to shout "One-two-three, Lakers!" Nick Van Exel shouted, "One-two-three, Cancún!" At this implication that Van Exel was looking forward to vacation when his team still had pressing business, Shaq complained bitterly to management, and Van Exel's vacation from the Lakers became permanent.

If you mentioned this chain of events to Shaq, he smiled a little half-smile, because it portrayed him in his idealized self-image. This was Shaq as the watchdog, the captain, the drill sergeant. It was Shaq protecting his turf and, beyond that, protecting his claim to being the biggest, baddest, toughest dog to ever play the game.

But Shaq was not bringing what he had brought before. His defensive edge was lost. Last year Jackson had sold him on transition defense, but this year he couldn't seem to finesse its speedy retreat.

Ever since Shaq arrived in the league, there had been those who suspected that he wasn't serious, that he coasted on his size and talent. He should be practicing free throws, they said, instead of making movies and cutting rap albums. True, Shaq had sold a million albums. But what use was it to be the first professional athlete to earn a gold record when he'd never won a championship trophy?

"If I could just get that one championship . . . ," Shaq used to say. Hearing this, the guys never thought he meant that he wanted only *one*. But they were beginning to wonder if that was exactly what he meant.

The championship season had been Shaq's answer to every doubter, every critic, to everyone who claimed he didn't work hard enough, didn't care. He was so dominant that year that even Sarge, who had never once complimented his game, put an arm around him midway through the play-offs and told him, "You're doing pretty good."

As Kareem Abdul-Jabbar had before him, Shaq engendered hopelessness in the opposition. When he was on the court, you saw fear in his opponent's eyes. Now that was changing. There was no fear, no hopelessness. And suddenly teams that had buckled when confronting the Lakers saw that Shaquille O'Neal was no longer the player he once had been. And they knew that the game had changed and that they had a chance.

Shaq's season was getting harder for him, even as what he referred to as his "knick-knack injuries" were healing. His improved health was the result of acupuncture treatments, which had produced a classically Shaq statement: "Thank God for the Chinese."

But he still suffered the incalculable effects of what he called "my free-throw thing." From the start, this inability to make free throws had plagued him. Now Jackson was saying that unless he got a handle on it, the Lakers couldn't win. Opposing teams were committing to the Hack-a-Shaq defense, forcing him to the free-throw line, where he generally blew it. For a proud and insecure man who had emblazoned the Superman logo on his front door, whose motto was the acronym T.W.I.S.M.—The World Is Mine—the "free-throw thing" was destined to be what Jackson delicately called "a very sore spot for him."

In fact, it was an ongoing humiliation. And he must have dreaded going for a shot, knowing he would be fouled and forced again to betray this glaring weakness. Every action of every player enhanced the team's sense of well-being or chipped away at it, and Shaq's free-throw shooting chipped away at it insistently. Players grumbled that a man earning his salary should have his basic skills intact. Watching Shaq miss free throws was a tedious, enervating staple of team life, one that other players handled by assuming as cavalier an attitude as possible. As Shaq approached the line, guys on the bench would elbow each other, saying, "Hey, check this out." The coaching staff tried to help him, but he wouldn't work with them. In college he had tried to get help, but his coach told him to shoot underhanded, and he was mortified. "This is a granny shot," he had told him. "Please don't make me shoot them like this." Now, nearly a decade later, the problem was so excruciating that he could not face it long enough to make it better.

Shooting free throws could daunt even the purest shooters. Jerry West once said he'd rather take a shot in the most hopeless situation than shoot when the game reached a dead stop and every eye in the arena was on him. When it came to making free throws, players adopted individual and eccentric form, and many high-percentage shooters were wedded to elaborate rituals that involved dribbling in place, stepping forward or back, knee bending, or sharp breaths in and out.

Kobe was an 87 percent free-throw shooter and not about to comment on Shaq's problem except obliquely. "Everybody has a weakness," he observed. "It's just who hides theirs the best."

Shaq's weakness, out there for the most uneducated eye to see, inspired a surprising number of people to send him healing crystals and amulets and to approach Phil Jackson on the street, telling him they had the answer for Shaq. Each day Shaq's mail was filled with the business cards of psychologists and physical therapists, of hypnotherapists and Scientologists. Even his three-year-old daughter had advice for him, telling him during the 2000 play-offs, "Good luck. Bend your knees."

And now, the more Shaq faltered, the more Kobe stepped into the breach, which only exacerbated the battle brewing between them.

It had become a sports reporter's commonplace to say that Shaq was the dominant player in the game and that Kobe was the most dynamic. Beyond that, assessments of their relative worth depended on who did the assessing. Some believed that Shaq was resentful because he needed Kobe more than Kobe needed him. Others said that you could duplicate a Kobe more easily than you could duplicate a Shaq. Either way, the irrefutable facts were that Kobe had never played on an NBA team that Shaq wasn't on and that Shaq had never won a championship until Kobe became a great player.

Their current battle was an extension of the battle that had, two years earlier, prompted Shaq to conclude an argument that he and Kobe got into during practice by slapping Kobe across the face. It was the battle that surfaced during the Lakers' championship year when Shaq stated in a team meeting that Kobe was playing too selfishly for them to win. Before, the battle had been about containing Kobe. Now it was escalating into a battle over who would dominate the team. Kobe was posting a career-high scoring average, leading the team in assists, and grabbing a fair share of rebounds.

Even though Jackson insisted that the offense run through Shaq, Kobe figured he might as well take the shot himself rather than pass to Shaq, who, likely as not, would be fouled and miss his free throws.

There was a way to work with Shaq, and every player on the team knew it. Shaq depended on other players to get him the ball, and if you did this he would kick it out to you all day, glad to reward teammates who showed him respect. But if he thought you were trying to take something from him, he got nasty.

Shaq had been taught to be a leader. He was not about to cede that position. If Kobe showed him respect, he was more than ready to enhance his play as second option, to be the big brother, to give their partnership cozy nicknames like "The Dynamic Duo" and "The Combo." But he was not about to do the dirty work, to be out there like a grunt defending the pick and roll, running the floor, taking on the rebounding and shot blocking, while Kobe scored big numbers and seized the glory.

Taking a cue from Jackson, Shaq waged his battle through the press. "If you want the big dog to guard the big yard," he told reporters, "you've got to give the big dog something to do. You've got to give him toys. You've got to feed him. You can't have him sit and do nothing."

During practice he called for the ball with his eyes, sending messages to freeze Kobe out. As Kobe led the league in scoring, while Shaq was relegated to fifth place, rumor had it that during games, Shaq was using hand signals to keep the ball from Kobe. "If I am," said Shaq, "they sure aren't working."

10

THE BEGINNINGS

Shaquille O'Neal and Kobe Bryant owed their presence on the Los Angeles Lakers to one individual, Jerry West: mythic player of the sixties and seventies, general manager of the Lakers during the eighties and nineties, and the only person that both men admired without reservation.

For as long as there had been a team called the Los Angeles Lakers, there had been the Lakers player named Jerry West. The association began in 1960, when the Minneapolis Lakers abandoned the Land of the Lakes and went west, literally and figuratively.

No one ever shot the ball better than Jerry West. His career average of 27.0 was fourth only to Elgin Baylor, Wilt Chamberlain, and Michael Jordan and did not even hint at his prowess because West played the game before the 3-point shot was instituted in 1979. This was more significant in his case than in Chamberlain's or Baylor's because West was a brilliant outside shooter, scoring from considerable distances with a frequency that would have increased his average by as much as 30 percent, enough to easily outstrip Jordan's record of 31.7.

He was known as Mr. Clutch and would forever be the embodiment of a certain type of basketball machismo and the essential ethics of grace under pressure, cool under fire. West never feared taking a key shot. Shooting late in the game was easier, he said. It was when he concentrated best because late was when a single foul, a single miscue, meant so much. For all that—and despite his cockiness on the court—West was a nervous player. It was nerves, he said, that gave him his energy. But nerves did not deter him from firing off shots like the one from 55 feet that tied the third game against the Knicks during the 1970 finals, a shot still recalled as the most spectacular clutch shot ever.

Jerry West was born and raised in a dusty West Virginia town too small to have a post office. The nearest was in Cabin Creek, which later prompted Elgin Baylor to nickname him "Zeke from Cabin Creek," a moniker that stuck and that West hated.

He was another player who came to the game because it was one of the few pastimes available to him. Soon what began as a stay against boredom became his one true love and later, his ticket to a better life. His college career with the West Virginia Mountaineers would become a legend. For the next generations of rural boys and girls, Jerry West, son of a mine electrician, would be proof that the American Dream was viable.

But when he retired in 1973 and his Number 44 jersey was ensconced high in the rafters of the Great Western Forum, he was neither happy nor satisfied. Some of his frustrations were owed to timing: in college, he was MVP of the NCAA Final Four, but the larger prize, player of the year, went to Oscar Robertson. As a Laker, he had shared the credit and glory with Baylor, then with Wilt Chamberlain. But the wound that could never heal resulted from those nine times that he went to the finals and came away with a single trophy. To be the only player named finals MVP while playing on a losing team was like a slap in the face, he said.

You had to go through it to understand what it was like to get so close but not get there, to have time running out and every fiber in your body straining to win the game while the fans of the other team are chanting, "We're number one! We're number one!" It was as if everything in the universe was against you: time, fate, the referees. "They didn't even call the time-outs right," West said after his sixth trip to the finals. How could you give so much, he kept thinking, and play until there was nothing left in your body to give, and still not win?

The unfairness of it never left him. He never made peace with it, never stopped obsessing over what might have been had he gotten just one more chance at the basket. Others viewed his career as illustrious, but for West the losses would always outweigh the wins. Looking back, he would say that his years as a player had "sort of been on the tragic side of everything."

Later his image was chosen to grace the NBA logo, a tribute to the skill and achievements that set him above and apart. But it was his disappointments that bound him to that mass of players who never quite get what they came for, and this imbued the logo with a rich, if unintended, meaning.

By the mid-1970s, the Lakers were languishing, a situation not helped by Chamberlain's departure in 1975 or by the fact that the sport's popularity was, more generally, running a distant second to that of baseball. It was a difficult transitional time, as a white sport became a predominantly black sport, and a game that thrived on star players lost a generation of older stars before the next generation had emerged.

In the interim, the NBA was reduced to a single icon. The good news was that this icon was Julius Erving, otherwise known as "Dr. J," originator of acrobatics and hang time. As he soared toward the basket, dropping the ball from impossible angles, Dr. J transformed basketball into an above-the-rim experience and made it astonishing. He never tried to put on a show, though the crowd's ecstatic reaction affirmed that this was what he was doing. And maybe, he thought, people took vicarious pleasure from seeing him act out on the court with an abandon that life didn't allow them.

For a time, Dr. J was basketball's saving figure. His game, like the game of every truly great player, was not simply exciting; it had a resonance that extended beyond basketball, that left observers with the ennobling sense that a man can do what cannot be done in the ordinary course of things.

Erving came to the NBA from the ABA in 1976. He was still at his peak in 1979 when ESPN became the first television channel dedicated exclusively to sports. At the same time, the American press was taking a cue from the personality-driven journalism pioneered by *People* magazine, which had been launched five years earlier. These factors combined to create a media poised to celebrate sports' larger-than-life figures, to exploit and worship Great American Archetypes like the two that showed up for the final NBA draft of the decade. Larry Bird was a white man from rural Indiana who would become the greatest forward since Bob Pettit. His college opponent, Earvin Johnson, nicknamed Magic, was a black man from East Lansing, Michigan, whose gifts would reinvent existing notions of how the game was played. Both were leaders, both were team players, both had a game and a work ethic that gave their teams something to which they could aspire. These were the great new stars the game and the fans had been waiting for. The NBA was waiting for them, too, and together they led basketball to a popularity it had never previously enjoyed.

With his huge, great hands and no-look passes, Magic was a playmaker like none before him. He floated down the court, flanked by the wing players, a vision of grace and speed that was at once beautiful and scary. Magic arrived weeks after Jerry Buss wrote a $67.5 million check to Jack Kent Cooke for the Lakers, the Los Angeles Kings, and their home arena known—for this was Los Angeles—as the Fabulous Forum. With the arrival of Magic the Lakers quickly became more popular in Los Angeles than the Dodgers or the Rams, and Buss knew that he had not squandered his money.

By then, Jerry West could have disappeared into the sunset, resurfacing as an honored guest at the occasional game or testimonial. Instead, in 1982, after a few seasons of coaching and consulting for the Lakers, he signed on as their general manager, turning his considerable energy to making them the champions his own Lakers teams had too rarely been. West was not given to half measures. His job inevitably became a mission, a quest to find and draft the right players, to nurture and develop them and, in the largest sense, to heal the wound he carried by putting together a team that could not be bested.

Throughout the eighties, basketball's popularity grew exponentially. The Lakers led the charge, armed with the two things television coverage thrived on: a lot of flash and a bona fide star. If Jerry West embodied the Lakers' spirit, it was Magic who embodied its success.

Later, West would say that Magic surprised him, that he took the game to a level no one could have anticipated, and that this proved you could never really know what was inside a player. The only thing you knew for certain was what your eyes showed you when that player was on the court, and what you saw might be all you got, or it might be the tip of an iceberg, the visible part of something deeper and more daunting. Magic fit West's estimation of that rarest kind of player, one blessed with the mental toughness to weather the hard losses and compete the next night.

Magic's smile melted the distance between the great star he had become and the fans who adored him. It left them with the warm feeling that they knew him. They didn't, of course, not as a basketball player or as a man. As an athlete, Magic was terrifically disciplined, terrifically driven, the smile not at all in evidence as he pushed and prodded everyone around him. As a man he was testimony to Oscar Wilde's line "I can resist anything except temptation." The area just beyond the locker-room showers became his private singles club, where his after-game activities were another kind of showtime and the reason he was always the last player dressed and always smiling when he appeared in the locker room for his postgame interviews.

In November 1991 he announced that he was HIV positive. Everyone on the team and in the organization adored Magic Johnson. He was their son, their brother. The news devastated them all, from Jerry West to Lee Moore, the security guard who had worked for the team for twenty-four years and remembered West and Baylor as players but would always tell new guys that he had never seen a player quite like Magic. "The man was just good; you had to give it to him. He had eyes in the back of his head."

Once retired, Magic made several attempts to return, but that was not to be. Other players did not want to be on the court with him and were vocal about it, leaving West to do what he would have eventually done in any case: begin scouting for the future and constructing a new team that could equal the brilliance of Showtime.

The player West most wanted for that new team was Shaquille O'Neal, center on the Orlando Magic, whose mention was generally preceded or followed by the legend "one of the most dominant big men in the game." Shaq was about to become a free agent and was letting it be known that he was not pleased with the Magic's record, its coach, or what he perceived as a lack of support from the front office.

To get Shaq, it would be necessary to loosen up a considerable amount of money, so a roster purge began that grew extensive enough to prompt the Magic to investigate whether they could file tampering charges.

First to go was Vlade Divac, the popular, congenial 7'1" center from Yugoslavia who'd been with the Lakers since 1989. Divac was well regarded by the front office, but several factors militated toward his being traded: he played the same position as Shaq and played it less convincingly while earning a hefty $4 million a year, with more years to go at bigger money. The trick for the Lakers' front office was to lose Divac's salary without taking on someone else's big salary. The one way to accomplish this was to trade him for a draft pick. In the upcoming 1996 draft, the Lakers had the twenty-seventh pick. The Charlotte Hornets were holding the thirteenth pick and needed a center, which seemed serendipitous to everyone but Vlade Divac, who loved L.A.'s beaches and weather and had a wife who dabbled in acting. He would rather retire, he said, than leave Los Angeles for Charlotte, North Carolina.

But Divac relented, and the deal was set in motion. "We just traded away our starting center," commented assistant coach Bill Bertka, "to shoot for the moon."

There was, in fact, a certain cushion in these high-risk maneuvers. If Shaq didn't sign with them, the Lakers would still have their choice of Dikembe Mutombo or Dale Davis, big men who could enhance any team they played on. In the worst case, they could play their power forward Elden Campbell at center, but Campbell was a lumbering fellow, and this option was not one for which anyone had much enthusiasm.

While waiting for Shaq to decide, West analyzed the coming draft. The 1996 draft would include some of the youngest players in NBA history and some of the most exceptional since the 1984 draft, which produced Michael Jordan, Hakeem Olajuwon, John Stockton, and Charles Barkley. There was Allen Iverson, leaving Georgetown after his junior year; Stephon Marbury; Marcus Camby; Ray Allen. And there was Kobe Bryant, the best high school player in the country, whose intention to skip college and go straight to the NBA had been criticized by everyone from the usual claque of cynical reporters to Marty Blake, the NBA's director of scouting services. "He's kidding himself," wrote Blake. "Sure, he'd like to come out. I'd like to be a movie star. He's not ready."

Kobe worked out for several teams, including the 76ers, who wanted a look at this hometown product who already had legions of fans and a stellar reputation. But the Sixers, with the first draft pick, planned to take Iverson and saw, in Kobe's workout, nothing that changed their minds.

Jerry West saw something more when Kobe worked out for him. Simply, unequivocally, he saw the best workout he'd ever seen. He called Mitch Kupchak, his assistant and a former Laker, whose knee injury had forced an early move from the court to the front office. There was a kid, West said, that Mitch and Coach Del Harris ought to look at. So they watched Kobe go one-on-one against assistant coach James Worthy, one of Showtime's great players. Within minutes, Kupchak and Harris glanced at each other in recognition of the fact that they were watching something extraordinary. And Kobe seemed to be such a good, happy-go-lucky kid, obviously well raised, saying "yes, sir," and "no, sir." West's teenage son Ryan was at the workout, and he and Kobe hit it off. Later, when they all went for sandwiches at the local Subway, Kobe talked to Ryan and not to the men, and this brought home the fact that this incredible talent was a seventeen-year-old.

A few days later West called Kobe's agent, Arn Tellem. He was going to figure out a way, he said, to bring Kobe to the Lakers.

With the roster duly cleared of big salaries, the Lakers offered Shaq $98 million for seven years, an offer he nearly accepted although the Magic were offering a million more and were willing to front-load the arrangement with $20 million. But the issue, Shaq insisted, wasn't money. He had come into the NBA thinking he'd be satisfied to have a supercool car and to be able to buy a house for his parents. Instead, at age twenty-four, he was set for life, with his 18-carat white-gold and diamond-encrusted crosses and bracelets, his twenty-car garage, his mansion overlooking the lake in the gated community of Isleworth, where Tiger Woods also had a place. "Man, I mean I got money," he said. But then he learned that Alonzo Mourning was signing with the Miami Heat for $110 million, and Shaq was not about to make less than Alonzo Mourning. The frantic last-minute dealings gave West an opportunity to reinvent his Mr. Clutch persona and to bring new meaning to the phrase "fancy footwork." The offer Shaq accepted was for $123 million for seven years. West said later that if Shaq hadn't agreed, he would have jumped out a window of the highrise office of Shaq's agent.

That was hyperbolic, of course, but an index nonetheless of what was by then obvious: to Jerry West, acquiring Shaquille O'Neal was not simply a deal, and Shaq was not simply a great player. West knew value, he knew talent, and he knew a lot about players' hearts and minds. He would never make the kind of blunder that the ham-handed Jerry Krause of the Bulls had made when he informed Michael Jordan that Jordan was the Bulls' "property." Shaq was not property to West, that $123 million notwithstanding. He was "this prize," and obtaining him, West said, might be "the single most important thing we've ever done."

So it went: Shaq in, Divac out, the roster purged to such a degree that only five of the sixteen players for the new season had been on the team the previous year. Kobe came in on a three-year contract for about $1 million a year while picking up major endorsement money from Sprite and Adidas. With their second draft pick, the Lakers acquired a 6′1″ guard from Arkansas named Derek Fisher.

With the arrival of Kobe and Shaq, a sense of excitement returned to the Forum that rivaled the excitement generated by the Showtime Lakers, who had the crowd reverberating even at moments when they weren't playing. The roar of the crowd, Kobe would say later, made him run wild. Shaq, too, fed off it, basked in it. For he loved nothing more than being, as he now described himself, a big fish in a big pond.

Jerry West kept refining the roster. Having promised Shaq that he would surround him with first-rate players, he was intent on keeping that promise. In 1997, when the starters included Eddie Jones and Nick Van Exel, he signed Robert Horry and Rick Fox. But the on-court performance never quite equaled the potential of the roster. The team took to calling itself "the Lake Show," to make the point that they no longer were the Showtime Lakers, something that anyone watching them could figure out. If they had the force and power that came with youth, they lacked the qualities necessary to balance it, the steadiness and player intelligence that come from maturity.

Kobe's presence had been unsettling. Players resented him. He was green. And when he made mistakes that cost them the coaches would say, "He's young; be patient with him." The word *patience* was not a favorite word with players. Shaq, in particular, resented it. No one provided a cushion for *him* when he came to the NBA after his junior year of college. No one told the team, "Cut him some slack," or said, "You have to allow Shaq a certain number of mistakes." As far as he and the others were concerned, once Kobe and his family made the decision to come to the NBA, the rules had to be the same for him as for everybody. You have to sleep in the bed you made.

Kobe's teammates had complained about him since he turned up at camp four weeks after his eighteenth birthday, a kid whose preferred game, they quickly decided, was one on five. They told him to pass the ball, and when he didn't they yelled at him to pass it, and when he didn't pass it then either, they got angry. Kobe was fluent in Italian and Spanish but could not hear, they said, in three languages. In one game, he ignored a teammate who was open under the basket. "If you ever do that again," the player told him, "I'll break your motherfucking ass."

Midway through Kobe's second season, 1997–98, Del Harris cut Kobe's playing time by nearly seven minutes a game. He would take Kobe out, Harris stated, whenever Kobe didn't play team ball. But the flashy plays that so annoyed the coach and the team were thrilling to the fans, and Harris's decision did not sit well with Jerry Buss, the Lakers' owner. Still, Harris was adamant. Kobe didn't know how to play a team game, he said. "He didn't learn it in high school, and he didn't go to college, so he has to learn it here."

It was all new to him, the pressure, the visibility, the applause. Here's this kid in a man's game, thought Harris, and he's not ready. He should be on a team that isn't expected to win right now.

Watching him dribble, hanging on to the ball while he searched out an opening in the defense, Jerry West wondered, How in the world can this kid do this?

My God, West would think, as he drove home in his black Mercedes after games, is he ever going to learn to use his teammates better? Is he ever going to learn situations in games? Is he ever going to learn to value the basketball?

But Kobe had his own notions, his own scenarios. If there was a moment when he made that all too plain, it came during his appearance in the All-Star game in 1998. He headed toward the basket with the ball, and there in the pivot was Karl Malone, the Utah Jazz's power forward, one of the league's fifty greatest players and the most prolific forward in NBA history, ready to set a pick for him. But Kobe waved Malone away, clearing the space to drive and dunk. "When younger guys tell me to get out of the way," an irate Malone told George Karl, who was coaching the west's players, "that's a game I don't need to be in."

Months later, the Jazz swept the Lakers in the Western Conference semifinals. The year before, the Lakers had faced the Jazz in the semifinals. They were down 3–1 going into the fifth game. With eleven seconds left in the fourth quarter and the score tied, Del Harris told the players to spread the floor and let Kobe go for it, a stunning responsibility to place on a teenager whose minutes had yet to number in double digits. Kobe took aim from sixteen feet. The ball went up and never met the rim or the backboard. He fired off two more air balls in overtime, and when the game ended the Lakers were officially on summer vacation. Shaq hurried over to Kobe and put an arm around him as they walked together off the court. "Hey, you're gonna be a great one," Shaq told him. "Don't let this bother you."

But afterward, Harris caught a lot of flak for his decision. Even the Jazz's fabled guard, John Stockton, said pointedly that Kobe was young, that the game was new to him, and that he'd been asked to take a very tough shot. All season long, Harris complained, he'd been criticized for not playing Kobe enough, and now he was being criticized for playing him. If he had it to do again, he maintained, he would still give the ball to Kobe, and the one person who did not doubt the wisdom of that assertion was Kobe himself. True, he was very young, but either because of this or despite it, he was not hampered by fear of failure. Sooner or later he'd manage to succeed at whatever he tried, and this meant that he defined failure as not trying. In the end the only thing that would have bothered him, he said, was if he hadn't had the guts to take the shot.

By the end of the next season, even within the ongoing soap opera that is the life of a basketball team, the Lakers were notably divided, unmoved and uninspired by a coach who no longer had their respect and was mired in his own frustrations. "Can anybody fucking guard this guy?" Harris had demanded after Maurice Taylor made two 3-pointers with Shaq right in front of him. "We're playing the fucking Clippers."

Still, they made it to the Western Conference finals, where they again faced the Jazz. They were swept in a humiliating series, and afterward Shaq could not contain his anger. He had scored 38 points, 18 of them in the fourth quarter. His adrenaline was still pumping when he stormed from the court to the weight room and proceeded to tear it apart, hurling everything but mirrors because he was superstitious enough to worry that breaking mirrors might bring him seven years' bad luck. Finally, Jerry West was sent for. He entered the weight room moments later, a study in the unruffled cool that crisis tended to produce in him, the quality that had made him a clutch shooter. "Yes," he told Shaq, "the team let you down. We don't have it together yet, but we will."

"You know," West said then, "I went to the finals seven times before I won."

West always seemed to know the right thing to say. Those words seized Shaq's attention and cast his own frustrations in a whole new perspective.

Yet the next year, the season of the lockout, the situation worsened. West was still altering the roster, but each change seemed to make the team shakier. Dennis Rodman was signed at the insistence of Jerry

Buss, who knew Rodman from the clubs and haunts they both frequented. Rodman made a good start but soon seemed less concerned about playing well than about upholding his status as the league's leading eccentric. Most traumatic was the departure of Eddie Jones, the shooting guard traded to the Charlotte Hornets in March for Glen Rice. No player had been more beloved than Eddie, by the team, by fans, by women and men who worked at the Forum. Until lately, Del Harris was playing Rick Fox at small forward, with Kobe as backup to him and to Jones. Kobe was not ready to be a starter, Harris determined, and in any case you don't send Eddie Jones to the bench. But when Robert Horry missed the opening home game of the '99 season to attend the birth of his son in Houston, the lineup was reshuffled and Kobe was put in as a starter. That was Scottie Pippen's first game as a former Bull, and Kobe destroyed Pippen that night. A performance on that level meant that he would someday be a starter, and, in fact, he started every game after that, setting the stage for Jones to go. There was a bitter irony in this since when Jones was attending Temple University in Philadelphia he had become something of a big brother to Kobe, always checking up on him, driving him to pickup games. Eddie Jones was Kobe's only friend on the Lakers. He left the team angry and possibly feeling that no good deed goes unpunished.

But Jones was not forgotten by the many who regarded him as such a fine young gentleman, with so much charm. Wilma Dennis, head usher at the Forum for seventeen years, had seen a lot of players come and go. She often missed them, but her feelings about Eddie were more intense. When he was traded, she would say, something went out of the game for her that she never got back.

Twelve games into the season it became clear that Del Harris had lost control of the team. He was fired. The Lakers' management turned to Kurt Rambis, the assistant coach. Rambis possessed the same fierce dedication as a coach that he had had as a player for the Lakers, when his coach, Pat Riley, called him "our Rambo." That doggedness, combined with easy charm, had made him a favorite of the fans. Rambis had a degree in psychology and was very smart about people and about the game. He was just beginning to make his name as a coach, attracting attention as a serious talent. To take on a divided team, in the middle of a truncated season, was by definition an impossible task with scant prospect of a happy ending. But Rambis had cast his lot with the team ever since joining them in 1981. He took the job, in the process taking a bullet for the Lakers.

They made it to the play-off semifinals, where they were swept by the Spurs. That loss brought to the surface all the bad feeling within the team and among the fans. Toward the end of the final game, when Rice missed a key shot, an angry crowd began chanting, "Eddie! Eddie! Eddie!"

That series decimated the Lakers, crushing them emotionally and physically. Those four losing games were their final games at the Forum before their move downtown to the Staples Center. When the players returned to clear out their lockers, all the disappointments and all the losses overwhelmed them, and they packed their bags in silence, tears in their eyes.

The championship hovered in the far distance, unobtainable. Jerry West took to observing games from the enclosing safety of the north tunnel. He had always watched games uneasily—pacing outside the Forum, or after seeing part of a road game on television, storming out of his house insisting that he couldn't take it anymore. Finally, when the team he had built was on the cusp of victory, he could not watch at all. As the Lakers went up against the Trail Blazers in the 1999–2000 Western Conference finals, Jerry West drove the 405 Freeway, heading north, then south, then north again, taking in the occasional update on his cell phone. A few weeks after the Lakers team he had brought together became the World Champions, Jerry West retired.

In his absence, the hopes of the team still rested on the two men on whom he had bet the farm, the only players on the Lakers known by their first names, a distinction that only Wilt Chamberlain, Kareem Abdul-Jabbar, and Magic Johnson had achieved before them. Shaq and Kobe were so versatile, Pat Riley would say, that the Lakers had, in effect, not two but four great stars.

And these great stars were bound together for the duration, whether they liked it that way or not.

11

THIS LEGENDARY COACH WE HAVE

A championship team is a team with a lot to prove, but if the Lakers proved anything in the first month of the 2000–2001 season, it was the wisdom of something Pat Riley used to say when he was coaching the Showtime teams: there is a difference between winning a championship and being a championship team. An equally big difference existed between how good your team was and how good it could be, and you could never know exactly how much of your success or failure was attributable to attitude or to technique. As the 2000–2001 season progressed, no team illustrated this better than the World Champion Lakers.

On November 30, 2000, the Lakers played the Seattle SuperSonics and came away with 88 points to Seattle's 121, having converted only one of twenty attempts at 3-pointers. This was their worst loss since 1995, which meant that, for every member of the team, it was their worst loss as a Laker.

They still led the league in scoring but had lost sight of Phil Jackson's imperative that defense wins championships. In points allowed, they had dropped from sixth the previous season to twenty-sixth and had plummeted in opponent field goal percentage from first to eighteenth place.

Offense is talent, players always said. Defense is will and heart. A defensive player has to take something away from his man, and you could do that only when you were dead set on doing it. "Anybody can play offense," Horace Grant said in a team meeting. "It takes a hard guy to go out there and play defense. And nobody here wants to do it." Grant had honed his defensive game on the Bulls, where he, Michael Jordan, and Scottie Pippen defended so ferociously that an assistant coach, Johnny Bach, called them "The Dobermans." But Grant also knew that what fires you up to play defense are those offensive touches, and players weren't getting enough of them.

Last year they had maintained a champions' confidence in what they did night after night, and that confidence took on its own life, its own energy. They had won the championship because they were a very good team, but also because they believed they could win.

That belief was gone. The players were subdued, their spirits tamped down. Watching them in practice, in the locker room, on the bus, Jackson read in their demeanor a sense of embarrassment, of disappointment, of resignation. In that condition you can't muster the psychic energy to go up against a man you're supposed to stop.

They were starting to realize that champions have to work harder. Being the champions meant that you had a bull's-eye on your back, that every team you faced was geared up to knock off the champs. These teams brought their best game to play against you. They looked at you and remembered that one shot, that one possession that could have put them in your position. They considered you pretenders to the throne rather than kings and echoed the bitter sentiment of Jalen Rose of the Indiana Pacers: "I feel like Kobe, Shaq, those guys, are walking around with my ring."

Players like that came to the dance totally juiced, bringing everything they had. But the defending champions, getting hit hard every night, didn't necessarily take that attitude or bring that energy. Robert Horry, with his three championship rings, knew all about the effect that rings had on players. It's a funny thing, he thought, but when you're the champions, from day one, it's like, *let's just get to the play-offs*.

So while other teams tried to bury you, you tried to get through the regular season without expending the energy you would need at the end. Maybe you played just hard enough to go into the play-offs with home-court advantage, but it wasn't easy to gauge exactly how hard that was, and certain games slipped away from you.

The regular season was a traveling show from one end of the country to the other, with one eye on the matter at hand, the other on the next game, the next opportunity. It was _let's play the Nets so we can get to Boston; let's play the Kings so we can get to Denver_. For a lot of guys, focusing came later, in May and June.

Jackson was well aware of this. The team was playing, he thought, like they were waiting for the NBA finals. This was potentially self-defeating since your chances of doing well in the play-offs increased if you played well all season. He said this on many occasions, to the players and to the press. With each repetition he sounded that much wearier, because the point was so obvious and Phil Jackson did not like to waste time being obvious.

In the fall of 2000 Phil Jackson was poised to become the most successful coach in the history of a league that effectively banished him at the end of his playing career. Jackson had played with the New York Knicks for eleven years. The Knicks were an immensely popular franchise, and the particular teams that Jackson played on captured the heart of a city too driven and cynical to give its heart easily. In the bitterly divided political climate of the late sixties and early seventies, the Knicks were the right team at the right time. They had something for everybody: Willis Reed for the purists, Bill Bradley for the Ivy League. And, for the hippies, there was Phil Jackson, Number 18, with his shoulder-length hair, his loft in Chelsea, his Spiro Agnew dartboard. A young man blessed with unusual amounts of intelligence and curiosity, he was in the process of building what would become a permanent reputation as a walking lava lamp.

The counterculture was not widely represented on team rosters, and Jackson was an early emissary of a trend that would go on to include headbands, moustaches, Bill Walton's beaded necklaces, Dr. J's Afro, Darryl Dawkins's shaved head and earring. Though known as well-mannered, he was neither retiring nor shy. In a milieu that revolved relentlessly around star power, he was perhaps the only role player to publish his autobiography. He did this in 1976, at the tender age of thirty-one, in a volume that heralded his distance from the NBA's eagerness to convey a clean-cut image by its title, _Maverick_, and its lush details of the Maverick's acid trips and marital infidelities.

This was no way to commend oneself to the existing powers of a great American sports league, especially when that league was embarking on a mission to win the same corporate sponsorship that had enriched the coffers of the NFL. Even Jackson's great, unmistakable love of the game may have worked against him, for it spoke of intensity, and intense individuals are viewed as emotional and therefore unreliable. So, after his retirement as a player, Jackson settled for coaching a CBA team, the Albany Patroons, for $18,000 a year. He was an impatient man awaiting an NBA mentor with sufficient vision either to ignore or to appreciate the idiosyncratic nature that would become central to Jackson's tremendous achievements.

That visionary turned out to be Jerry Krause, general manager of the Chicago Bulls, interesting in itself since it was Krause's eventual, grudging acknowledgment of Jackson's contribution to the Bulls, as enunciated in Krause's bywords, "Management wins championships," that would play no small part in driving Jackson from the game in 1998 after he and the Bulls had won their sixth championship together. Krause had hired Jackson in 1987 as an assistant coach to the Bulls' head coach, Doug Collins, a four-time All-Star who had played on Dr. J's 76ers. Collins accomplished a great deal with the team taking shape around Michael Jordan, but his commitment, passion, and competitiveness did not always serve him well. There is such a thing as wanting to win *too* much, in which case your attempts to stir and rally your team may fall flat. After three years Collins had lost the ear of his players, and in 1989 Krause determined that Jackson should replace him.

Later, Bill Bradley, Jackson's friend and teammate on the Knicks, would say that there were many signs in Jackson's playing days that he would make a good coach. There was his analytical approach to teams and players, his commitment to teaching and learning, his understanding of the team concept, and his appreciation of the value of strategy on the court and off. Jackson had honed these qualities during the two seasons with the Knicks when he was recovering from a back injury and became something of an apprentice coach to Red Holzman, who had transformed him from what he called a "me-first hotshot" into a player who understood the importance and meaning of selflessness in the game of basketball.

Jackson had a good amount of the coach's essential obsessiveness and tunnel vision, though he was neither as obsessive nor as tunnel-visioned as most. He had a life outside the game. He had a vast knowledge of books and movies. He liked music, especially bluegrass. He could carry on a conversation that wasn't about basketball and enjoy it. He did, however, have an abundance of the coach's salient feature, a mania for control—though his particular ways of asserting control were generally so subtle or so bold that they could only bring about the desired result or backfire in ways that would have dire consequences. In the '91 play-offs, when the Bulls went up against the Lakers, Michael Jordan had reverted to his early penchant for winning the game by himself. During one game, Jackson made the point, not delicately, that Jordan's teammate, John Paxson, was open. Then, in hearing range of the entire team, he told Jordan, "Get him the fucking ball."

That demand and the fact that Jordan complied with it signaled that Jackson had a sense of self equal to that of any of his players. Sense of self did not appear on a coach's job description, but it was crucial, and a coach who lacked it could not maintain his hold on his players. That sense of self allowed Jackson to be both unbending and pliant. His willingness to admit his own mistakes amazed players whose experience with other coaches had left them convinced that being a coach means never having to say you're sorry. There were, his players knew, two Phil Jacksons: the one in the suit who shouted and whistled through two fingers from the bench and the guy in the worn jeans who encouraged them to be rabid with opponents and gentle with one another. In neither case was there any doubt about who was in charge. "If Michael and Scottie never talked back to me," he told the Lakers when he began coaching them, "none of you guys should ever say shit to me. Period."

In nine years as head coach of the Bulls, Jackson won six championships, a dazzling record that some would dismiss as the good fortune of coaching Jordan and Pippen, just as Red Auerbach's championship seasons were often dismissed as the inevitable bounty of coaching Bill Russell and Bob Cousy. To win with Jordan, these people said, called for the amount of talent you'd need to sell water in the desert. Jackson was just lucky, his detractors said. But Jordan did not win until Jackson became head coach; he did not win without Scottie Pippen or without the A-list supporting cast constructed around him and nurtured first by Doug Collins and then by Jackson. And when Jackson won another ring in his first season with the famously underachieving Lakers, those detractors were forced to uphold the unlikelihood that one man can get lucky seven times.

In any case, a great talent can be a liability that daunts and dwarfs a team. The essence of Jackson's achievement, as David Halberstam noted in *Playing for Keeps*, his classic book on Michael Jordan, was to pull off the high-wire act of channeling Jordan's greatness without discouraging it, of retaining his goodwill without acquiescing to him in ways that would cost Jackson the respect of the team and, ultimately, of Jordan.

Still, if you didn't win entirely because of a stellar player, it was also true that players of that caliber were few and that without them you didn't win at all. Coaches blessed with such players admitted this readily. After his first championship season with the Lakers in 1981, Pat Riley, who would go on to win more play-off games than any other coach, asked a friend to guess the two words responsible for his success. The friend suggested a string of flattering adjectives, but the two words Riley had in mind were "Magic Johnson."

And so, the question lingered as to whether Jackson was a brilliant coach or had simply coached brilliant players. Answering it inevitably became something of an avocation for reporters. "Is Phil Jackson driving this train," Bill Plaschke wondered in the *Los Angeles Times*, "or simply flashing peace signals out a passenger window?"

"Sometimes, I think Phil's full of crap," said a reporter who had known Jackson for some time. "Otherwise, I think he's the wiliest coyote to come out of the Dakotas."

Phil Jackson was raised in Williston, North Dakota, where great stretches of open land extend to the horizon. This was Indian country, and the white people who settled there brought with them a faith as harsh and punishing as prairie weather.

Jackson's mother and father were ministers in the Assembly of God Church, a Pentecostal sect whose members speak in tongues and believe that dancing, smoking, movies, and television are tools of the devil, that believers ascend to eternal life and that nonbelievers are consigned to hell. Theirs is a world of stark blacks and whites, unburdened by irony or ambivalence, a world of rigid, evangelical certitudes that he came to perceive as bogus and man-made. It was a world so distinct from the world of other young men that Jackson could rebel against it simply by embracing the bounds of normalcy. His path to a normal life came through playing sports, one of the few worldly pleasures that his parents' church did not regard as sinful. Sports permitted him to engage with the world instead of observing it from a distance, though his time as an observer lent him an unobstructed view of human behavior that would serve him later.

If physiognomy is fate, then Phil Jackson was fated for basketball. He grew to 6'7" with an arm span enabling him to sit in a car with both front doors wide open and pull them shut at the same time. He called this his car trick, and it played a part in convincing Coach Bill Fitch to recruit him for the University of North Dakota's Fighting Sioux.

Phil Jackson left home at the age of eighteen in pursuit of the two things he would need from then on: a life in basketball and a spiritual system that he could embrace and believe in.

The Knicks drafted him in 1967. He was their backup forward/center, with a strong, vigorous game coming off the bench. He was not a great shooter, but he was a fine, serviceable player thanks to his respect for skills like passing and rebounding, which allow players to help their teams in ways other than scoring.

When it came time to stop playing, he didn't want to leave the game. His mother always hoped he would become a minister, and when he came to New York to play for the Knicks, he told Red Holzman that this was his intention. But his journey had taken him too far from the religion of his youth. He was on his own path to faith—blending the Zen perspective, with its emphasis on mindfulness and being in the moment, with those aspects of Christianity that emphasize love and compassion. Coaching had, in fact, many similarities to preaching. Its goal was to uplift, to inspire, to engender harmony and a willingness to cleave to the greater good. As inspirational coaches do, Jackson raised life questions: What is generosity? What is community? What is selflessness? He spoke of playing with an open heart, of love as the force that binds the team and ignites its spirit.

He came to describe himself as a "Zen-Christian," leading his teams in meditation sessions and, before Sunday games, in recitations of the Lord's Prayer. If any single tableau illustrates the way coaching synthesized the life Jackson was born to and the life he created to escape from it, that tableau is a team of basketball players praying together.

Like his players, Phil Jackson did not merely love basketball. He needed it. He walked away from it in 1998, when his time with the Bulls hit a dead end. He had been looking forward to a new life, but there was a dead spot where the old life had been that he could neither ignore nor fill. He missed the players; he missed the camaraderie on the team bus. For men who love basketball, nothing can equal the engagement of the game: of being on the court, joining with other men in a war of wits and speed, hearing the crowd, feeling your heart pound and adrenaline course through you. You felt alive, captivated and free in equal measures, immersed in the absolute, centering sense that nothing mattered but this moment, this play, this victory.

The women who loved these men had to accept that everything else came second to this passion and that this was the way it had to be when you engaged in a sport at this level. That acceptance did not come easily. When, after a year's absence, Jackson returned to the game, knowing that he needed in his life the passion that the game offered every player, his marriage of more than twenty years came to an end. The divorce rate in the NBA was said to be 92 percent, and even if this figure was wildly inflated, it was telling that it seemed entirely plausible to players.

Phil Jackson came to the Lakers established as that most revered of American figures, the self-created individual who heeds the sound of his own drummer. His odyssey had taken him an impossible distance: from a family in which movies and all other entertainments were forbidden to a life in Los Angeles, that most public of cities, where reporters asked him about matters like his appearance on the "Tonight Show" and who would win the Oscars. At the heart of this impossible journey was the Old West notion *a man's got to do what he's got to do*, which, translated into Jackson's new-age terms, became a belief in the sanctity of each man's journey.

That belief had served him well, and never better than when Michael Jordan told him that he was renouncing his status as the game's greatest player to become a shortstop in baseball's minor leagues. Jordan feared that Jackson would try to talk him out of it, but Jackson spoke only of how Jordan's playing brightened the lives of so many everyday people. This, in itself, was an enormous gift, he told Jordan.

It was a classic Phil Jackson construct, the idea that what matters, in the end, is that a man assume his God-given place within the greater community.

12

FREE THROWS AND SIXERS

Two disparate threads ran through the Lakers' season: Shaq's decline and Kobe's ascendance. Both came into sharp relief in early December, when Shaq exceeded and Kobe matched a record set by Wilt Chamberlain in the 1960s.

Chamberlain had been another big man with a "free-throw thing," but Shaq managed to outdo his epic 0-for-10 showing at the line by going 0 for 11. What was especially humiliating about this was that it happened in a game the Lakers lost to the Seattle SuperSonics by 8 points, 103–95, numbers allowing anyone with a working knowledge of arithmetic to calculate the cost of his deficiency.

Shaq operated on the saving principle that when you can't salvage your game you salvage your pride, and this he did days later, poking fun at himself with a litany of player clichés. "Anytime you can replace a guy like Wilt, it's an honor," he said. "I'll tell my sons 'Your daddy beat out Wilt.' You know, when you try real hard, anything can be accomplished. I'll always be remembered in this game."

The record Kobe broke was for two players scoring more than 50 points in the same game. In 1962, when Chamberlain was playing for the Golden State Warriors, he scored 62 points during a game in which Elgin Baylor scored 51 points for the Lakers. In the year 2000, the Warriors had another high-scoring player in Antawn Jamison, who had posted 51 points against the SuperSonics the night before his team played the Lakers.

Going up against Jamison, Kobe took off on a shooting spree, racking up point after point, leaving other players to speculate that he cared only about outdoing Jamison. When he missed a dunk, he turned to one of the guys in the huddle. "Watch what happens when I get the ball next time," he said. Then he took off from the free-throw line and dunked on five players.

When the game went into overtime with the score tied at 107, Kobe had 39 points. Shaq ran the pick and roll, but Kobe wouldn't get the ball to him. "Drop it off," Shaq told him during a time-out. Instead, he scored another 12 points, sinking jumpers from 16, 18, and 19 feet.

"What does Kobe see?" Derek Fisher wondered, not for the first time. "Does he feel this is the right way for us to win? Or is it all about him?" Maybe Kobe wasn't as interested in a second championship ring as in leading the league in scoring and other individual achievements. That wouldn't be wrong, thought Fisher. We could work around it, but then say that, and let the organization make whatever decision they want to make. Everybody's cards have to be on the table.

In the game's final seconds, with the Warriors ahead by 3, Kobe passed to Horace Grant. But Grant wasn't expecting the ball, figuring that Kobe would take the shot himself. Like any player, Grant saw the game as operating on a simple rhythm: you think the ball is coming to you, you get it, it goes in. That's how it worked. It was what put you into the flow, and nothing interrupted that flow more quickly than uncertainty. Kobe made them all uncertain. He shot the ball when you thought he would pass. He passed when you thought he would shoot, so you fell out of shooting mode and then, if he passed to you, you weren't ready. And so Grant faltered and missed a final layup. The buzzer sounded. The score was 125–122 for Golden State. Jamison had scored 51 points, and so had Kobe.

As the Lakers dressed, the locker room was silent. There was a right way to play, they all believed. You help your teammate's game, and when you do, your own game gets better. But some players never believe that, they thought resentfully, especially not those who prove the axiom *the bigger the talent, the bigger the greed.*

In college, Shaq worked briefly with a coach who had made a virtual science of free throws. His name was Ed Palubinskas, and he was a near-perfect free-throw shooter, winner of countless shooting contests in which he sank all but 3 of 15,575 attempted free throws. As a college player Palubinskas competed against Shaq's agent, Leonard Armato. With Shaq's problem accelerating, he called Armato. "I can help him," he said.

Palubinskas arrived at HealthSouth a few days later, heading into the facility with the purposeful gait of a man on a mission, which he was. The object of this mission was seated with his laptop computer, reading E-mail. "I don't even want to do this," Shaq said, his eyes fixed on the screen. "I'm just doing it because they want me to do it."

This was Shaq's way of testing, of determining his new coach's mettle, a crucial exercise for an embattled player in need of answers and able to respect only those who proved tougher than he was. Palubinskas didn't look tough. He was a blond-haired, forty-something Australian, neither tall nor especially muscular. In Shaq's repeated incarnation as the Big Aristotle he was wont to observe that image is reality, but he was about to discover that this is not necessarily the case. Palubinskas looked at Shaq. He waited until Shaq looked back. "I don't care how much money you make," he told him. "I just know you suck."

They would work together every day after practice, Palubinskas continued, and Shaq better get serious. "You need to wake up thinking about me," he said. "I want you to dream about me. You won't make your shots until you're dreaming about me."

In December another player with an eye on becoming the leading scorer headed into the visitors' locker room at the Staples Center. Allen Iverson, point guard for the Philadelphia 76ers, gave his height as 6 feet, though he was more likely 5′11″. Iverson had entered the league five years earlier, the same year as Kobe, the number-one draft pick on his way to becoming Rookie of the Year. He brought with him a rage rarely seen in basketball, the kind of roiling anger that generally precludes sustained or productive activity.

Iverson was a natural athlete and a rebel by nature and choice, battling with his coach, hanging out all night in clubs, curling up in a locker-room closet eating tacos, skipping practice. These behaviors would be intolerable in a minor player; they were even more egregious in a star looked to by the rest of the team as an example, although Iverson maintained that he was less of a truant than was generally believed. "I'm not even brave enough to miss that many practices," he said.

If Iverson was one of the NBA's more troublesome figures, he was also one of its most compelling, with a persona flashier than that of any player's since Dennis Rodman. But he was more controversial than Rodman, whose stylistic quirks were so over the top and so particular as to pose little real threat to the mothers of America or even to the NBA's efforts to cultivate an acceptable image. America's young men were less likely to streak their hair green or to cross-dress or to turn up at gay bars than they were to affect the hip-hop, gangsta-rapper style and attitude that Iverson epitomized, a style sufficiently worrisome to the NBA that he was featured on the cover of a league magazine with most of his many tattoos airbrushed.

Iverson was a flashpoint for the NBA's burgeoning identity crisis and for its corollary, the question of whom—to use the lingo of Madison Avenue—the game was targeting. Basketball had become an increasingly black sport since 1950, when the league made its first tentative steps toward integration. By the early eighties this color shift, and the resultant sense that the sport was too black to appeal to white America, hindered the NBA's initial efforts to secure corporate sponsors. Those sponsors came onboard in the mid-eighties once Nike began making fortunes as a result of the handsome, princely Jordan, who occupied that useful marketing zone known as "color neutral." In those days NBA players, following Jordan's lead, were coming to games dressed like bankers—or failing that, like bankers out for a day of cards at the country club. Their beautiful clothes signified that they were not dumb jocks but serious professionals for whom these vast arenas were offices, men savvy enough to conduct themselves appropriately outside those arenas.

Hip-hop was emerging then, its keep-it-real ethic an antidote to the synthesized squealing of the disco music it mercifully replaced at the end of the seventies. As the fixations of the culture in general grew more relentlessly material, hip-hop gave black America a culture with

Kobe Bryant came into training camp eager to show how much he'd improved over the summer. He was frustrated to find that everyone expected him to remain the player he'd been the season before.
(© NBA ENTERTAINMENT. PHOTO BY ANDREW D. BERNSTEIN)

Shaquille O'Neal had been through other power struggles within his team. Disputes in Orlando forced him to leave the Magic (where he played with Horace Grant), all but ending Orlando's hopes of a dynasty.
(© NBA ENTERTAINMENT. PHOTO BY ROBERT MORA)

Rick Fox had come to the Lakers to win and to play the way he had dreamed of playing. He wasn't about to settle for anything less.
(© NBA Entertainment. Photo by Andy Hayt)

Isaiah Rider was brought in to be the third option. He was popular with the players, but his habit of self-sabotage was hard to break. (© NBA Entertainment. Photo by Andrew D. Bernstein)

Phil Jackson had more mystique than any coach in the NBA. In a world that measures credibility and status in championship rings, he came to the Lakers with eight—two for playing and six for coaching. (© NBA Entertainment. Photo by Andrew D. Bernstein)

Robert Horry was a clutch player with nerves of iron. Sometimes he played like he didn't care; at other times he was unstoppable. (© NBA Entertainment. Photo by Andrew D. Bernstein)

At the first home game of the season, Shaq and Kobe get their championship rings before the Lakers lose that night's game.
(© NBA Entertainment. Photo by Andrew D. Bernstein)

Mark Madsen was gentle off the court. On the court, he was every inch the embodiment of his nickname Mad Dog. "A dog that doesn't want his rabies shots," Shaq said of him.
(© Donald Miralle/Allsport)

Ron Harper was a wily veteran who'd played on the Bulls, getting the ball to Michael Jordan and Scottie Pippen. Now he was team captain and team father.
(© Jeff Gross/Allsport)

They started the season, in Brian Shaw's words, "fat, happy, and content." Here, Robert Horry, Brian Shaw, Shaquille O'Neal, Horace Grant, and the injured Derek Fisher have a laugh on the bench.
(© NBA Entertainment. Photo by Andrew D. Bernstein)

Early-season game against the Dallas Mavericks at the Staples Center. The tensions are showing. (© NBA Entertainment. Photo by Andrew D. Bernstein)

Few players challenged Kobe like Allen Iverson. Here they go at it again. (© Donald Miralle/Allsport)

Shaq unable to stop Iverson, a player described variously as "this wisp," "a blur," "a tornado." (© Donald Miralle/Allsport)

Kobe against Golden State. He and Antawn Jamison both score 51 points, but when the Lakers lose 122–125 there are hard feelings among the team. (© Tom Hauck/Allsport)

Phil Jackson's mounting frustration with his players is plain to see. (© NBA Entertainment. Photo by Andy Hayt)

Shaq on Christmas Day against Portland. No team confounded him more, but even at that, he had his moments. Looking on is Scottie Pippen. (© NBA Entertainment. Photo by Robert Mora)

Kobe and Shaq together, but not in the ways that matter. (© NBA
ENTERTAINMENT. PHOTO BY ROCKY WIDNER)

Shaq against Golden
State, looking to get
past Erick Dampier.
(© TOM HAUCK/ALLSPORT)

The Lakers lose to the Clippers for the first time in sixteen games, an embarrassing defeat and an unmistakable sign of trouble. (© NBA ENTERTAINMENT. PHOTO BY ANDREW D. BERNSTEIN)

At the All-Star Game. Kobe, Chris Webber, Tim Duncan, and Gary Payton. (© NBA ENTERTAINMENT. PHOTO BY ANDREW D. BERNSTEIN)

Kobe and Iverson have a word at the All-Star Game. (© NBA Entertainment. Photo by Andy Hayt)

Shaq promised his teammates that he would come back in the second half of the season "with a vengeance." And he did. (© NBA Entertainment. Photo by Andrew D. Bernstein)

Shaquille O'Neal makes a point—a verbal one.
(© NBA Entertainment. Photo by Robert Mora)

Kobe versus Vince Carter. A matchup between two of the best in the game. It was, Kobe thought, one of the hardest games he had ever played.
(© NBA Entertainment. Photo by Robert Mora)

David Robinson, Shaq's nemesis, scores over Rick Fox and Horace Grant as the Lakers lose to the San Antonio Spurs in their last meeting of the regular season. (© NBA ENTERTAINMENT. PHOTO BY ANDREW D. BERNSTEIN)

The next-to-last game of the season. The Trail Blazers' Arvydas Sabonis and Kobe Bryant. (© NBA ENTERTAINMENT. PHOTO BY SAM FORENCICH)

Kobe soaring high despite his injuries, as Ray Allen looks on. Minutes later Kobe would fall and injure himself again. (© NBA Entertainment. Photo by Andy Hayt)

In the Western
Conference finals,
Kobe is unstoppable.
(© NBA Entertainment.
Photo by Andrew D.
Bernstein)

David Robinson
and Tim Duncan
see their hopes of a
championship
evaporate. (© NBA
Entertainment.
Photo by Andrew D.
Bernstein)

Kobe, Shaq, and Rick Fox before the last practice in Philadelphia. (© NBA ENTERTAINMENT. PHOTO BY ANDREW D. BERNSTEIN)

Shaq and Kobe, united, victorious. (© NBA ENTERTAINMENT. PHOTO BY ANDREW D. BERNSTEIN)

its very own marketing imperatives and became a bandwagon that white America was eager to jump on. The eventual result was that Iverson, as part of the first NBA generation to grow up with hip-hop, would do his gangsta-rapper imitation in Reebok ads.

Take away Iverson's silver Bentley, take away his posse, and what you had was a young man with the 'do-rags and cornrows and heavy jewelry, the oversized T-shirts and jeans, that were signatures of a street style popularized by rappers.

This made Iverson something rare and contradictory. It made him an accessible icon, a multimillionaire who dressed and talked the way young men dress and talk when they live in poverty. Iverson's style was something these young men could attain now, rather than something to which they might aspire. He was one of them by birth, and now that money had supplied him with infinite choices, he was one of them by conscious selection.

This season he was leading the Sixers to a 9–0 start, better than they had gotten from Dr. J, Wilt Chamberlain, or Charles Barkley. For all his toughness, there was a wide-eyed, innocent quality to Iverson, the aspect of Dorothy awakening in the land of Oz. "You don't think about this in your wildest dreams," he said of the new season.

There had been faster players and smarter players, but rarely had there been a player as fearless, who operated from a reserve of such emotion. Iverson's unrelenting toughness daunted and demoralized his opponents. His quickness allowed him to blow past defenders, to create shots against almost any impediment. Kobe had cut his defensive teeth guarding him, and there were few players he would rather play against.

And on December 5, before the Lakers came onto the floor to face the Sixers, one word emanated from their coaches. That word was *defense*.

The Lakers came out and smothered the Sixers, with Shaq totaling a season high of seven blocked shots and Kobe holding Iverson to 27 points that he took 27 shots to get. The crowd at the Staples Center was impassioned, as if sensing that this opponent might be *the* opponent, the one that would dog the champs to the bitter end. As Kobe pulled off Jordanesque fallaways, outrageous alley-oop dunks, and flashy 3-pointers, they roared, "Kobe! Kobe! Kobe!" As Shaq took a charge against Tyrone Hill and landed flat on his back, they stood and burst into an ovation.

The Lakers defeated the Sixers 96–85 and left the Staples Center with a spring in their step that hadn't been there all season. In the wake of the victory they felt united and hopeful. They felt like champions again, at least for a moment.

13

CHRISTMAS

If Kobe was growing up, he was doing it slowly and in the manner that his team did everything that season, which is to say by taking two steps forward and one step back. When the Lakers played a losing home game against the Milwaukee Bucks, he played terribly, shooting 8 for 31, a baffling and woeful percentage. Every player had nights when the ball didn't make it into the basket, and on those occasions they relinquished it to guys who had a little more of a stroke going. Jackson thought that Kobe's unwillingness to give up the ball could be due to any of a number of factors: because he'd fallen below a 30-point scoring average, because in a recent game Vince Carter had scored 35 points, because he wanted to show up the Bucks' young star, Ray Allen. "It could be anything," said Jackson. "He's a kid. A twenty-two-year-old kid."

After a game, you could gauge the mood of the players by the sound level in the locker room. Less sound equaled more unhappiness. On this night the room was silent. The person who finally spoke was Kobe: "Fellas, that was my fault." The guys turned to him, surprise evident on their faces.

"I missed a lot of shots," he said. "I missed shots I normally make. But I took some bad ones too."

According to the code that players live by, an error admitted is an error forgiven. But bad feelings toward Kobe ran too long and too deep for a few words to dispel them. In the ensuing silence, Kobe tapped his chest with his hand. "It was my fault," he repeated. He started from the room.

"Kobe," someone said.

He turned. It was Rick Fox who had spoken. "You made some mistakes. So what?" said Fox. "If you're responsible for tonight, you're also responsible for the fifteen wins we got."

Their eyes met. Kobe nodded, the slight gesture brimming with appreciation. That night Kobe may have understood why Phil Jackson often quoted two lines from a Kipling poem:

"The strength of the pack is the Wolf, and the strength of the Wolf is the pack."

An hour later the Lakers boarded the team plane and flew to Portland, disembarking at 1:30 in the morning. There are teams you want to beat and teams you need to beat, and the Portland Trail Blazers were both for the Lakers. Portland was the team they measured themselves against, and this meant that a game against Portland was a jousting match for pride and confidence. The next day they dragged themselves from their beds and onto the bus for practice, anticipating the kind of intense practice you have when you've just blown three games out of four.

The coach was usually the last to arrive, as he was on this occasion. Jackson had always believed that the source of leadership is vision, that what you envision lends your dreams a structure and a starting point. It was his habit to envision not simply what he desired but how to bring those desires into being. Now, as he stepped inside the bus, the driver pulled from the curb. "Stop the bus," Jackson told him. He turned to the players. "We're not practicing," he said. "Everyone here must mentally visualize what he can do to help this team." He turned to Kobe. "Especially you," he said. "You need to bring it in a little. Tone it down." Then he walked off the bus and disappeared into the hotel, leaving behind a stunned group of players.

That night at the Rose Garden it was apparent that no other team confounded Shaq like Portland. He was stopped by Shawn Kemp, by Dale Davis, by Arvydas Sabonis, double-teamed by Rasheed Wallace and Scottie Pippen. As he made 7 of 21 shots from the field, the millions of dollars the Blazers had invested to nullify him paid off. Kobe, playing with a sprained right pinkie reinforced with gauze and medical tape, had 6 assists and 35 points, more points than the rest of the team, apart from Shaq, totaled collectively. It was another enervating night, with the game ending 96–86 for Portland.

This time last year the Lakers had been on a sixteen-game winning streak, with the best record in the league. Now, Jackson was telling them that they didn't know how to win on the road. They left the arena wondering what was wrong and figuring that, whatever it was, it would take more than visualization to fix it. For all that, they were still only a game and a half out of first place in the Pacific Division of the Western Conference. "There's no reason to panic," Jackson told the press. But privately he was saying that the team had to find a way to stop the bleeding.

A week later the World Champion Lakers returned to Houston. They had won their last three games—at home against Vancouver, at Miami, and an overtime victory at Toronto against Vince Carter and the Raptors, in which Kobe played a fierce fifty-two minutes and scored 40 points. On their day off, before they faced the Houston Rockets, Kobe slept the entire day, so worn out from hard play that he woke just long enough to eat a single meal before falling back into bed.

Shaq barely slept at all. He was pondering his changing fortunes since the day seven years earlier when he came to the league an instant star, surrounded by quantities of praise and expectation that exceeded those heaped on any player—including Jordan.

In a game that called for taking advantage of any mismatch you have, Shaq was always mismatched because, quite simply, there was no match for him. He was more than a player. He was a force, basketball's equivalent of the neutron bomb, and he relished these roles that cast him as a real-life superhero. Other players watched with amazement as he battled defenders. *I'm doing my man the same way*, they would think, *but the mismatch is not as dynamic.*

In his early days as a player, he loved the attention the press gave him, loved the public events heralded on billboards that read "Shaq

Here Soon." Some players viewed such things as distractions, but when the Magic's staff offered to take these tasks from his shoulders, he said, no, it was good for him, it got him going. Now he recoiled from reporters. When they asked about his game, he stuck his thumbs in his ears and refused to talk.

It's just time for me to get my game back, he told himself. I just gotta get it back. I gotta get focused.

He decided to make a ritual offering to a better game. He shaved his head, ridding himself of the slight Afro he was growing to "Kobe-ize" himself, as he put it, and returning to the style and feel he had when he'd won it all the year before. In the next game, against the Houston Rockets, he displayed a punch he hadn't shown lately, as he posted 25 points, 12 rebounds, and helped break a 97–97 tie for a Lakers win.

Kobe too played a dazzling game. Afterward, he was elated and playful with reporters who asked, yet again, about his relationship with Shaq. "We get in fistfights every day," he said, feigning sincerity. "We throw chairs at each other, water coolers at each other. You know what I mean? I hit him with a stun gun yesterday. That was at the free-throw line. Shook him up a little bit . . ." Then he loped off to the team bus, laughing, a twenty-two-year-old kid having the fun of a twenty-two-year-old.

The next day the Lakers went up against the Dallas Mavericks, a team that Shaq regarded with particular venom because their coach, Don Nelson, was the man credited with devising the Hack-a-Shaq defense. Nelson was one of basketball's genuine eccentrics. He had played for the Boston Celtics when Jackson played for the Knicks, and Jackson recalled him as a crafty player who put pine-tar resin on his fingers to make the ball adhere to his hand when he faked a shot.

In Shaq's last encounter with the Mavericks weeks earlier, they had used the Hack-a-Shaq defense to force him to the free-throw line nineteen times. He had made just five of his shots and was taken out of the game at crunch time to Nelson's evident delight. Now when they tried the same tactic, Shaq didn't get rattled. He took it as an effort to embarrass him. When he felt beleaguered, he often sulked, but when he got angry, he got mean; and this time, the meanness returned him to a game he hadn't played in some time. The Mavericks were playing clown basketball, he thought, an opinion he would repeat later to the press, adding that it should be clown basketball coming from a clown coach like Don Nelson.

He scored 28 points and got 9 rebounds. He made 11 of 15 free throws. After each went whooshing through the net, he stared at Nelson, eyes narrowed, shaved head high. He was the villain again. He loved every minute of it. When the game ended 108–103 for a Lakers win, Shaq stared at Nelson a final time. Having proved his point, he left the court thinking, They know who the biggest bad man is.

On Christmas morning, Kobe was with his fiancée, Vanessa, the beautiful young woman he had met and fallen in love with the year before. One of his gifts to her was a Pomeranian puppy that they named Gucci. She gave him a rectangular watch edged in two rows of tiny diamonds.

Shaq spent Christmas morning in Watts, a visit unannounced to the community or to the press, during which he knocked on doors and handed out five hundred gifts that he had personally purchased. Then he headed for the Staples Center for the afternoon game against the Portland Trail Blazers.

His game that day was oddly dispirited. The trouble, he insisted, was back spasms, and he asked off the court at the start of the second quarter. Jackson let him go to the trainer's room to work with the massage therapist. When he returned to the game, he asked for a sub a couple of times. In the second half, he took a total of 6 shots. Given his activities earlier in Watts, Shaq seemed less a candidate for MVP than for the J. Walter Kennedy Citizenship Award.

All season, whenever Shaq left a void, Kobe had tried to fill it. Now, with the Lakers trailing 107–104, he zipped around Steve Smith and into the paint, flipped up a layup, and collided with Rasheed Wallace. He heard the referee's whistle. "Three-point play," Jackson muttered on the bench. Kobe thought so, too, but then he glanced at Portland's bench and saw the Blazers jumping up and down. What the hell are they cheering for? he wondered.

They were cheering the call, which was for an offensive foul, one of many dubious calls that left Jackson raging and incensed over what he called a "mired, ugly, clock-stopping game." When it ended, Portland was ahead 109–105 and their coach, Mike Dunleavy, was declaring the win one of those season-changing victories, like the Lakers' unexpected February win over the Blazers the season before. Jackson had to take a breather to cool down before meeting with the press. When reporters asked him about Shaq's fatigue, he said it could not have been physical. He had not played that kind of game. "I think he's mentally fatigued," Jackson said.

If Shaq was wearing himself out, he was doing it off the court, where he stewed and fretted over Kobe's ascendance. There had been no question about what the Lakers' game plan was to be since Jackson had stated it at last year's training camp, in words that Shaq had not forgotten. "The ball is going in to Shaq," Jackson had said, "and he's going to have a responsibility to distribute the ball. It's going to be good for the team and good for him." And now Shaq could not comprehend why Kobe refused to play within the offensive system that won them the championship and, not incidentally, kept the big dog fed.

Shaq had always been a "bigger is better" kind of guy, by necessity, if nothing else. Now he could hear Kobe getting louder cheers. He looked at the newspapers and saw Kobe getting more headlines, more ink. Kobe was about to become the NBA's Player of the Month, while Shaq was making 37 percent of his free throws. "I feel like a token center out there," Shaq told Jackson.

And he could see what everyone else could see: that the torch had been handed off to a new icon. If he was unprepared for this turn of events, he had, in a sense, anticipated it. A few years earlier, asked who would supplant Michael Jordan, he said it would never be a big guy, that big guys might be feared, might be respected, but they would never be worshiped.

Yet Shaq had been worshiped. The 1999–2000 season had been his season, a season of fans in Number 34 jerseys, a season when his spectacular moves were greeted by chants of "MVP! MVP!" It was the season when he led the Lakers to a championship with such force and fervor that fans were stunned when the vote that made him MVP was less than unanimous.

Now Kobe's Number 8 jerseys were outselling the Number 34s nearly two to one, and the throng of fans waiting at the bus for Shaq had become a throng of fans waiting for Kobe. Reporters circling Shaq for postgame interviews would see Kobe enter the locker room and hasten toward him like birds flitting from one wire to another, leaving Shaq in midsentence.

And guys like Derek Fisher could understand how Shaquille might feel robbed of his victory. Almost any human being would feel that way, thought Fisher, would feel like, "After all I've helped you accomplish, after all I've done for the team, not only for myself . . . and it's only been a few months since that happened."

With nearly a third of the season gone, the Lakers headed to Phoenix, where they beat the Suns 115–78, a 37-point margin of victory, their biggest of the season and their fifth consecutive road win since Jackson had told them that they didn't know how to win on the road. "Shutting Phil up felt good," said Kobe.

Kobe scored 38 points, converting all three of his 3-point attempts and 11 of 11 free throws. He was in the flow, and when efforts to stop him yielded a 4-inch gash across his forehead and a longer gash across his arm, it merely confirmed his sense that he couldn't be stopped. "Guys just want to scratch me, man," he said. "It's pathetic, really."

Shaq scored 18 points, but to get them he played a quarter of garbage time. He was not happy, but he knew what bad form it would be to complain about a game you won by 37 points, so he went on to reporters about what a great game it was, a real team effort, everybody pulling together. In truth, he was fed up with Kobe trying to take everything over. He remained in the locker room long after the others had left, thinking about the game. The Lakers' general manager, Mitch Kupchak, came walking through. Shaq looked over at him. "If that's the kind of shit you're gonna put up with," he called to Kupchak, "why don't you just trade me?"

Kupchak knew Shaq pretty well. He could see how angry Shaq was, but he didn't give his words serious consideration. Shaq was just venting his frustration with the offense in general and with Kobe in particular. Shaq is a character, thought Kupchak. He says and does the most outlandish things.

14

MALAISE

The 2000–2001 season was becoming testimony to the significance of that state of being that Jackson called team wellness, a critical aspect of playing that goes uncharted on stat sheets. With thirty-one games played, it was clear that the Lakers had a distinct wellness shortage, a lack that left Phil Jackson with a sharp sense of disappointment.

Years of coaching the Bulls had accustomed him to players who placed the team's interest above their own, who came out and practiced like they were playing a game. But the Lakers conserved energy during practice and, in games, displayed too little heart. It was getting very difficult, which wasn't to say that Jackson ever thought it would be easy. No season was easy. Still, he hadn't anticipated this much trouble.

What could be done about it? Not much. In an eighty-two-game season you had to be selective about the issues you brought to your players' attention. You couldn't cry wolf too often. You had to parse your warnings, decide what had to be dealt with urgently and what could wait. A coach needed to sense which battles he could win so as not to squander credibility on hopeless causes. From that perspective it made no sense to declare a state of emergency over things happening in December—or not happening. Players responded when a situation seemed like an emergency to *them*, and most players didn't see an emergency until the play-offs started. So Jackson approached the issue in another manner. The only players going for it, he told reporters, were Kobe and Rick Fox.

"Are you aware," a reporter asked, "that your comment might strike fans as critical of Shaq?"

"Yes," said Jackson.

His assessment came as no surprise to Foster or Penberthy or Tyronn Lue or other players who spent games on the bench, watching the action and asking each other, "What the hell is going on?"

But Shaq was devastated. Nothing mattered more to him than the approval of his father, and he regarded Jackson as his white father. "I never wanted to let my father down," Shaq often said. And on those occasions that he did, he recalled that the punishment had been swift and violent.

"I can never let Phil down," Shaq had said at the start of the season. Now he was left to grapple with the fact that he *had* let Jackson down, despite his intentions. But Shaquille O'Neal was a champion player with a champion's pride and a champion's ability to maintain composure in tough situations. Asked what he thought of Jackson's words, he said simply, "The coach is always right."

This measured statement blanketed an anger that manifested itself in the next two games when Shaq fouled out. His words on those occasions, as noted in the newspapers, were accompanied by the word "expletive" several times per sentence, as in "the expletive referees," "the expletive Clippers," and "the expletive Utah Jazz."

For a team already overburdened, a new cloud was drifting onto the horizon. Kobe had recently vented his own frustrations in an interview with Ric Bucher, a senior writer for *ESPN the Magazine*. As the article's publication date neared, he warned his teammates about it, hoping to minimize its impact on a group of men among whom the reserves of wellness and community were swiftly diminishing.

An index of the precise degree of trouble besetting the World Champion Lakers presented itself at the start of the New Year, when they lost a game to the Los Angeles Clippers. The Lakers had beaten the Clippers in their last sixteen encounters, including in a close contest the week before. This meant they had beaten them on the watch of Del Harris, when they were struggling and downhearted; that they beat them in the chaos of the lockout year on the doomed watch of Kurt Rambis. Nor did they simply lose. They lost by 23 points, a rout in which the Most Dominant Player in the Game returned to the bench and covered his head and face with a towel, while the game's most storied coach, head in hand, assumed the aspect of a man trying to shake off a nightmare. It was, said Chick Hearn, the Lakers' play-by-play announcer since 1965, the most embarrassing Lakers game he had ever seen.

The year before, despite phases of sluggish, ineffective play, Jackson believed they had the stuff to win. His opinion had not been shared by the Lakers' principal owner, Jerry Buss, who had perhaps seen too many losing seasons to let himself hope in the absence of irrefutable evidence. Buss was an interesting figure, a Horatio Alger with southern California overtones. He began his career digging ditches in Wyoming, then went on to secure a Ph.D. in physical chemistry. After a brief career in aerospace, he invested $1,000 in a nondescript apartment building and parlayed it into the fortune that bought him the Lakers. Buss's impressive journey, like that of Phil Jackson, was navigated by exceptional radar for opportunity and trouble. Now, in the wake of the Clippers' victory over the Lakers, trouble was all too apparent, and Jerry Buss was reduced to a single conviction: "We've got to get ahold of this sucker."

After the loss, Phil Jackson awoke in the middle of the night. The hardest losses, he always said, were the games you knew you should have won. It was a coach's job to distill those experiences, to learn from them and not dwell on them longer than was useful. Still, you felt them. His own NBA coach, Red Holzman, used to say, "I'm a coach, but I've got an ego too." Jackson had quoted this bid for human recognition to his players on several occasions. They might not be sure what he was getting at, but they knew it was important to him because he kept repeating it.

The point of coaching, bottom line, was to make your players better. When you didn't see them getting better, it didn't feel good. If he had expected this year to be hard, he had also believed that they had a winning formula, that in the end, the worst that would happen was that they'd get off to a bit of a late start because Fisher wasn't playing and because they were integrating Fox and Grant into the starting lineup.

Maybe, he thought, because they were the champions, he'd started out the season too loose, too soft. Or maybe this situation wasn't right for him. Players could fall beyond the reach of their coach. They were willful. Force of will brought them to the NBA and kept them at the exceptional physical and mental level required. Jackson respected that. As he often told his players, he too was willful. Maybe my personality is not capable of reaching these guys, he thought. Maybe someone else can reach them.

The next morning he said as much to his assistant coaches, adding that the team might do better with someone younger than he was, or with someone less intense or lower profile. But Phil, the coaches said, they've already had those kinds of personalities.

A critical loss calls for a critical reaction. Some twelve hours after they had lost to the Clippers, Jackson met with the players in the team meeting room at HealthSouth. For years he had sought to imbue his players with the spiritual grounding he found so moving and impressive in the Lakota Sioux. With this in mind, he had decorated this room with a tomahawk and a white headdress and named it the "Warrior Room."

Lakota warriors were known as holy men. They believe that all things in life are sacred and are as one with all other things. This was allied to Jackson's own belief that there is a profound spiritual connection between players that is not communicated verbally. On this occasion, to foster that connection, he invited George Mumford, a psychologist affiliated with the Massachusetts-based Center for Mindfulness in Medicine, to lead the team in a basic meditation exercise. The players remained seated, spines straight, eyes cast down, keeping their attention on their breath as it moved in and out. If they became distracted, they were to note the source of that distraction, then focus again on their breathing, the idea being that a team breathing as one functions as one, at least ideally.

The next day, to refocus them in a more physical way, Jackson gave them an hourlong session in the balancing exercises called *tai chi*. He had faith in these tools but also knew that they were just tools, that they were not the team's ultimate answer.

"What was it that you guys had last year?" a reporter asked. "Was it a player?"

"It was esprit de corps," said Jackson.

15

THE FEUD

The next day, *ESPN the Magazine* published Ric Bucher's cover story on Kobe. "Kobe's gotten even better," read its subhead, "and that's a problem for Shaq and the Lakers."

If Kobe was hoping to minimize the story's impact, his hopes were lessened when ESPN promoted it on their website using the article's most provocative line, in which he speculated about playing for other teams.

By the time Kobe and Shaq arrived at HealthSouth for practice, the facility was overrun with reporters in numbers generally seen only during the NBA finals. Rumors had Kobe calling an undisclosed team to ask them to trade for him, on the grounds that his ambitions to be scoring leader and MVP could not be realized with the Lakers. Other rumors had Shaq returning to the Magic and Kobe being traded to the Vancouver Grizzlies.

For readers of local papers, the Kobe-versus-Shaq struggle was familiar to a point approaching tedium. Since their first season together five years earlier, the *Los Angeles Times* columnist Mark Heisler had been noting troubles between the players he called "the Golden Child" and "Shaq Daddy." The difference, and it was a crucial difference, was that Kobe never commented on any of it. Now, in Bucher's article, he was voicing things that everyone suspected he believed but never expected him to utter. In the tradition of Lenny Bruce's standard query, "Is there any group I haven't offended?" he also addressed the issue of his teammates, saying that he trusted them but trusted himself more. This was a comment that all great players could make if they had the honesty to make it. But the words rankled with other players, who reduced his statement to something harsher and more radical, as in "I don't trust my teammates."

Jackson was furious with Kobe, with Shaq, with the press. "This is our business. It isn't your business," he told reporters.

The real issues, Jackson told the team, were a sense of focus and self-discipline, things they had achieved in the past, but not lately. Maybe it was his fault, he said, for giving them too much room because they'd won the season before. In any case, they were not nearly as disciplined as they'd been during their championship year.

"I tried to let you guys figure it out," Jackson went on. "Now I'm going to have to instill more discipline. I'm going to sit on you like I did last year all the time. You don't get the respect of being champions."

The players headed onto the court, except for Derek Fisher, who was still recuperating from foot surgery and spending practices working in the weight room adjacent to the court. That day Fisher heard a lot of shoes making a lot of noise on the court's polished maple floorboards. Whoa, he thought, we're really getting after it.

The degree of disruption the magazine article caused would depend on how Shaq reacted to it, whether he took it seriously or laughed it off. Shaq was in no mood to laugh anything off. He had a tendency to hoard slights, whether real or perceived. He felt deeply slighted by Kobe. Now he was angry, an anger Jackson detected in his voice, his demeanor. After practice, reporters found him at the edge of the court, seated on a huge rubber medicine ball, talking with his bodyguard, Jerome, who had worked as a policeman in New Jersey before Shaq hired him to watch his back.

"Did you know they pay more taxes in Canada?" he was telling Jerome.

"Like in Vancouver?" Jerome asked.

"Hmmm . . . Vancouver . . . ," said Shaq. "Isn't that where Kobe's gonna get traded to?"

If Kobe thought there was a way to win besides the way they won last year, Shaq was not going to help him prove it. "I don't know why anybody would want to change," he told reporters, "except for selfish reasons. Last year we were 67–15 playing with enthusiasm. The city was jumping up and down. We had a parade and everything. Now we're 23–11, so you figure it out."

"Clearly," he added, weighting each word, "if the offense doesn't run through me, the house doesn't get guarded. Period." Having thrown down the gauntlet, he got up and ambled across the court to practice free throws with Ed Palubinskas.

Kobe emerged from the locker room moments later, eyes obscured behind new Gucci sunglasses. "Things change, things evolve," he said to the cluster of reporters. "You have to grow with that change. I improve as a basketball player every day, and I want to show that I improve." His words were punctuated by the plunking sound of the balls that Shaq was tossing toward the basket, if not into it. The two tableaus, Shaq with his coach, Kobe with his sunglasses, reinforced a prevailing image of Kobe as the aloof, glamorous figure and Shaq as the remedial plodder.

"Have you ever thought of playing on another team?" a reporter asked Kobe.

"That's what the whole article's about," Kobe answered, "so, yes, I have."

In the next days both Kobe and Shaq made dark allusions to unnamed people. Shaq cited "people who were jealous of me and wanted to take me down," while Kobe spoke of "people who wanted to level off my playing."

That week, Kobe instructed the Lakers' DJ to play a few bars of an Eminem song each time he scored. The song was "I Am," a defiant anthem that served as Kobe's way of conveying that he really didn't give a damn what anyone thought.

As the controversy went on around them, Kobe mentioned to Horace Grant that he and Shaq were speaking only through reporters. This was, potentially, a tricky business for players who tended to share Phil

Jackson's view that the press puts words into players' mouths. Whether or not this was true, there was no question that young players, unaccustomed to being interviewed and vulnerable to the seductiveness of the press, were known to say things they came to regret. Horace Grant was one of those players. Grant was playing for the Bulls when Michael Jordan turned down President George Bush's invitation to the White House after the team won its second championship. Jordan's decision had nothing to do with politics; he was, in fact, determinedly apolitical. (A few years later Harvey Gantt, the black mayor of Charlotte in Jordan's home state of North Carolina, ran for Jesse Helms's Senate seat, and Jordan, fabled Nike pitchman, declined to support him. "Republicans buy sneakers too," he said by way of explanation.) When newspapers quoted Grant taking Jordan to task for his proposed White House nonattendance, Jordan never got over it, and neither did Grant. Now Kobe told Grant that he wasn't sure he should believe the words attributed to Shaq in the papers.

"You know what, Kobe," Grant replied, "you can't even believe things that *you* say in the paper."

Grant's view of Kobe's situation was derived from having won three rings alongside Michael Jordan. When you played with Jordan, Grant told Kobe, you had to put your ego aside and accept that Jordan was the man. "In Chicago we knew what we had to do to win," Grant told him, "and that was to play together. You can't have two Batmans. You have to have one Batman and one Robin."

Phil Jackson had seen it all before, seen men pull together and refuse to be derailed until a particular goal was attained, only to lose the unity and spirit that had made their goal achievable. "Success turns *we*'s into *me*'s," Michael Jordan said after the Bulls' first championship team devolved from a merciless winning machine into a giant weakened by exhaustion, injuries, mental and physical fatigue. "Last year was a honeymoon," Jackson had said when they finally repeated. "This year was tough and filled with travail."

The championship Bulls had survived their share of internal struggles, many initiated by Jordan, as when he told his teammates not to give Bill Cartwright the ball and told Grant to stop shooting and get back to defending. Jackson never confronted Jordan on these things. Confrontation was his choice of final resort.

Jackson was a new kind of coach for the Lakers. Before him, high-priced, high-profile coaches had been anathema to Jerry Buss, who promoted from the inside, as with Pat Riley and Kurt Rambis, or hired low-key outsiders like Mike Dunleavy and Del Harris. But with the team moving from the Fabulous Forum to the vastly larger Staples Center, Shaq's suggestion that Jackson be hired became an idea whose time had come. The power of Jackson's considerable celebrity—the very thing that Buss had always sought to avoid—would be one more big draw to fill those twenty thousand seats.

Kobe had endorsed Jackson's hiring. He was, in fact, so eager to meet him that just before the press conference at the Beverly Hilton to announce the appointment he arranged to meet Jackson in his suite, avoiding the press by taking the freight elevator. Shaq introduced himself to Jackson in Montana, arriving unannounced at his new coach's summer home where, after a cursory greeting, Jackson won him over by leaving no question as to who the boss would be. "See that tree?" he said, pointing to a dead tree that had washed up on his property. "Move it."

Jackson knew, of course, about the problems between his two star players. "That's why I'm here," he said early on, "to deal with this situation." He seemed uniquely positioned to do this, for he too was a star, a well-paid star, and then there was the additional leverage of those eight championship rings.

Often as not, Jackson used that leverage to maintain his famously hands-off stance, something that less storied coaches would have difficulty getting away with. He was renowned for letting players find their own way through situations that sent other coaches screaming for time-outs. Coaches of that sort amused him. They were NBA stereotypes, calling every play, jumping up and down, shouting, trying to orchestrate everything. Jackson viewed coaching as a kind of parenting, with the parental goal of guiding its subjects toward independence. True, if he stopped the game and told players what to do, they might have more faith in him. But it was more important for them to develop the faith in themselves that comes from making your own decisions.

Similarly, dealing with problems off the court, Jackson did not presume to think for other men. He respected players too much for that, and the idea of one man forcing his ideas on another was something he had soured on while attending the church he was raised in. As few people with power do, he understood that the things that are most crucial to know must be learned rather than taught.

And so, when Shaq asked him, early on, to stop Kobe from going one-on-one, he said he wouldn't. "Let him go," he told Shaq. "Let him learn by himself."

What would Jackson do now? players wondered. Would he do what Coach Bill Sharman had done when he persuaded Chamberlain to play defense and paved the way for thirty-three Laker wins in a row and a championship? Would he do what Pat Riley did when he gave Magic the reins, telling him that his time had come? No, he would not do those things, nor would he do anything else. What was called for was not a change of strategy but a change of heart, something that could be neither decreed nor legislated. For basketball was a metaphor, and what pertained on the court pertained in life as well. "In this game," said Jackson, "you don't change people. They change themselves."

He had no thoughts of trying to bring his two feuding players together. And when he said that he did not even want them in the same room right now, the remark set some reporters saying, only half-jokingly, that Phil Jackson never really did anything, that if he got up from the bench during a game it meant that he had a cramp.

"When we listen to your comments," the columnist T. J. Simers said to him, "and by the way, they're not always easy to understand . . ."

"Yes, they're cryptic," said Jackson.

"There's a perception that you're paid six million . . ."

"Yes, it's a very generous salary."

". . . to sit around. Are you more a psychologist than a coach in fact?"

"The philosophy I teach," said Jackson, "takes a great deal of execution."

"Do you plan to sit Shaq and Kobe down," asked another reporter, "and have them work it out?"

"Not everything can be worked out," said Jackson.

Perhaps it took a practitioner of Zen to apprehend that *not* acting is also an action, that, at times, the most radical and most comprehensive thing to do is nothing.

In the next days, Jackson was inundated with letters from psychologists, mediators, counselors, Scientologists, all with suggestions for how to heal the rift. But for Jackson the most interesting response was that of the other team members, who refused to side with one party or the other. Not that the matter didn't have its fallout. The younger guys had the anxious quality of children who fret about their parents not getting along, tracking Kobe's and Shaq's behavior, eyeing them uneasily, telling each other, "They walked right by each other and didn't even say anything." And it was clear that the battle had certain undertones of class and style: young players who wore large diamond-studded crosses tended to secretly favor Shaq. Experienced players had no favorites and no use for what Robert Horry dismissed as "the so-called feud between our two big hot dogs." Shaq and Kobe were forgetting their teammates. It's all me-me-me-me, thought Horry.

Yes, Kobe played a self-centered game, but Shaq's demand that Kobe be less selfish was also rooted in self-interest. Both had oversized egos and ambitions, and that's what you would get on championship teams as long as conventional wisdom decreed that winning required two players of Hall of Fame quality. Players of that stature knew their outsized egos and ambitions were among the ingredients that made them great players. They were more apt to place their own interests ahead of the team's, even if this decreased their standing with teammates who knew that truly great players make their teammates better than they would be normally. The fact was, both Kobe and Shaq needed to change. Kobe needed to trust his teammates and stop hogging the ball. Shaq needed to stop talking and start playing.

You'd think, they'd say, with all the drama going on, that Kobe and Shaq were the first teammates to not get along. But they weren't. No love had been lost between Kevin McHale and Larry Bird, as Brian Shaw witnessed during his rookie year with the Boston Celtics. That was another case of opposites: Bird so taciturn, so tough, all business; McHale so talkative that they nicknamed him 411. Bird, with his perfectionist's work ethic, so scornful of McHale for not working harder, for not being better when he could be so good. But when it came time to play basketball and they put on the same uniform, they set aside every consideration but winning and were joined in the knowledge that if they played together there was no way to stop them.

But there were cases, too, where personalities destroyed everything. Shaw had seen that on the Orlando Magic with Shaq and Penny Hardaway. That situation was almost identical to Shaq and Kobe, thought Shaw, two great young players who could only benefit from getting along. And whatever went wrong, whether it was egos or people on the outside in their ears, you ended up losing.

As days passed, players aired their thoughts in the Warrior Room, the place they saw as a haven where they could voice their grievances. In the Warrior Room they were a team, an angry team that feuded and got fed up and disgusted but was still a team. As such, what they said in the Warrior Room mattered less than the fact that it could be spoken.

Two days after the article on Kobe was published, a second controversial article appeared in the *Los Angeles Times*. Written by Tim Brown, the reporter covering the Lakers, it was headlined "O'Neal Was Frustrated Enough to Seek Trade" and included Shaq's "trade me" remark to Mitch Kupchak. That night, an hour and a half before the Lakers were to play the Cleveland Cavaliers, their first game since losing to the Clippers, Magic Johnson strode into the Lakers' locker room to talk with Shaq and Kobe.

Magic was now a vice president of the Lakers and watched home games from a courtside seat a few yards from the team's bench. When Magic signed with the Lakers in 1979, the team had been dominated by Kareem Abdul-Jabbar, a great player and the Lakers' center figuratively as well as literally. Magic's talent left no doubt that he would be the team's most significant player, but until Coach Riley told him to do otherwise, he deferred to Kareem, always speaking of the Lakers as Kareem's team. "We were like best friends on the court," he told Shaq and Kobe. "One thing about us, nothing ever interrupted winning and what's best for the team."

Magic had only his own dazzling experience to go on. "One of you," he told them, "is going to have to defer to the other; that's all. There's enough shots out there for everybody."

Magic did not attempt to address the crucial matter of which player should do the deferring. "They've got to work that one out," he said.

A good index of how out of control the situation had become was that it was making Isaiah Rider look like one of the saner, more sensible guys on the team. "The two main guys need to cut that stuff out," Rider was saying. "They're too good to cry about the things they're crying about."

Shaq's agent, Leonard Armato, was a fixture at home games, where he often conversed with Tim Brown, whose paper was the one Los Angeles newspaper with clout in the sports world. That night he talked to Brown longer than usual. The press might be a pesky annoyance, but it was useful to anyone with an agenda to promote. And Armato's particular agenda had to do with the fact that Shaq was committed to the Lakers for the next six years, when he would be thirty-five, while Kobe's contract expired in four years, when he would be a mere twenty-six. In the next days word circulated in both the *Los Angeles Times* and the *New York Times* that Shaq's people believed that in this dispute between their two leading players, the Lakers' management was favoring Kobe.

Kobe's agent, Arn Tellem, was rarely seen at games but appeared at this one. Many of Tellem's clients were baseball players, and Brown, having written about some of them when he was on the baseball beat, had reason to assume that he was not Tellem's favorite individual. But Tellem walked over to him and put his arm around him, a gesture suggesting to Brown that the battle was on for the hearts and minds of those with influence.

Before the game against the Cavaliers, the locker room was strangely quiet. This kind of stressful situation, Kobe told himself, can increase your focus or decrease it. What will happen, players wondered, when Kobe and Shaq come onto the floor? What if one gets booed and the other gets cheered?

But when they appeared, cheering for both men echoed throughout the arena. The crowd was enthused, to the point of giddiness. "This has a play-off atmosphere somehow," Kobe said to Horace Grant.

Kobe had thought a lot about this game and about the entire situation. The only thing to do, he had concluded, was to grow from it and leave it behind. By the time the announcer called the starting lineup, he had woven that intention into a plan. He would get the ball to Shaq as often as possible, get him going early in the game, and take just a few shots himself in the first half. "At 6'7", 210 pounds," he heard the announcer saying, "from Lower Merion High School . . . Kobe Bryant . . ."

Kobe rose. As he headed onto the court, he turned back to Shaq. "Yo, let's go," he said.

That night Kobe kept Shaq fed. In the first quarter, after he sent him a flashy behind-the-back pass for a dunk, they slapped hands for a high five. When Shaq hit his free throws, he gave him a quick pat on the butt. By the end of the game, the Lakers had won 101–98, with Kobe scoring 32 points, most in the second half, and Shaq playing his best game in weeks, with 34 points and 23 rebounds, a virtuosic display that reestablished the dominance he thrived on and needed.

"We can't have the Big Fella be unhappy," said Kobe. They still weren't talking, but Kobe didn't think it mattered. The most important communication between them had always been nonverbal.

In fact, Shaq wasn't talking to anyone—not to the press, not to the rest of the team. A few nights later, after the Lakers went flat in a loss to Utah, he kept his silence, leaving the locker room wearing a leather jacket emblazoned with the Superman logo and listening to music on the earphones hidden beneath his gray stocking cap. As days passed, he remained silent.

But he could see that Kobe was trying to do things differently; there was no question about that. When Jackson told Kobe that it was more important to get a triple double than to score 20 points, he went out two days later, against the Vancouver Grizzlies, and got his first triple double, the first for a Laker since Vlade Divac got one in 1996, and his way of proving that he could do much more than score. He sent the ball to Shaq with a showy pass off the backboard for a dunk. He jumped for what he called "every damn rebound." In overtime Shaq hit two free throws and made the winning shot with seconds to go. "He's fine," Kobe told reporters. "He's just not talking to y'all."

The person who wasn't fine was Jackson. Yes, they had won, but they had also gone into overtime, barely beating the Grizzlies, hardly a team that should pose a challenge to world champions. He had talked to the players repeatedly about focus and discipline. You're running out of time, he told them. Get it together. Basketball is a 94-foot game, which means that defense and offense are equally important. He was still talking, but with the resigned thought, he would say later, that if you throw enough shit against a wall some of it's going to stick.

Did they know, he asked one day, what kind of government was thought best by certain Greek philosophers? Democracy? they asked. Anarchy? No, said Jackson, the answer was benevolent dictatorship. That was not the way he wanted to run the team, but he would, he said, if it became necessary.

Four nights later, before they went up against Houston, Jackson gave the team a simple instruction: feed Shaq. They did, and it set Shaq sweeping across the court like an avenger, a scoring tornado, posting a season-high 41 points. A spirit was in the air that had been absent, and it spread through the players, sending starters like Fox and Grant and Shaq onto their feet from the bench to cheer when Mark Madsen and Tyronn Lue made two baskets each. Suddenly the Lakers seemed united.

As Kobe left the court, a reporter asked if he'd heard that a tabloid had paid a psychic to analyze his body language and Shaq's. Kobe shook his head, amazed. "I guess they've got a lot of free time," he said finally.

In the locker room, Shaq made a show of straightening the few items in his locker, as if oblivious to the fact that a horde of the reporters he hadn't talked to for days waited just behind him. Finally he turned to them and faked a startled look. "Oh my," he said.

16

DEPRESSED BASKETBALL

The Miami Heat was the league's second-worst team in scoring and last in rebounding. In late January the World Champion Lakers lost to the Heat 103–92 in a Sunday game broadcast to millions on NBC. With a team total of 11 assists, with Kobe shooting 13 for 27, with Shaq hitting 7 of 16 free throws and getting no blocked shots, the game was another textbook example of the observation made by the Heat's coach, Pat Riley, when he was coaching the Lakers: there is a difference between winning a championship and being a championship team.

Afterward, Ron Harper was seething. "I'm team captain," he told the players when they returned to the locker room. "I'm gonna say what I see. We stink. If this team scores 100 points on us, we gotta stink. If you don't like what I'm saying, I don't care."

In fact, the players seemed unwilling or unable to take in his words. As they showered and dressed, the atmosphere was strangely upbeat. Isaiah Rider hummed Bob Marley tunes while Brian Shaw and Shaq's bodyguard, Jerome, debated whether the suede dress shoes Jerome was wearing with his suit were dark blue or black. Nothing fazes these guys, thought Harper. They're not broken up over anything. They need to go home and just sit down and think about what we're doing as a team. They need to look at themselves and ask, Are we on the same page? Are we here to help this team out? Or are we here for ourselves?

Harper had four championship rings, enough to know that winning teams operate as a united community guided by a purpose the whole team agrees to. Basketball isn't played just on the court. To be a good team, he thought, you got to take your job home. These guys don't.

The one player not joking that afternoon was Kobe. His misgivings about his teammates at the start of the season had solidified into convictions. These guys were in no shape to play defense, not even against the Heat, and that was pathetic. "It's not like we don't know what we have to do," he told reporters. "It's a matter of conditioning. We have so many old legs, old bodies, it's hard for them to run all-out every day in practice. We run out of gas. We can't sustain intensity for forty-eight minutes."

He said "we," but the older players knew damn well he meant them. They didn't appreciate it. Kobe's attitude, they thought, was the arrogance of youth, which everybody got over soon enough. That was why Horace Grant was always saying that he needed to apologize for laughing, when he was young, at his teammate Bill Cartwright, an older player whose multiple injuries prompted the writer Peter Vescey to give him the nickname "Medical Bill."

Grant was now thirty-five, and Brian Shaw was weeks away from his own thirty-fifth birthday. "I played with your father," he reminded Kobe the next day at practice. Shaw's first year as a player was Jelly-Bean Bryant's last, and this was something Shaw thought about when every muscle in his body was aching. "What that's like," he told Kobe now, "is if my son grows up and plays in the NBA and you play with him."

"This is my thirteenth season," Shaw went on. "That's saying a lot for what I'm doing right now. When you get to the point where you can say you played thirteen seasons, then you'll be saying something."

In late January, the Lakers were 27–15. This meant that forty-two games into the season they had lost as many games as they lost after playing eighty-two games the season before. We just don't play with the selfless bent that it takes to be a good basketball team, thought Jackson.

At times, he told the players, he considered breaking up the team, trading for a player who might get the team more active, more motivated, who might shake up the troops a little bit. Not that this was a realistic option given that Shaq's and Kobe's combined salaries next season came to $32 million and Jerry Buss had no intention of exceeding the salary cap. That did not leave a great deal of money with which to seduce another player, a fact that led the billionaire owner of the Dallas Mavericks, Mark Cuban, who had recently bought the Mavericks an airplane equipped with a state-of-the-art weight room and shower, to refer to the Lakers as "Shaq and Kobe and the Merry Minimums."

The team, Jackson allowed, was for the most part neither youthful nor quick, nor particularly athletic, and these shortcomings had been compounded by the enervating effect of Shaq and Kobe's feud. Jackson watched the team at practice, on the road, in the locker room. Everything about them, from their facial expressions to the way they ran the offense and barely helped each other on defense, brought Jackson to an uneasy conclusion.

"The feeling I'm getting," he told his assistant coaches, "is that they're playing in a depression. They're playing depressed basketball."

Being a team member was not the same as being a star on a team, and being a star on a team was different from being *the* star, the player who drove the team by force of example or force of will or ambition or, as it happened in most cases, by all these things.

That leader would have been Shaq had he not been hobbled by circumstances of his own making. By late January, Shaq was beaten down, his name entered onto the injured list as the result of a strain in what Tim Brown called the "Most Valuable Arch in Basketball."

A rest would do him good, he decided. "It can't get any worse mentally," he said, "and physically I can only get better."

Because he lacked that core of confidence that facilitates taking criticism in stride, Shaq's first reaction to any hint that he had a problem was to deny it. But his great strength was an ability to take his own measure, if not at first, then at last. You can do one of two things, he told himself now. You can think, I'll show you. Or you can wimp out.

But wimping out was not an option; his father never let him wimp out, and he was grateful for that. I've always showed people, he thought. I'll always continue to show people.

In the end, for all his protestations and sulking, it came down to his fierce champion's pride. "I can't let people see Superman like this," he said. "It's an ego thing." He smiled as he said it, but he wasn't kidding.

"When I come back in the second half," he told the team, "I'm coming back with a vengeance."

Shaq was not the only player needing to get himself together. As Jackson pointed out, the team's savvy players were all in a slump. The usually reliable Brian Shaw was in an 0-for-7 slump, and Robert Horry had missed his last 12 shots.

The player on the upswing was Isaiah Rider, who was having moments that prompted other guys to tell him, "That looked like the old you out there." In the first three weeks of January, he was on time for every game and practice. But by the end of the month trouble was brewing for him again. He had refused to take a drug test, an NBA requirement for players known to have used illegal substances and required for Rider because he had been accused of smoking pot in a hotel room the year before. Rider was nothing if not perverse, and the night the story broke about his refusal to comply, with its subsequent implication that he was about to be suspended, he had a breakthrough performance. From the minute he got onto the court, Rick Fox felt him coming on strong, and as the crowd shouted, "Rider! Rider! Rider!" he scored 24 points against the New Jersey Nets, his season high, no pun intended. The next morning Rider missed the team's chartered flight to New York, arriving at 9:07 for a 9:00 A.M. takeoff, two minutes too late to conform to Jackson's rule, "We wait five minutes, then we're gone."

The next day they played the Knicks, a game the injured Shaq sat out, while the *New York Times* speculated that he was doing so to teach Kobe a lesson. Kobe made 15 of 27 field goal attempts, trying hard to win, but uninspired defense left the Lakers vulnerable even as it signaled a lack of that sense of community essential to well-being.

"This time last year was our lowest time," said Jackson. "I think it corresponds to the weather."

Shaq's absence gave Kobe a taste of what it means to carry a team, of the way that mental and physical pressures can wear you to the nub.

Taking that on was right up Kobe's alley, and the team knew it. The tougher things got, the more he enjoyed them and the harder he battled. That was his way. What was an obstacle to you was, for him, a challenge. His determination to spend himself, to push beyond what the body could tolerate, was a hallmark of his playing, a reason his coaches kept cautioning him not to place himself in needless jeopardy.

As they watched him, his teammates wanted to say, Just know that you don't need to carry the whole load yourself. But you couldn't actually say that unless you were playing well, and they weren't playing well, in part because Kobe's lack of trust was undermining their confidence.

Of the many differences between Kobe and other players, one of the more telling was that while most players regarded basketball as a career, Kobe saw it as a destiny. The others didn't mind his being a player of destiny. What they couldn't handle was that his destiny was being carved from their touches, their statistics, and, most importantly, from their basketball manhood. Your manhood was the measure of your worth, and even guys who considered this attitude hopelessly shallow couldn't help but subscribe to it. Each time you stepped onto the court, your manhood was on the line. You had to play like a man and win like a man and lose like a man, and this meant you had to be calm off the court and, on the court, play like an animal.

NBA basketball was a kill-or-be-killed sport, a human jousting match played without benefit of armor. The sweat, the near-naked bodies barreling into one another, the clashing against other men there to contain you, to stop you—all these things had a primal aspect. They hearkened back to when men competed to be the best hunter, the best warrior, when being a man was about who brought back the biggest fish or had the most kills. It was a battle over prowess and territory, and in their particular ways they all romanticized it. "Strength and honor," Brian Shaw would say in the pregame huddle, quoting from the movie *Gladiator*. Mark Madsen could recite from memory the Wordsworth poem that Tex Winter had presented to him, "Character of the Happy Warrior," an ode replete with references to "noble deeds" and the uplifting assertion that "what he most doth value must be won."

And when a player wouldn't pass you the ball, it was your manhood that he was violating, and this cut into your confidence and your pride and left you wondering about your game's viability. It would open a window of doubt, and from then on you'd be fighting a downward trajectory because the more you felt doubted, the more you doubted yourself. How many times, thought Rick Fox, had he been out on the wing, watching his man, who was supposed to be defending him but had so little respect for him and his place on the team that he went to Kobe instead. Seeing that made you feel degraded. The idea that you were not respected, that you were unworthy—these were terrible, subversive notions, the very notions that players came to the game to redress. These notions could take hold of you, hobble you, dull your sense of daring.

So they watched Kobe, and wondered, Are you willing to give it up a little so the rest of us can accomplish what we want to accomplish? But when they sat down in team meetings to discuss what was wrong, they could see from what Kobe said and, more importantly, from what he didn't say, that his trust of them was minimal at best. Kobe didn't believe, Rick Fox felt, that veterans like him, Grant, and Harper were worthy of shooting the ball. Fox had been around long enough to understand the psychology of the game, and he knew about the absolute correlation between confidence and winning. He kept hoping Kobe would acknowledge that they, too, had a role in any prospective victory, because what the team sorely needed was the confidence that Kobe had confidence in them.

With Shaq out of the game, Kobe drew double and triple teams but hung on to the ball as his teammates eyed him with renewed resentment. OK, they thought, if you're shooting all the shots, then you do all the defense and you get all the rebounds. He charged through one cluster of opponents, then another. Watching him, assistant coach Jim Cleamons thought, Is learning ever going to take place? Or if you are learning, it's at a very slow rate.

The tried-and-true formula was: if you're open, you shoot it; if you're covered, you pass. The players called this "unselfish love," and they all subscribed to it. Every guy on the team, Robert Horry thought, had sacrificed some part of his game to play with the Lakers. Every guy but Kobe.

Without Shaq, they had gone 1–1 when they lost to the Timberwolves, 95–83. Led by Kevin Garnett, their 6′11″ forward, the Timberwolves were all business, a team on the verge of becoming a challenge to the Lakers. The Lakers' other four starters combined for 20 points, with Mark Madsen the only player other than Kobe to score in double digits. After the game Ron Harper hurried toward the team bus as a reporter hurried after him. "What's up, Harp?" the reporter asked.

Harper grinned. He kept walking. "Suck my dick," he said.

Pressures were building on Phil Jackson, from within the team and from outside it, pressures to do something about the situation, to do anything, but it was not Jackson's way to respond to external pressures. "I don't want to put a gun to the head of either one of those young men," he said. A coach blessed with great players needed those players to have faith in their own abilities, just as he also needed them to understand that the team is more important than individual efforts. These were tricky and opposing concepts, and you could not force them on anyone; you couldn't mastermind or plan. You could only allow things to take their course, in the process freeing space for inspired things to happen. This was the way he had always proceeded. Now, in adversity, he stuck to this approach with a tenacity reserved for fools and true believers, and Jackson was not a fool.

Pressure was building on Kobe, too, and it was getting to him. He knew the question reverberating through the Staples Center was: is Kobe selfish, or is he inspired? Everyone in the arena seemed to have an opinion. There was the elderly lady who insisted, "That child gives everything he has," and the twelve-year-old boy who remarked, "He lights up the game." For each of them, there were others who shouted at him, "Take it back to Philly, man," and still others who muttered darkly about his "needing to learn a lesson." How had it happened, Kobe wondered, that public perception of him decreed that he was either an angel or a devil?

That Kobe Bryant would evoke such impassioned views was predictable in a nation that worships success but is deeply suspicious of ambition.

The circumstances that would change Kobe's season began at a February 2nd home game against the Charlotte Hornets. Before it began, Jackson warned Kobe not to forget his teammates. But he scored 44 points, shooting 15 for 30 from the field, going 14 for 14 on free throws, taking 9 rebounds, while no one else on the team made it into double figures.

Horace Grant was furious. When Kobe gets double-teamed, he told Shaw, he has to pass. With 40 seconds remaining, the Lakers were ahead by 5 points when Kobe got the ball again. Grant yelled that he was open, but Kobe hurried a spinning fallaway jumper.

Brian Shaw headed over to Kobe. Was he aware of the shot clock? he asked. Did he know that Grant was open? Kobe walked away, angry, refusing to answer.

"Hey, I'm on your team," Shaw told him. "I'm not trying to chastise you or anything like that. I'm just pointing something out. Just relax and take in what I said, and next time we'll make whatever adjustments we need to make."

Kobe left the court feeling battered in a number of ways, including in his right hip, which had been bruised toward the end of the game when the Hornets' P. J. Brown shoved him into the basket stanchion. This added a sore hip to a roster of injuries that already included bursitis in the right hip and left elbow, a sore right shoulder, and a sore right pinkie.

The next day, Saturday, was a day off. Kobe always practiced on his days off. That day he felt so bad he didn't shoot the ball. When was the last time he'd gone all day without picking up a basketball? he wondered. Then it struck him that since he started playing when he was five, he'd had a basketball in his hands every day of his life.

When he was placed on the injured list, Shaq watched games from the trainer's room. He didn't appear in the arena until the Lakers played Charlotte on February 2, Groundhog Day, prompting the reporter Howard Beck to compare Shaq's presence to that of "a weather-predicting rodent."

Shaq did not read sports pages, but his bodyguard, Jerome, did. "You called my man a mole, man," Jerome said to Beck the next day with a grin. "You called him a mole."

Two days after beating Charlotte, the Lakers played the Sacramento Kings. Their best player, Chris Webber, was making the most of his abilities to dominate down low, to hit the outside shot. With the softest hands of any big man in recent memory and a generosity with the ball, Webber was a prime candidate for this season's MVP. He had come into the NBA after making one of the greatest sports gaffes ever, calling a time-out for University of Michigan when they were out of time-outs, a move that cost them the NCAA title.

As the game started, Shaq watched from the bench, face impassive, as he noted the toll that Kobe's latest injuries had taken. Kobe's shots were flatter. He couldn't make hard cuts. His leaping ability was diminished. Other players needed to step up, Shaq thought. And they did—first Greg Foster, another player not having an easy time this season.

Foster had been on the team less than two months when he began hearing rumors that he would be traded. The Lakers were Foster's eighth team in ten NBA seasons, and from day to day his mood, hopes, and confidence shifted. Sometimes he felt it was a privilege to stay in the game at a high level. At other times he thought the NBA was just a show. It was a business, and you were a number.

Foster learned long ago how hard it was to come off the bench and charge into the game with the right level of energy. As a bench player, you walked a thin line between staying poised enough to play and getting so psyched that if the coach didn't call your name the disappointment was unbearable.

This season had been especially frustrating for Foster. The Lakers were in need of a leader, and he couldn't see why Shaq and Kobe didn't set their own problems aside. He tried to contribute what he could to this team wellness Jackson was always talking about, making suggestions to new players, offering insight and his own mantra for shooting: if you don't let go, you'll never know. This game is about consistency, he told them. No one cares what you did before, though he admitted that he himself wasn't playing at the level he'd achieved during his four years with the Utah Jazz. In those years he had been a vital member of the team and had gone twice to the finals. The last shot that Michael Jordan made in a Chicago Bulls uniform had ended Foster's second chance for a championship. Now with the Lakers, his career had come down to waiting for O'Neal to get tired and finding ways to stay useful on the bench. "Fold towels, bring water, whatever," he said. "Just give me the damn ring."

But he was a starter against Sacramento, scoring 11 points in the first eleven minutes, more points than anyone but Kobe had scored in the entire game against Charlotte two nights earlier. For the first time since he'd been on the Lakers, he thought, the team was playing with some heart, some emotion. Grant got a double double. Harper scored 11 points, 2 with a dunk that left Shaq so amazed and pleased that he laughed till he nearly fell off the bench. Robert Horry, on his way to scoring 20 points, made three 3-pointers in a three-minute span. When he sank a left-handed finger roll with 1:21 left in the fourth quarter, the shot sent Grant, Madsen, and George from the bench to the sidelines, waving towels and cheering while the crowd chanted, "Horry! Horry!" energized by the game of an exceptional player lately operating on wheels that Chick Hearn described as "underinflated."

That afternoon, on their way to beating the Kings 100–94, the Lakers were united, helping each other on defense, with the result that Chris Webber made only 12 of 32 shots, scowling at referees every time Horry or Grant stuck a hand in his face, while Fox kept their other scorer, Peja Stojakovic, to 7 points. As they pulled together, their collective mood brightened. Kobe high-fived Grant and Harper each time they stopped Webber. Brian Shaw gave Kobe an affectionate poke in the ribs. When Grant argued with a referee who gave him a technical foul, Kobe came over to him and placed a restraining hand on his chest. They had turned a corner energy-wise and defensively, thought Jackson, and were playing harder than they had all season. Shaq was so impressed that he couldn't wait to get back for the second half of the season. "I'm ready to go," he told Mitch Kupchak. And Kupchak could see that he was brimming with life and enthusiasm, that his demeanor was entirely different from when he made his "trade me" statement in Phoenix.

In the locker room there were winner's words, winner's smiles, as players talked about hard play and joked about their near success in getting the fans the free chalupas awarded to them when the Lakers scored 110 points. "You guys really wanted to redeem that coupon," said Jackson.

The press gathered around Horry, who replied to questions while running a hot pink Afro comb through his hair.

"You looked like you were about fifteen years younger," a reporter told him.

"I wish," said Horry.

Across the room Brian Shaw answered questions while inserting a ¾-carat diamond earring in his left earlobe. This game, with everyone pitching in the way they did, was, he said, the funnest way to play.

But in the next days some of that pleasure evaporated as he went around town. "Hey," people kept saying, "that was great the way you guys beat Sacramento."

Like we're some scrubs, Shaw thought, bemused and irritated, and that it was a big deal. Like when the Clippers beat us.

The particular troubles besetting the Phoenix Suns made the Lakers' troubles seem benign and insignificant. In addition to an array of drunk-driving and marijuana-possession charges, their guard Jason Kidd had recently hit his wife and subsequently been arrested in their home, located in the section of Phoenix known as Paradise Valley. Before the Suns played the Lakers, one of their coaches wrote on the white greaseboard in the visitors' locker room: "Transition. Get below the line of the ball. CONTAIN KOBE. He will take it 1 on 4."

This he did, going up against all defenders while also making 9 assists that included feeding the ball to Madsen, who was on his way to scoring 13 points. Every season there was a player the crowd loved especially, and this season that player was Madsen. He was a lot like Kurt Rambis had been, a white player with as much heart as anyone on the court, the player that a predominantly white audience identified with most readily. As hard as Madsen played, as much as he loved being a Laker, he had no trace of player macho when he wasn't playing. "There'll be many more," he had said when he hit his first 3-pointer, "in my dreams."

He cheerleaded the crowd with energy as abundant as it was contagious. The fans returned that energy to him. He felt it. It nourished him, but as much as he loved it, he was determined not to be ruled by it. That night the cheers were even louder than usual. Madsen was in the flow, thrilled to be getting the ball from a player as great as Kobe. This is magical, he thought. I don't ever want this to become a job.

With 11.5 seconds left in the game, the score was tied at 83. Harper pulled Kobe aside. "If I get Jason Kidd down low," he told him, "and you don't throw a pass to me, you and me are gonna fight."

"With the game on the line? We're just gonna have to go to blows," said Kobe.

Kobe was struggling to trust his teammates. He needed to do it, he knew it, and he tried. In this game he had 9 assists. But when push came to shove, he trusted himself more.

Now he started from the right wing, took a jab step to the left, a single dribble, and with Shawn Marion in his face, shot from 17 feet, the ball sailing just beyond Marion's desperate reach. Harper followed the ball's progress from his inside position on Kidd. It arced above him and into the basket. Kobe balled his fists and thrust his arms into the air. Mark Madsen enveloped him in a bear hug. Brian Shaw turned to the Suns' coach, Scott Skiles. "You're no match for him," he shouted.

Harper, ever the team player, was thrilled with the win. "You know what the best thing is?" he said to Madsen after the game. "We've become a good team again."

From then on, Madsen knew how to reply to the many people who asked him what was wrong with the Lakers. "I don't know," he would tell them. "But we're working through it, whatever it is."

17

ALL-STARS

The All-Star break is a breather in midseason, offering an embattled team the chance for a new start. But this break was not starting auspiciously for the Lakers. Shaq insisted that his locker be moved away from Kobe's and said in an interview that he wanted to return to Orlando and play with Tracy McGrady, while Kobe said that his choice for MVP was Allen Iverson or Chris Webber.

Shaq wasn't playing in the game, and Kobe didn't want to. He would have preferred to rest, but if he didn't play he risked a five-game suspension, so he was in Washington, teasing Chris Webber on the bus to the MCI Center about the Kings' loss to the Timberwolves the previous weekend.

Kobe had played in the All-Star game since his second year on the Lakers, when he was sixth man on a team that had many reservations about him and his playing. But the fans adored him, and when they voted him All-Star they made him the youngest starter in that game's history. This, in turn, jolted the NBA's substantial mythmaking machine into high gear. Soon the letters K-O-B-E were spelled out across the marquee of Madison Square Garden, and full-page newspaper ads were proclaiming, "Kobe versus Jordan," heady stuff for a nineteen-year-old still living with his parents.

As requests for interviews and cover shoots poured in to John Black, the Lakers' public relations director, Coach Del Harris worried that it was all putting Kobe under too much pressure. "Take it easy with this kid," Harris told Black, who was caught between this reasonable caution and a sports world so dreading the retirement of the man Larry Bird described as "God disguised as Michael Jordan" that it was already gearing up for a second coming.

"What do you think about it?" Black asked Kobe. "You want me to downplay this stuff?"

"Bring it on. I can handle it," said Kobe.

Bring it on. I can handle it. That said it all for a player who did not know the meaning of fear or ambivalence. And if there were those who questioned what Kobe was made of, Jordan made clear that he knew precisely where Kobe was coming from and where he was going. Though he outplayed Kobe that day, he had entered the game with a more modest ambition. "I just wanted to make sure Kobe didn't dominate me," he said later, a remarkable, telling comment coming from the greatest player in the history of the game.

Now, three years later, Kobe was surrounded by reporters, and he was patient and resigned when asked to address the issue of trusting his teammates. It was not that he didn't trust them, he repeated. It was just that he had put in so much hard work that he felt he could make any shot in any situation. "Not to say your teammates don't work hard," he said, "but you feel that you work harder. So you trust yourself a little bit more." These remarks were aired that evening, causing the team's veterans to think that maybe you had to be older to realize that certain questions are better left unanswered.

The All-Star game heated up in the fourth quarter, with Stephon Marbury, Vince Carter, and Allen Iverson going for it forcefully enough that the East overcame a 21-point deficit. In the final minute, with the East leading 111–110, Kobe got the ball for a final shot. Dikembe Mutombo moved in front of him. Kobe lobbed the ball to Tim Duncan, who missed the shot, losing the game for the West as the buzzer sounded.

Watching the game at home in Oakland, Brian Shaw smiled wryly. You can pass to your All-Stars, he thought, but not to us.

After the All-Star break, Shaq returned to the game, armed with arch supports in his shoes and jokes that he was going to get a tattoo reading, "For those who know me, no apology is necessary; for those who don't, none will do."

By then both he and Kobe could see that the controversy was draining them and everyone else. They were ready to end it, and each offered a final word in his own style.

"The things that don't kill you only make you stronger," said Kobe.

"I'm ready to stop answering these stupid questions," said Shaq.

Last year, going into the All-Star break, they'd had a three-game streak going and they had won their next six games. Now with a tough road trip ahead of them, Rick Fox was thinking, We've got to repeat that kind of effort. This year's record isn't all that different from last year's.

Their first game was against the New Jersey Nets, a team with a 17–34 record and an exceptional player in Stephon Marbury. That night Marbury was on fire, scoring 50 points. But Shaq was back. He had a lot to prove to a lot of people, thought Horace Grant, and he was starting to prove it. He scored 32 points, got 14 rebounds and 5 blocked shots, and made 12 of 24 free throws.

Still, the moment that mattered most for the Lakers' future occurred early in the fourth quarter, after Kobe fed Shaq for a vicious dunk. In the ensuing time-out, Kobe sat on the bench. Shaq stood nearby, and when he thought no one was looking, he turned to Kobe and stared at him until Kobe felt his gaze and returned it. Shaq raised his eyebrows a fraction, gave a slight smile and a nod. Then Kobe nodded. In that moment, they acknowledged how brilliantly their games meshed together.

The game went into overtime. In the final seconds, with the score still tied at 110–110, Kobe barreled through four defenders, drove the lane, flipped the ball into the basket, and was fouled. He fell to the floor and sat there, arms crossed, eyes wild. Shaq came over to him, put his hands under his arms and raised him up, then nudged him toward the free-throw line, where he made his 38th point toward a Lakers win.

No matter where the Lakers traveled, whether they went by bus or by plane, the players had particular seats they sat in. On buses Shaq sat in the back on the right side; Kobe took the seat farthest back on the left. Each player sat alone, the seat beside him empty. But then basketball players need room. Even on college teams where everyone got along, players sat with an empty seat beside them.

As they traveled from East Rutherford, New Jersey, to Philadelphia, Jackson gave each player a book. This was something he did each year, the gift of a book being, in itself, an expression of respect. Last year Shaq's book was Nietzsche's *Man and Superman*. This year he was given Hermann Hesse's *Siddhartha*. Phil always gives me these damn Harvard books, thought Shaq. Why can't he give me a simple book? He knows I don't have a big vocabulary.

But Jackson was not known for random acts, which occurred to J. R. Rider when he began reading his gift from Jackson, *Cookie Cutter*. "It's about a deranged guy," he whispered to Horace Grant.

"Phil's playing psychological games with you," Grant told him.

"I've got to respect Phil," Rider replied. "I think he gave it to me for a reason. He wouldn't give me a book about violence just like that."

And there was indeed an intention in these gifts. It was Jackson's way of saying that he knew them in ways that were real and profound, and cared about them not simply as athletes but as men. In that sense it would be hard to find a better book for Shaq than *Siddhartha*, with its exploration of the search for self, of the necessity of turning from hatred and choosing love.

Kobe's book was *Corelli's Mandolin*, the story of an Italian army officer who goes from being an outsider to incorporating himself into the community. "You know I'm not going to read it, man," Kobe told reporters. That was Kobe for you, thought Jackson; he's not willing to let someone else's ideas penetrate his mind.

Both Shaq and Kobe had family in the East. Shaq spent a day with his great-grandmother—looking through family albums, taking a nap on her sofa. It feels like when I was getting baby-sat, he thought, like when I was little. Kobe went to see his grandmother dressed in a gray suit, pink shirt, pink print tie. "Grandma loves me in a suit," he said.

At the First Union Center in Philadelphia the Lakers went up against the 76ers in front of the fifth-largest crowd in Sixers history. It was a big game for the Sixers. A win would be meaningful, especially now, when they held the best record in the league, had given their coach, Larry Brown, his thousandth coaching victory, and Allen Iverson had passed Kobe as the league's high scorer. Early on, Jackson saw that they were bringing an intensity to the floor that the Lakers couldn't or wouldn't match.

Plainly the marathon in New Jersey had taken its toll. Rick Fox's back was in spasms, his solid game so off that a fan, seeing Fox's wife, the singer Vanessa Williams, in the crowd, held up a sign that read, "Bring your game, not your wife." Kobe, playing in his hometown, heard himself booed during the introductions, then jeered by a crowd that greeted Iverson's every move with chants of "MVP! MVP!" Iverson was set on overwhelming the Lakers. In a game that would see Tyrone Hill score 12 points, George Lynch with 11, and Eric Snow with 9, Iverson noted that his team was a closely bound unit, with no ego issues about who gets to shoot. He went about scoring 40 points, and when Harper talked trash to him he was dismissive. "Whatever, girlfriend," he said. "Whatever." After the Sixers won, 112–97, the Lakers left the arena downcast and exhausted and headed to their hotel. As they walked off their bus, a bystander approached Rick Fox. "Are you basketball players?" he asked.

"Sometimes," Fox said.

Then they were on the upswing again. In Charlotte, North Carolina, playing the Hornets, Kobe made it clear that Shaq was not the only player on the team able to take his own measure. "If I get doubled, I'm going to give it up," he told his teammates, his first statement of intent to include them, to adhere to the triangle's basic premise of passing to the open man.

That night Kobe got his second career triple double, with 10 assists, 10 rebounds, and 25 points. Shaq posted 38 points and 12 rebounds, a game closer to his real game than any he had played all season. Toward the end of the fourth quarter Kobe heard someone saying "Pssst . . . pssst." He turned to see Shaq cocking the ball above his head, waiting for him to go long for a pass the way they sometimes did in practice when they ran football patterns.

"Dang, Shaq," Kobe told him in the next time-out, "you didn't throw the pump fake. You need to throw the pump fake; then I can spin out and go." They both laughed. This is the nice thing about the NBA, thought Kobe. Whether it's trusting your teammates or playing with Shaq, you were always faced with a challenge.

It was in Kobe's nature to mull things over, then come to a decision and stick to it. Now he decided that the time had come to push through the obstacles they'd been facing and move on. He was ready to do it, ready to step back a little now that Shaq's game was changing for the better, his free-throw percentage rising from 37.2 to 56.4, which dissuaded other teams from hacking him so much.

Shaq had not forgotten what his coach Ed Palubinskas told him when they met: you won't make your free throws until you're dreaming about me. After the game in Charlotte, he told Palubinskas, "You S.O.B. You were in my dreams."

Since losing the championship to the Lakers, the Indiana Pacers had also lost their coach, Larry Bird. Under the new leadership of Isiah Thomas they were a diminished team. But Thomas, who spent his college career as Bobby Knight's brilliant problem child and went on to be one of the NBA's greatest and most rabid guards, knew about winning. When he came to the Detroit Pistons in 1981, he had asked his friend Magic Johnson what made a championship team. He would have to find out for himself, Magic told him, and as Thomas recognized that winning teams are distinguished by their single-minded, unshakable focus, he led the Pistons to two championships. The Pacers' leader, Reggie Miller, also knew about focus, and now his focus was sharpened by the memory of the Pacers' loss to the Lakers in the sixth game of last year's NBA finals.

You could never underestimate the power of bitterness, and a team that felt displaced was a team that would either fold or fight to the bitter end. The Lakers had their moments against the Pacers, as when Kobe made a left-handed reverse layup to give them a 5-point lead, then zipped a pass out of a trap and sent it to Grant for a dunk, a play prompting Madsen to call to him, "You the man!" But the Pacers refused to go away. Miller was unstoppable, freed by the fact that Ron

Harper was on the bench in street clothes. Harper's swollen left knee deprived the Lakers of a defender who had dealt for a dozen years with Miller's bag of tricks, many illegal, but effective nonetheless. With Kobe guarding him, Miller managed to score 18 points in the fourth quarter, getting open for a 3-pointer by stepping on Kobe's foot, then breaking away to shoot. As the game reached the final seconds, the Pacers led 110–109. Kobe got the ball, released a 22-foot jumper that missed, then landed off balance, straining his left ankle as the buzzer sounded.

In the face of that loss, the Lakers were downcast again. Indiana was a team they were supposed to beat, and they all knew it. Jackson gathered them together. It was time, he told them, to start thriving on the adversity.

Perfect, thought Shaq. I love that stuff.

18

RECOVERY AND INJURY

The Lakers' next game was against the Dallas Mavericks, a team that Shaq always wanted to trample. On the morning of the game, he was all business as he headed out of the shootaround. "I'm gonna go to work tonight," he told Mark Madsen.

But before the game there would be a moment of another nature, as Nelson made his first appearance in the arena since his recent surgery for prostate cancer, striding onto the court to a standing ovation. Sneaking up behind him, Shaq enveloped him in a bear hug, saying "I love you, Don Nelson." Then Nelson took a plastic clown's nose from his pocket and put it on, in remembrance of Shaq's describing him as a "clown coach" at their last meeting.

Then the Lakers went for it. As Shaq made one free throw, then another, Nelson was forced to scrap his Hack-a-Shaq tactic. "Foul him," he told his players, "only when he's in a dunk kind of situation."

Late in the first quarter, Kobe and Shaq went to the bench. The Mavericks relaxed their defense, creating the opportunity for Grant, Fox, Rider, Madsen, and Penberthy to go 9–0 on them. Back in the game, Shaq cut loose. By the time the final buzzer sounded, he had finished with 11 for 15 from the line, posted 29 points, 11 rebounds, and 5 blocked shots, and led the Lakers to a 119–109 win.

This, thought Rick Fox, was the Shaq they'd been missing all season. To be this, Shaq had to do more than play. He had to withstand terrific punishment, to absorb more poundings than anyone in the NBA. Referees rarely fouled players who pummeled him, assuming that he could take whatever they meted out. To reporters who sat just off the court, this was particularly apparent. Tim Brown was in his first year on the Lakers beat, and what Shaq put up with amazed him. Still, referees never called a flagrant foul, not even when undertalented opponents played him like the game was happening in a dark alley. Shaq's rage had been known to separate doors from hinges. At times Brown was certain Shaq would retaliate, lashing out against these players. But he didn't. At least not yet.

Kobe, too, played a complete game, with 19 points, 6 rebounds, and 7 assists. But as he crossed the court with two minutes and thirty-three seconds left in the game, he tripped over Shaq's size 22 EEE shoe and tumbled to the floor. His foot rolled. He heard a pop in his right ankle. "Suck it up, man," he told himself. "This is not happening. This is not going to happen."

Then he got up and kept on playing. That was all there was to do: play through the pain and deal with the consequences later. He left the court wincing, his ankle swelling.

Shaq left knowing what he needed to know. He knew that he could turn it up, get the job done, make it happen. Buoyed and triumphant, he turned to the courtside table where the L.A. beat reporters were seated and called to them, "Who's the fucking man?"

After the game, the players could hear him singing in the shower. "Shaq . . . he's the greatest in the universe. . . ." He sang very loudly, a little off-key, to the tune of Queen's Flash Gordon theme song.

Yet the pall over the team did not disperse. Like a cloud blackening the sky, it hovered, threatening and useless. The trouble between Kobe and Shaq, Rick Fox confided to his workout partner, had drained the team's reserve of wellness. This was insupportable in a team that, from the beginning of the season, had been missing vibrancy and commitment.

If how you play is who you are, then a team that had been supremely confident in the previous season was now tense and unsure. Last year, thought Brian Shaw, you always knew that somebody had your back. This year they didn't always have each other's back. Last year they came onto the floor convinced that no team could beat them. This year they were so erratic that they had to get out there and play a while before they could register the reassuring thought, "OK, we can handle this."

Shaq's revitalization did little for the team. To them, his efforts to take better care of himself, to be the Shaq of last season, were just another case of a premier player having individual thoughts.

Now, Kobe's ankle had been diagnosed as a sprain and he was out of the lineup, which meant that they would be missing about 30 points on any given night. The fact was that Kobe and Shaq were the only guys on the team with scoring averages in double digits. And the reason for this, thought Rick Fox, was that the supporting cast not only recognized their go-to guys but deferred to them relentlessly, passing to them instead of taking their own shots, or even worse, shooting whenever they got the ball because they got so few touches. They didn't play the game the way it was supposed to be played, moving the ball to the open man. Jackson kept telling them that they had to be more assertive with the offense, and they all knew it.

From Dallas, the Lakers went on to San Antonio. To Jackson, going up against the Spurs without Kobe or Harper—whose left knee was still acting up—was like going into the woods to fight a bear with a club instead of a gun. But on the first play Fox moved in for a driving layup, establishing an aggressive tone and releasing a sense of exhilaration that carried from player to player as seven guys played their way into double digits. They missed Kobe's speed on the defensive end just as they had missed Shaq's size in the post. But what mattered was that in both cases, to their considerable surprise, they were finding ways to make up for it.

Nothing could be more encouraging to players who had long ago tired of hearing that the Lakers were a two-man team. This was a troubling, sensitive issue, one that Jackson tried, at times, to treat lightly. In mid-December, Shaq had missed a game against Vancouver to attend his graduation ceremony at Louisiana State University, flying there in a private jet that he chartered for $3,000 an hour to get his degree in a field of study he described as "crayon biology." "And," he had declared, "I'm valedictorian."

That same night a young, promising player, Devean George, was sidelined due to a minor health problem. George was averaging fewer than two points a game. "The question isn't whether we can play without Shaq," Jackson joked before the game. "The question is: can we play without Devean George?"

This had offered little in the way of amusement to players who won that game without Shaq, not that it was a big deal to beat the Grizzlies. A week later they had won their first meeting of the season with the Los Angeles Clippers, albeit another weak team, in a game that saw Shaq fouling out and Kobe ejected on a technical foul.

"How did you feel with both your premier guys out of the lineup?" a reporter asked Robert Horry after the game.

"Like we didn't have a chance in hell, man," said Horry, his voice thick with sarcasm.

The Lakers, Horry often insisted, had no role players. They had two superstars and a lot of stars. Each of them had been a star at one point or another, he noted repeatedly. This was true, and they all had moments when they remembered what it was like to be the main man, and missed it. "It's just that you're something for so long that it's hard to change it," Shaq told his bodyguard, Jerome, by way of explaining how the other guys felt. "It's like if I get a wild coyote puppy, I can bring him in the house and brush him and perfume him and make him a Beverly Hills dog if I want to. But once he be back outside he's a wild coyote."

Kobe had been injured many times before, but this time the pain was more intense. It was pain that keeps you awake, and each night he was sleepless till four in the morning. At games he sat on the bench, an elegant observer in suits by Armani and Zegna, watching impassively, forced back to the inborn restraint from which playing freed him, the unwilling prisoner of his own body. As the Lakers played the Orlando Magic, he seemed lost in another place, and when the many TV cameras projected his live image onto the huge screens above the arena, he did not respond to the resulting cheers and applause. Possibly he didn't realize that the cheers were for him; possibly he was not in a state of mind to accept the cheering.

Kobe's exhaustion was more than physical. He was animated only when Tyronn Lue made a 3-pointer and when the Lakers' DJ played "Hit the Road, Jack" as the Magic's power forward, John Amaechi, retreated to the bench after fouling out.

Amaechi's presence in the game was a special spark for Shaq. Amaechi was paid $600,000 a year to play with the Magic, but last summer he had turned down an offer from the Lakers for a six-year, $17 million contract, an offer, that is, to play beside Shaq, and Shaq did not forgive such disinterest easily. Inspired and methodical, he led the Lakers to a come-from-behind victory, posting 37 points and 19 rebounds, leaving the court with nineteen seconds to go as gold and purple streamers rained down and Kobe joined in a standing ovation.

When the buzzer sounded, Kobe applauded the Lakers' 106–100 win. Then he hurried from the arena, his camel-colored cashmere coat draped over his shoulders, a surpassingly graceful figure despite his injuries.

The Lakers had seventeen games scheduled in March. This is the stretch, Jackson told them, that we have to play well. That would be harder to do in the absence of two of their starters, one of whom, Ron Harper, at age thirty-seven, seemed out for the long haul given that his knee would require arthroscopic surgery. One afternoon, after playing hard in practice, Harp could barely walk. Before the next game he sat in the locker room eating steak from a silver foil take-out container, listening to music through headphones. "I ain't playing no more basketball," he announced to no one in particular. Sometimes he thought about the conversation he'd had with Jackson at the end of last season, when he asked if he could retire and Jackson told him to hang around. Now, he joked, if he asked the same question, Jackson would probably say, "Yes. Please do."

If Jackson had been waiting for players to feel a sense of urgency, now, with the season three-quarters over, that sense seemed to be awakening. In practice, in the locker room, you could feel the hustle of guys getting down to business. Maybe somehow, the younger players thought, it'll all come together. They had won six of their last seven games. "Yeah," they told each other, "we can do this thing."

What they needed was momentum. Win one game, then another, and suddenly you're feeling invincible. That was why Jackson placed so much value on winning streaks.

Kobe came back in a road game against the Denver Nuggets. His ankle was still giving him a lot of pain, but he was walking and jogging on it. You just have to suck it up, he told himself. If this is as bad as it gets, you can play through it.

Against the Nuggets he paced his energy more carefully than usual, finishing a first-quarter breakaway with a hop and a finger roll instead of a jam. He made 16 of 28 shots, pulled down 10 rebounds, dished out 6 assists in forty-five minutes. But even that effort, combined with solid showings from Shaq, Grant, and Fox, was not enough. In the fourth quarter the Nuggets recovered from a 9-point deficit, then pulled ahead. Kobe was weary. He tried to tie the game with a 3-pointer, but his balance was off and he missed. Then Nick Van Exel sank a 3-pointer with thirty-six seconds left to seal a 107–102 Nuggets win.

On the team plane Kobe sat in his usual seat, across from the card-playing table, ankles taped to keep them from swelling. He wasn't going to let his problems get him. He sat back, adjusted his DVD player. I've always been able to play with one sprained ankle, he thought, but till now I never had the challenge of playing with two of them.

A few nights later, before the Lakers played the Golden State Warriors, Kobe was in so much pain he could barely sleep. He wasn't much for dwelling in the past, even the recent past, but during that long night he found himself thinking back three months earlier, to the Lakers' losing game against the Warriors, when he and Antawn Jamison scored 51 points each. Considering the present condition of his hip and shoulder and ankles, 51 points was a number he wasn't aiming for now.

Against the Warriors he scored 22 points, but the strange thing was that the Warriors' Jamison didn't score at all. That, thought Kobe, kind of put his own problems in perspective. Bad as he felt, not scoring was something he just couldn't relate to.

Two days later Shaq celebrated his twenty-ninth birthday. Jackson told Penberthy and Madsen to lead the team in singing "Happy Birthday," and during the song guys looked over to see if Kobe was singing. He was.

Shaq was still a big kid. "You know what I really want for my birthday?" he said. "Anna Kournikova."

But later, when talking about Kobe, there were signs that he was growing up. "I don't hate the guy," he said. "It's like being married. We need each other."

19

DRUGS AND MONEY

J.R. Rider had many skills: he was a spot shooter, a post-up guard, a defensive guard, a one-on-one player. This meant, potentially, that he could fill a number of holes for the Lakers. He was not doing this, however, for the simple reason that the burden he had hoped to shed by joining the team was nothing more or less than himself. He maintained that he played better when he was a starter, ignoring that Jackson was a stickler for earning minutes and not about to reward a player who was regularly late, who drifted away from the bench during games and simply disappeared. One evening he stood courtside directly in front of one of the team's more devoted fans, the actress Dyan Cannon, obscuring her view, immersed in his own world, neither noticing nor caring when her assistant tried to get his attention by tugging repeatedly on his arm.

Rider had his own way of looking at things, and he stuck with his viewpoint no matter what. He still refused to heed the NBA's demand that he participate in its aftercare program. He had never tested positive for drugs, he pointed out, so why should he have to join a program he shouldn't be in? It was believed that Rider had spent hundreds of thousands of dollars fighting to stay out of the aftercare program, fighting what he called "the power of the NBA coming down on me."

In early March he lost that fight when the league announced that he had been suspended for five games, information relayed in a dryly worded statement that did not obscure that here was another sexy story for that substantial segment of the press that showed up in force only for melodrama and play-offs.

Players and substance abuse was a topic that the Lakers' announcer, Chick Hearn, referred to as "that doggone subject." It had long plagued the NBA, particularly since the sudden, tragic death of Len Bias, who died on the court in 1986 as a result of cocaine abuse days after the Boston Celtics made him the number-two draft pick in the country. Rider's suspension added credence to a recent remark by Charles Oakley, who had stated publicly that 60 percent of the NBA's players used drugs. This was widely believed simply because it affirmed what many suspected about self-indulgence and arrogance among players.

In the wake of the Rider announcement, Jackson could not have been much in the mood for his pregame press conference. His willingness to use the press for his own reasons did not mean that he respected it. He might befriend certain reporters at certain times, but as an entity the press was, he believed, increasingly hostile, scandal-driven, and distant from the press he had known in his own playing days, when reporters functioned largely as extensions of a team's publicity machine. But Jackson's pregame and postgame conclaves with the press were mandated by the NBA, and though he shared Rider's distaste for being told what to do, he also appreciated the value of responsibility and discipline—concepts, he would observe later, that had no meaning for J. R. Rider. So Jackson made his way through a tangle of reporters and cameras and took his place at the podium that was wheeled into position just outside the locker room for these occasions. He looked around at the assembled mob. "Flies on a manure heap," he said.

Rider's situation, said Jackson, "doesn't endear Isaiah to us, obviously." Still, he seemed inclined to give him every opportunity. A man who had titled his autobiography *Maverick* might have a soft spot for a rogue player, just as a man who had planned to be a minister might seek to rejoin the prodigal to the fold.

Jackson knew that Rider wanted to play more and be more productive. "You can make or break this team in the play-offs," he told him the next day. "You need to work out every day, be prepared, and come back with a vengeance."

Rider was out for five games. During that time his locker was empty aside from a fishnet bag stuffed with dirty laundry, a nice touch for those inclined to the symbolic.

Every man has three lives, a public, a private, and a secret one, and sometimes, as Jackson learned when coaching the Bulls, the thread connecting private and public life could be read easily. For example, Horace Grant was a twin. He took the view that everyone ought to be treated equally, an assumption endowing him with a generosity that made him one of Tex Winter's favorite players.

Similarly, Jackson had always thought that what made Scottie Pippen such a team-oriented player was that sharing came naturally to him because he was the youngest of twelve children in a poor family. Then you had Kobe, less ready to share, the only son and unrelenting focus of his family.

But players were also affected by unseen things, those feelings of shame or weakness or unworthiness they were inclined to leave unspoken. Rider might be one of those cases, though Rider himself had another view of what caused his troubles, one that made some sense to those with an intimate view of players. "All my problems happened," he insisted, "when I started getting money in the NBA." He'd come into the league so young and clueless, he pointed out, that when he got his first paycheck he couldn't understand why they'd taken half of his money.

The impact of money on NBA players was too enormous to calibrate. Basketball was the ultimate "Mine Is Bigger Than Yours" world, where players were always trying to one-up each other, vying over who had the most cars, women, square footage.

Few jobs allowed a young man, a poorly educated young man at that, to make so much money so quickly while having so much free time. Then there was the fact that once you became an NBA player you were expected to be much more than an athlete. There was always someone who wanted your name on a guest list or a board of trustees or on a new product that cured teenage acne. People wanted you to bank at their bank, to front a land deal for them, to be the life of their New Year's Eve party, to invest in a great new company that imported cutting-edge furniture from Japan.

Players entered the league as nice kids, expelling their energy on the court, leaving their aggression in the game, unprepared for the effects of the money, the adoration, the people sucking up to them. In ten years with the Lakers, John Black, the director of public relations, saw many of those kids become spoiled and ungrateful and full of themselves. That was why, he thought, when you encountered a kid like Kobe Bryant, a good, well-mannered kid, who insisted on calling you Mr. Black during his first years on the team—who was so good with the fans and with children that the Make-a-Wish Foundation brought to the arena—you'd find yourself thinking, Don't let this kid change.

Generally speaking, players changed. For most, the journey to the NBA was also a journey away from the communities they grew up in, where people knew and looked out for one another. And this meant that coming to the NBA forced them to grapple with the twin confusions of instant fame and instant anonymity.

Basketball players were travelers on that classic, mythic American road from poverty to wealth, obscurity to renown. It was no secret that there was a gaping pothole in this road marked "too much too soon" and that a lot of players fell through it. The fact was that basketball increasingly was not simply a sport. It was a culture, and like any celebrity-driven culture, it was based on a sense of entitlement that had a way of turning toxic. "The pure products of America go crazy," the poet William Carlos Williams wrote. And the pure American products of the NBA were defendants in paternity suits and owners of unregistered guns. In the 2000–2001 season, Rod Strickland would spend ten days in jail for drunk driving, Jason Kidd would be sentenced to "anger counseling," Charles Oakley would be suspended without pay and fined $10,000 for hurling a ball at Tyrone Hill's head, and Jason Williams would shout at several fans of Asian descent, "Remember the Vietnam War? I'll kill y'all just like that."

The NBA's commissioner, David Stern, was an eminently civilized man who grew up in New York City working after school in his father's delicatessen near Madison Square Garden. Like the players, he came to have far more than he was born to, though he retained a sensitivity to the millions of NBA fans who would not earn, in a lifetime, what some players made in a season.

David Stern did not need editorial writers to tell him what message was sent to these people when players threw towels in one another's faces or when Mark Cuban, owner of the Dallas Mavericks, ran onto the court screaming at referees. The NBA responded to these transgressions by imposing fines and suspensions, but these were not much of a deterrent. Mark Cuban had founded Broadcast.com, an Internet venture he soon sold for billions of dollars. He had plenty of money to throw at the fines levied by Stu Jackson, a senior vice president of the NBA and the league's enforcer. Cuban misbehaved so regularly that the going joke was that he'd earned a spot on Jackson's speed dial. The prospect of fines seemed to fill Cuban with the same level of concern and social responsibility they inspired in Shaq. "No man can control me with money," Shaq said. "I say what's on my mind whenever I want." In other words, the rules do not apply to people who can buy their way out of them, which was not exactly the kind of socially minded message with which the NBA sought to be associated.

The pressures on players increased along with their salaries, with the result that basketball was a very different game, played by a different kind of player, than the game and the players of 1967, the year that Phil Jackson signed a two-year contract with the Knicks for a grand total of $26,000. Even in those days stars made the kind of money that bought Jerry West his Ferraris and Mercedes-Benzes and houses in Bel-Air and Brentwood. But in the summer of 1982, the pay scale rose precipitously when Magic Johnson signed a twenty-five-year contract for $1 million a year. This was a significant change, setting the stage for a future in which big talent could be held to long-term deals for big money. Eleven years later, Michael Jordan was earning $6 million a year, a sum that Jerry Reinsdorf, the CEO for the Bulls, continued to pay him during his baseball sabbatical. Reinsdorf was also, not incidentally, CEO of the Chicago White Sox, on whose minor-league team Jordan was playing. When Jordan returned to basketball in 1995, Reinsdorf was given an opportunity to say "Welcome back" in the form of a $36 million annual salary.

In fact, there was a substantial argument to be made for this salary. Jordan was the rising tide on which an astonishing number of boats had been lifted, including those of the owners of sports arenas, purveyors of NBA souvenirs, and the National Broadcasting Company. In light of that, and considering what he had done to generate fascination with the game and respect for it, it was hard to argue that Jordan's salary was excessive.

But his payday had the effect of letting the genie out of the bottle so that players who had yet to lift anything, including their own scoring average, were demanding what one of the most popular NBA players, Kevin Garnett, called "the loot." And getting that loot was a dangerous thing, giving very young men a sense of arrival and power they had yet to earn. Garnett came into the league in 1995, the first player drafted directly out of high school since Moses Malone was drafted into the ABA twenty-one years earlier. Garnett was not averaging 20 points a game when he signed a $125 million multiyear deal. "I want the sky," he said at the time, "and I'm not going to stop until I reach the top."

Even a player at the end of his career, like Ron Harper, wouldn't come in for less than a couple of million, though this had to do with money only indirectly. As Harper pointed out, he had $10 million in the bank and didn't need money. If all this signaled a new America, it was still an America retaining the old equation that worth is counted in dollars.

In the 2000–2001 season, every eighteen-year-old coming to the draft with his mother and his agent was expecting millions and looking to augment lucrative new contracts with what Darius Miles, the NBA's youngest player that season, called "a lot of pub." The power of that publicity and money was such, thought Ian Thomsen of *Sports Illustrated*, that at the draft, in the twenty or so seconds between the moment that a young player's name was announced by David Stern and the moment he joined Stern at the podium, his life changed irrevocably. And there was no adequate preparation for it, no way for a young man to cope readily with great wealth when all of his previous struggles had been about having nothing.

The guys who'd known money before signing their first contract could be counted on the fingers of a single hand: Grant Hill, Mark Madsen, Steve Kerr, Kobe Bryant. Kobe enjoyed the beautiful clothes, the bedroom of his home in Pacific Palisades with its marble floor and huge windows looking out on the ocean, but the odd thing about money, he would say, was that once you had it, people were always pressing things on you for free.

Some players wanted an immediate payday. Others were willing to forgo the payday to play on a team that had a chance to win. Which choice you made depended on whether you saw the game as a proving ground or as a business. Most players went for the sure thing, which was the money, figuring they had a brief time in which to grab what might be the only brass ring they would be offered.

With that prospect in mind, Rick Fox had agreed, in the summer of 1997, to sign a new contract with the Boston Celtics. He was not happy there, but Rick Pitino had just taken over as head coach and offered him a $17 million contract. Fox was on his way to get his hair cut for the press conference at which the deal would be announced when Pitino called again to say he was relinquishing rights to him. Fox was very angry, of course, but more than that he was ashamed for having been so willing to sell out.

The Cleveland Cavaliers offered him $20 million, but by then money had become beside the point. His interest was in two disparate things, redeeming his earthly soul and winning, both of which could be addressed by accepting an offer from the Lakers for one year at $1 million. When word of this got around, Fox was swamped with calls from coaches and players, whose expressions of admiration were, he thought, an interesting index of the degree to which money had come to dominate all other considerations.

The NBA of the new millennium was where coaches tried to discipline men half their age making many times their salary. It was where players forged allegiances with companies that paid them endorsement fees exceeding their salaries and where lawyers and agents parlayed a player's status on a team into individual benefits. Addressing a team of players, John Salley once said, had become like talking to the CEOs of twelve corporations.

The money had spawned a generational tension as well. Older players viewed younger guys, who started out with the immense salaries they had struggled to attain, as spoiled and lazy, less team-oriented, less disciplined, and ungrateful. Not that gratitude had ever been a major impulse among older players, which was why, when Jordan's Chicago Bulls were looking bored and disinterested before a game, Jordan took it upon himself to remind them of what basketball had given them. "Let's go, millionaires," he said.

20

PAIN AND PLAYING THROUGH IT

By the end of the first week in March, five teams in the Pacific Division, including the Los Angeles Lakers, were within a game and a half of first place. The Lakers had some tough games ahead, including one against the Toronto Raptors, a team with considerable firepower led by Vince Carter, an exceptional player who shared Michael Jordan's Tar Heel pedigree.

Few players had been hyped more relentlessly upon joining the league, and in three years as a player Carter had discovered what Kobe was learning: that what gets caught up in the tornado of the sports world's hype machine is apt to be thrust back to earth with a vengeance. Kobe and Carter were inevitable rivals, though Kobe tended to wince at suggestions of competition between them. And both dismissed efforts to nominate them in the "Who Will Be the Next Jordan?" sweepstakes, especially now that rumors were circulating that Jordan would be returning to the game.

Still, in the last two years, with Jordan not playing, it was Carter who had ranked first in the All-Star voting, a fact not lost on Kobe. On the other hand, Kobe had a championship ring, while Carter, like the young Jordan, was on a team whose dismal record in the play-offs had increased the length of his summer vacations.

Somewhere early in the game against the Raptors, Kobe sensed that this was becoming one of the toughest games he'd ever played. He started forcing things, exceeding what the defense allowed, turning away, yet again, from Jackson's caution to let the game come to him.

He missed 12 of his 13 shots, while Carter scored 15 points, nailing one jumper after another.

During halftime Kobe lay down in the trainer's room, trying to get centered. He had been playing long enough to know how to read the crowd, to know when they were with him and when they weren't. And he knew what they thought tonight. They think I can't bring it to the table, he thought.

But he could. He would. This chance was too important to let it go by. It's an opportunity to kill two birds with one stone, he thought—win the game and win the individual matchup.

Coming back in the third quarter, he breathed deeply, shook off the fatigue, his heart pounding. He went for it, no holds barred, throwing down a pair of two-handed jams. He was aching, exhausted, but it didn't matter. Whatever he had to take, he could take. As a kid he had played until he vomited, then kept playing until he hit the wall. Still he played. And it taught him that you can push yourself beyond the point where your body shuts down, and from that he deduced that the game was mental, that mind could win out over matter. Too much of the time the game was too easy for him. He loved having obstacles thrown in his way. Not that he perceived anything as an obstacle. For Kobe there were no obstacles; there were only challenges. He pressed on, scoring 29 points to Carter's 28, as the Lakers beat the Raptors 97–85.

Afterward he was spent. That night, for the first time in two weeks, he fell asleep at 2:00 A.M. instead of 4:00. He woke up feeling almost rested from those extra two hours of sleep.

In the second week of March the Lakers found themselves in first place in their division as a result of a Spurs win over the Trail Blazers. Portland had lost the momentum achieved after their Christmas Day victory at the Staples Center, a decline owed in part to their leading player, Rasheed Wallace, now two technical fouls away from tying the record for technicals in a single season, a record standing at 38 and established the previous season by Wallace himself.

The Spurs were a different story, all play-off dreams and forward momentum. Generally acknowledged to have the best defense in the league, they were evidence that one key to success is peaking at the right moment. The Spurs were basking in the kind of late-season surge they'd enjoyed in 1999, when it carried them to play-off sweeps of the Lakers and the Blazers, then on to the championship.

This would be the Lakers' last game against the Spurs in the regulation season, their last chance to size each other up, take each other's measure, and to gather the confidence that would come from a win and would be critical in the looming play-offs. Kobe couldn't wait for the game, but he woke up that day feeling sick and decided he'd better skip the morning shootaround. He arrived at the Staples Center an hour and a half before game time looking weak and shaky and determined.

He went to the trainer's room and lay down until the game started. Then he dragged himself up and onto the court, where he pushed himself into a play-off level intensity to combat a Spurs lead that rose, in the second quarter, to 15 points. But there is such a thing as too much intensity, and by the second half his teammates could see that Kobe's aggressiveness was backfiring. He was edgy and seemed ready to take every shot.

When Tyronn Lue got the ball, Kobe looked over at him. The crowd chanted, "Lue! Lue! Lue!" as Lue held the ball while Kobe indicated with his eyes that Lue should shoot it. Kobe was always trying to light a fire in Lue, fire that Lue knew he lacked. Lue could not count the number of times that Kobe had encouraged him, saying, "Don't be afraid to take a big shot," or how many times he had warned him in practice, "They're gonna come after your little ass." But with ball in hand, Lue froze, positioned for a shot that he could make in any shootaround with ease. Kobe, frustrated, seeking to goad him, shouted, "Shoot that bitch."

Certain things are difficult to do without confidence. Lue shot and missed. But then no one was making their shots except Shaq and Kobe. Fox missed seven jump shots. Shaw missed three. Horry didn't get a single offensive rebound. Kobe kept pressing, hitting an 18-

footer to tie the score at 81 with eighteen seconds left in the game. San Antonio scored, then Kobe made 2 free throws to tie it at 83 with only a few seconds left.

In the first forty-seven seconds of overtime, Kobe made two baskets, followed by 2 turnovers. As San Antonio scored, he pressed his palms down, against the air, as if trying to tamp down his temper. Kobe's mood could be read by his hands. When things went right, he batted his fists in the air. When things went wrong, he knotted his fists into balls, as he did now when San Antonio pushed ahead, taking the score to 93–89 while the clock ran down. With thirteen seconds left, he missed a 3-pointer. Then the buzzer sounded. His fists were knotted as he walked off the court.

It was a miserable, embarrassing loss, a loss that Kobe blamed on weak defense and that Shaq blamed on Kobe. As they showered, Brian Shaw apologized to Shaq for the entire supporting cast, none of whom had scored more than 6 points. How and why this happened depended on who was doing the assessing. Maybe they played poorly because Kobe was taking over the ball. Or maybe he took over the ball because they were playing poorly. In fact, they were all distracted, and had been all season, taking their lead or not taking it from two leading players whose ability to play together remained in question.

Kobe left the floor exhausted and dehydrated. In the safety of the trainer's room, he collapsed onto a cot. After some time, the Lakers' assistant public relations director, Mike Uhlenkamp, went to check on him. He had a fever and was developing the flu. His rail-thin body was covered with towels. An IV protruded from his right arm. Uhlenkamp was not easily rattled, but Kobe's apparent frailty was startling.

"Are you OK?" he asked.

Kobe looked up at Uhlenkamp, weary, incredulous. "Do I look OK?" he said.

Everything that had been easy for Kobe suddenly became difficult. Just weeks before, he had angered the older guys by saying that the team had too many old legs. He had come to practice loose and limber and made fun of Brian Shaw, laughing at how stiff he was, at how long it took him to get warmed up.

Shaw might not like the attitude, but he understood it. When he was young, his attitudes weren't any different. In his rookie year on the Celtics, Shaw had played with the great Dennis Johnson, by then a veteran whose age was showing. Shaw would laugh when he saw Johnson in the training room after practice with ice on everything. "D.J.," he'd say, "you're an old man." In practice, when Shaw would be jumping and playing hard and trying to dunk everything, Johnson would look over at him, shaking his head. "It doesn't matter if you dunk or you lay it up," he would say. "It's still 2 points."

Now it had come full circle. Shaw was the old guy, an old guy lately amazed to hear Kobe saying the players he most identified with were him, Horace Grant, and Harper. For the first time, on the court, Kobe could not simply power his way through everything. "There's cracks and holes that I've always been able to get through," he told Shaw, "that I can't quite get through right now. I can't elevate the way I want to."

"That's how I feel every single day," Shaw told him. "So now this is where you grow up. This is where you say, 'OK, I have to rely less on my athletic ability and more on my smarts.'

"You have to put yourself in a position where you don't need to jump that high. I can get as many rebounds as you can because I know how to position myself to get them. I'm not just thinking, 'Oh, I'm going to jump over everybody.' "

Shaw could remember when Shaq felt indestructible too and got that Superman "Man of Steel" tattoo put on his arm. Then he tore his stomach muscle and found out that he wasn't made of steel. That awareness of frailty awaited them all. It was part of their reality, the terrible part.

Now Harp was trying to get back, practicing hard but then suffering pain. The fact was that to use your body the way they did was a barter. As an athlete you were fitter than anyone, but only for a time. That fitness allowed you to abuse your body, but the point always came when your body betrayed you. They had all been through it, had all experienced the agony that Rick Fox described as a pain that can't be remedied by all the Advil in the world. That kind of pain changed your thinking, it changed your game. It changed how you dealt with everything.

When he watched Harper on the court, Fox would think, only half-jokingly, Only dead people know how Harp feels. Some days Horace Grant looked in the mirror and had to remind himself that he was thirty-five, not seventy. Recently he had been hit in the face, and as the wound was being glued together so that he could get back in the game, someone asked what he was thinking. He laughed and said, "I'm thinking of changing professions."

You gave your body's soundness to the cause of doing something you felt proud of. But eventually you'd be fifty years old with bad hips and gimpy legs, walking around like Phil Jackson with the gait of a wounded animal. We're sacrificing the end up front, thought Fox. That reality prompted cautious players to take it easier, while others took a damn-the-torpedoes attitude and played harder, caught up in the moment or an excess of macho or a sense of fate.

One thing's for sure, thought Robert Horry. We all have to pay the price in this game.

Basketball was a sport of rising and falling fortunes, in which everything had a way of changing for the better or the worse in a single, unanticipated moment. Derek Fisher had missed sixty-two games. For weeks he had waited for the go-ahead to play. Now, at last, he was cleared to go, and he called his parents to tell them that he would play in that night's game against the Boston Celtics, although Jackson warned him that it would be impossible for him to rediscover his rhythm quickly. "I don't know how many minutes I'll get," he told them, "but whatever it is, I'll take them."

Anyone who came to the Staples Center when the doors opened an hour and a half before games had seen Fisher on the court, practicing shots with Jim Cleamons. With his movement restricted, there was little he could do to improve his game. But he could stand rooted to the floor to the right or the left of the basket and shoot the ball. He had never been much of a shooter, but the ceaseless repetition made something click, set him into the right rhythm, got the movement into his body.

So much about Fisher impressed Cleamons and moved him: his work ethic, his humility, his graciousness. Watching him shoot one ball after another, he thought, Derek should be very proud of the person that he is.

As word spread that D Fish was back, the gloom in the locker room lifted. "We need to start holding each other accountable," he told the team. "At this point we want to be the best team in the West." With the Lakers' record at 41–21, after sixty-two games of the eighty-two-game season, Fisher was still convinced that they could finish the season with 60 wins.

Even if in this case he was dreaming, as Jackson suggested, Fisher was a genuine leader, a voice of faith and hope. The team had never been more in need of what he brought to the game: the hustle, the grit, the all-out effort, the heart.

Every member of the team knew how hard he had fought to get back. Fisher was an integral part of their lives, the guy who had been there for them through tough moments on the court and off. He had been there for Tyronn Lue when Lue had surgery the year before. As Lue walked into the Staples Center and heard the good news, he thrust his fists into the air, face beaming, a generous response from a player who knew that, as the team's other small guard, it was likely his own spot on the roster that Fisher would get.

When you fight that hard to get back, you come back with passion and fire, qualities that Fisher had never lacked in any case. He went dashing onto the court so excited to play, and so thrilled by the ovation that greeted him, that he jumped up onto Robert Horry's back and hung there a moment, arms wrapped around Horry's neck.

He had taken thousands and thousands of shots, but even before he touched the ball that night he had transformed his game in his mind. He used to worry about what people thought of him. That didn't matter now. All that mattered was being aggressive, helping his teammates, and having as great a time as possible. In the first minutes he made 2 free throws, took a steal, a rebound, sank a layup. This is like an out-of-body experience, he thought.

Kobe, still sick with the flu, watched from his bed at home. He was moved to see Fisher playing with a fervor that he himself always tried to summon but lately could not. Fisher's presence proved that an inspired individual can lift a team, and now they all became tougher, more focused, as Fisher scored a career-high 26 points, made 8 assists and 6 steals. That's an incredible game, a remarkable game, thought Jackson. So much for training camp.

With its bursts of energy, sheer talent, and power, Fisher's victory was one of spirit, of determination, a victory that was compensation for the long months of frustration and gave purpose to his having been consigned to the bench for sixty-two games. Maybe, he thought, there was some value to his long, painful absence if, by returning, he had raised in the other players the fragile but essential hope that players and teams and seasons can be resurrected.

21

"YOU SICKEN ME"

The resurrection continued as the Lakers embarked on a road trip that had them telling themselves, "If we can survive it, we'll be back in the heat of it."

Kobe returned to play against the Detroit Pistons, emerging from the locker room before game time whistling for joy. He took it slow in the first half, so slow that when he got back to the bench he heard people muttering behind him, "Kobe isn't showing up."

"Don't think about it, Kobe," he heard a woman say. He turned and saw her sitting nearby, in a courtside seat. "Don't worry about it," she said. "Just play through it. Please play through it."

And he did. Ignoring the pain, he traversed the court, coiled, ready, shooting one shot, then another. Jackson wanted to take him out in the fourth quarter. But Kobe begged him to leave him in, insisting that if he had to stop playing his ankle would stiffen. So Jackson relented, and as the clock ran down, Kobe drove to the basket to seal a tie. In overtime he made one basket, then another, tapping his heart with his hand. The game ended in a Lakers win, 125–119. Kobe had played forty-eight minutes, scored 39 points, hit 16 of 28 shots. The determination and fortitude that kept him out there, scoring and playing, shouldering the responsibility, had brought them all to a win they badly needed. That's Kobe, thought Fisher. The things people question about him or hate about him are the same things that you have to love about him.

That night the Lakers flew to Washington, D.C., arriving in the small hours. Settling into his hotel room, Kobe called room service and ordered buckets of ice. He poured the ice into the bathtub, pulled up a chair, and sat there soaking his ankles, weary and emotionally drained. Each day things were getting harder. The season meant to be his season of achievement had become his season of physical therapy, his season of one injury after another, of grappling with the ever-widening chasm between the way it was and the way it should be.

There were two realms in the world, he was discovering, the realm of the healthy and the realm of the infirm, and these realms had little in common. In the world of the well, people were free to worry about frivolous things. In the world of the infirm, there was only pain and telling yourself, as he told himself that night, I have to get through it. I have to learn how to deal with it.

But by now he knew that he had lost more than facility. He had lost the youthful certainty that if he wanted something badly enough he could will it into being. For the first time in his life, he was finding that what he wanted did not necessarily have a bearing on what he would get.

One thing he was lucky about, he thought, was to have teammates who understood him. Teammates like Harp, B Shaw, and Horace. In the past, he had never sought his teammates' understanding, never valued it, never needed it. But that was then. This was now.

Kobe had always loved children because children have no sense of limits, and in that sense he had lived a child's life. His favorite children's book, *Curious George*, was the tale of a monkey who goes off on wonderful adventures. "The part of it that really gets me," he once told his fiancée, Vanessa, "is that he looks at the world through a child's eyes. He's totally innocent. It's the time for him to go out and do whatever he wants, to accomplish whatever he wants."

It was a telling description; that was how he felt too. His summary of the book might have been a description of the charmed life he had lived. If innocence is that time before you learn that things do not always go according to plan, Kobe was less innocent than he once had been.

The Washington Wizards were notable mostly for their president, Michael Jordan, lately rumored to have received a call earlier in the season from Kobe to discuss Kobe's possible trade from the Lakers. The Wizards had one of the league's worst records. They were a demolition project, wrote *Daily News* reporter Howard Beck, with Rod Strickland being handed $5 million just to go away, with Juwan Howard traded and Mitch Richmond injured and not playing.

The previous season, despite their weaknesses, the Wizards had managed to snap the Lakers' nineteen-game winning streak. "Hey, Kobe," a worker outside the MCI Center called out as the team disembarked from the bus, "they gonna get you like they did last year?"

"Naw, not this time," said Kobe.

The Lakers came alive against the Wizards, forcing them into 19 turnovers, with Kobe grabbing 5 steals, Shaq blocking 5 shots, Fisher taking charges throughout his third consecutive game in double digits. If they were looking for a sign that they were finding their rhythm, they got it as Shaq headed down the center of the court, dribbling almost to his shoulder, flipping the ball to Fisher, who returned a lob from 20 feet that Shaq sent crashing through the net.

The final score, 101 to 89, gave the Lakers their first rout since December 28 in Phoenix. They left the arena with the jaunty walk of world champions. They were supposed to dominate, to beat people, and they were doing it, though on the other hand they didn't want to make too much of it. It would be kind of a loser thing to make a big deal out of beating the Wizards.

Then it was on to Orlando and their fourth consecutive win. Orlando had become Shaq's hometown, where he was booed and cheered with equal vigor and where his stepfather shouted at Kobe from courtside, "Pass the ball. Pass the damn ball."

Kobe drilled a 23-foot jumper, but he was wearing down, making only 5 of the 17 shots he attempted. He dunked off a lob pass from Fisher, but he could barely get his hands over the rim.

He was exhausted the next day in Atlanta, where they were playing the Hawks, another weak team and one badly in need of their former center, Dikembe Mutombo, a defensive force traded that week to the Philadelphia 76ers.

Atlanta played a fast-paced game. The Lakers tried to run with them. It's not our game, thought Horace Grant. We're trying to match up with them, and we can't.

Players took off with the ball, failing to heed the admonitions that Jackson issued from the bench, speeding it up when he told them to slow it down, shooting when he told them to pass, ignoring him when he whistled to get their attention, pinkies stuffed in the corners of his mouth. Kobe was surly, out of control, snapping at Fisher when he turned the ball over, snapping at Fox, shouting at Jackson. He was raging, a rage that had nothing to do with any of them and every-thing to do with his own limits. In the past he had used his anger to notch up his game. When he was a child with a very bad temper, his mother had told him to channel his temper into basketball. When he did, he came to crave and need the release it gave him. Now when he felt unchallenged on the court, he found that he could fire himself up by thinking of something that made him angry, the way actors use memories to work up emotion. He had become a master at psyching himself. I'm gonna try to kill you, he'd think before a game. Don't matter who you are, man. I'm coming after you.

But he was too worn down to rechannel his anger. He was too worn to defend Jason Terry, who scored 36 points on him, too worn to make 4 of his last 5 shots, including a 19-foot jumper to tie the game with three seconds left, a shot that went clanging off the rim. The Hawks were left to a 108–106 victory. They did not need Dikembe Mutombo to defeat a team of champions who made 19 turnovers. It was a night, said the Hawks' Nazr Mohammed, when it could be said that it's great to be a Hawk—bringing the total of such nights, observed reporter Tim Brown, to one.

How in the world, wondered Derek Fisher, could the world cham-pions lose to a half-baked team like the Hawks? They were all shaken and disappointed, and no one was more disappointed than he was. The four-game streak that followed his return had gratified him, for he knew it signaled that he had lifted the team. Now those great feel-ings were dashed. Usually he had a lot to say after games, but as other guys chewed on the loss in the locker room, he said nothing. That spoke for itself, and the others knew it. Usually Fisher liked to grab a bite with them, but he wanted to be alone that night.

When the press was let into the locker room, it was empty except for Brian Shaw. "Everyone wants to bury their head in a hole like an ostrich," Shaw said.

Derek Fisher went back to his hotel room, ordered room service, and turned the television on. He didn't care what he watched. Anything would do as long it wasn't sports highlights. Somehow, he thought, the team's problems never reached critical mass. They got bad, they got better, they got bad again, but they never got to the point where the whole thing could be aired and dealt with and finished. Will it ever get better? he wondered. Will the trouble ever end?

The next morning Brian Shaw checked out the team's standing in the newspapers. The Western Conference was up for grabs. The Lakers would have been in first place if they'd won a few games they ought to have won. All the games we messed up like we did last night, Shaw thought. It's like they're trying to give us the championship but we don't want to take it.

On that road trip Jackson was publicizing his third book, *More Than a Game*, written with his friend Charley Rosen. At one point he spoke with a columnist for the *Chicago Sun-Times*, Rick Telander. They had a cordial relationship. Telander had edited Jackson's diaries for *ESPN the Magazine*, which they had contracted to turn into a book until Jackson decided against it. Now, they had a long rambling conversation, speaking of many things, including Kobe. Jackson mentioned that Kobe had been saddled with the playmaking duties that come with the guard position. And he said other, more damning things about him, assuming they were not for publication.

Some time ago, Jackson had posted a note on the washing machine in his beachfront house: don't let your successes go to your head or let your failures go to your heart. In the wake of the loss to the Hawks, that dictum was harder to live by, and Jackson spent another long night questioning whether he was the right coach for the team. He had never thought the season would come to this, never anticipated that it would be the most difficult of any season in his memory, a season when he wouldn't see improvement in the team or achieve the momentum he thrived on.

In eleven years as a head coach in the NBA, he had won seven championships. The 1995–96 Chicago season had been his best, with the Bulls going 72–10. The Lakers had lost more than twice that many, with more games ahead of them. How, Jackson wondered, do coaches get through a season where they lose sixty games?

At times he was asked if he could coach Kobe again. "Yes," he would always say, "if he wants to be coached." Now he wasn't sure that he could coach any of these guys after this season.

Recently the athletic performance coordinator he'd brought with him from the Bulls, Chip Schaefer, had told him a slogan he'd learned in the marines, and Jackson had shared it with the players. "Think about this," he told them. " 'Immediate, willing, obedience to order.' " It was a useful slogan, he thought, but some of the guys bristled. They weren't looking to be obedient to orders. Not to orders, he told them; it's *order*.

He expected communication gaps. He expected players to be willful. He, too, was willful. But he was also there to do a job, and he had to do it, in spite of everything.

All season he and Kobe had argued during games. He shouted. Kobe shouted back. Publicly he insisted that the only problem they had was with the people who wrote that they had a problem. Privately, his frustration with Kobe was showing, and he was noting with increasing frequency that there was a difference between being worldly, which Kobe was, and being mature, which he wasn't. Players were lately coming to the game too young, too green, he would say, lacking the maturity you get in college. Basketball is a man's game, and he often thought about something they said in the Bulls' locker room: that NBA stands for "No Boys Allowed."

Above all, he thought that the team's situation was out of hand. It couldn't go on like this, with every step forward followed by two steps back.

He called the players to his hotel room. In the past, they had seen him angry. They had seen him walk away after a game saying, "Don't talk to me. You played like Broadway whores; you let your defense be penetrated."

But what they sensed in him now was something deeper than anger and more disturbing. "I'm not coming to practice today," he told them. "I can't stand watching you guys. I can't watch you anymore. You sicken me."

They sat there, stunned and still. Devean George's eyes were as round as saucers. They had become accustomed to looking for subliminal messages in Jackson's declarations, for a purpose implied rather than stated. But this time it seemed there were no tactics, no psychological games, no secret meanings. There was only real disappointment, real frustration, real emotion. To see Phil this way, thought Fisher, when he's been so patient, so kind . . . it's just painful.

Jackson opened up the meeting. He looked at Rick Fox, waiting for him to say something. Fox had also come from a family of evangelical ministers. It was a bond between them, an upbringing that prompted them to look for meaning in the game, to see a spiritual component in the values of teamwork and fellowship, to look with awe at God-given talent. But Fox couldn't say anything. He was too disappointed, too upset to trust what would come out of him. When the players filed out of the room, he went to Jackson to apologize. He would have spoken if he could, he said. Yes, said Jackson, he was disappointed that he hadn't. They went downstairs together, then walked through the lobby, proceeding slowly in silence. And Fox could feel how intensely Jackson felt, how much he was hurting.

The thing was, said Jackson, that he really didn't know what would come out of what he'd said, if any good would result from it. He just knew that he had to do something.

"I don't know which way they're gonna go," he told his staff. "They could pull together. They could fall apart."

The team shuffled off the bus, into the arena. As they lifted weights and did a few drills, each of them wondered how it had gone this far. We enjoyed so much success the first year Phil was here, thought Fisher. We thought we already knew what winning takes. If you feel like you know something, you don't work hard to continue to learn. You just kind of shut the engines down and kind of cruise on in.

While the players were on the court, some of the beat writers were on the Internet reading Rick Telander's account in the *Chicago Sun-Times* of his conversation with Jackson. "Someone told me that in high school Kobe used to sabotage his own games," he quoted Jackson as saying, "so the game could be close. So he could dominate at the end. To sabotage the team process, to be so self-centered in your own process, it's almost stupefying."

In the next minutes, one of the Lakers' press officers would be dispatched to tell Kobe about it. Shortly thereafter the Lakers would receive a call from Kobe's attorney, threatening to sue Jackson for slander. Why Jackson would say such things became a guessing game among those who rejected the obvious conclusion that he had never intended the words to be public.

Jackson was always assumed to have an agenda. Because he seemed to know what he wanted from people and was clever about getting it, the prevailing belief was that he was not just controlling but in such control of himself that he never made mistakes or acted on impulse. These were notions fed by Jackson's inscrutability, his knack for being readable only when he decided to be readable, useful qualities in the big-ego world of the NBA, where it could be advantageous to keep people off balance and guessing. To most observers, the prospect that Phil Jackson could make a simple, human mistake was unimaginable.

Before that night's game, Kobe told himself, It's no time to panic, no time to be afraid. Just go out there and give it your all. At the start of the game he felt pretty good as the Lakers controlled the pace, keeping it slow, and he contributed to their 16-point lead with 5 assists. Then Horace Grant turned the ball over, Shaq rushed a few shots, and suddenly they all lost their rhythm. Fox sent a pass to Kobe for an alley-oop dunk that he couldn't jump high enough to get. He felt his ankles weakening. His teammates saw him struggling across the court with the pained, labored grace of a wounded deer.

With forty-four seconds to go, the Lakers trailed by five. Kobe jumped and dished to Shaq for a dunk, then landed sideways on his ankle. He fell to the floor and lay there as the game went on around him. The pain overwhelmed him. He focused on it to see if it would go away, but it only got worse.

Chip Schaefer came onto the court. He leaned down and raised Kobe up slowly. Kobe slumped against Schaefer. He had nothing left.

Schaefer helped him from the court and the buzzer sounded. For the first season in a decade, the Bucks had swept the Lakers.

In the trainer's room Kobe sat perfectly still, his ankles in buckets of ice, staring into the middle distance. Jackson looked on. "If it's broken," he said quietly, "then it's serious."

Kobe remained there for a time, left to deal with the pain and to ponder the price you pay to play the game, and to wonder, for the first time in his life, if it was worth it.

On the plane ride home Shaq was silent. The winning streak that would bring them momentum seemed a fading hope. Still, he thought, nobody beat us, really. The Spurs did, Utah did, but except for that we messed around, gave it away. Nobody beat us. It's just us.

"We just have to go home, take a day off," he told the team, "soul-search, and come back. We just have to keep fighting and try to win as many games as possible."

As they waited for their luggage, Jackson went over to Kobe, who stood apart from the others with his fiancée, Vanessa, who had come to take him home. He was sorry, he said, that Kobe had to hear his comments that way. Kobe nodded, but he did not have much to say, not to Jackson or to anybody.

The charge was ridiculous, Kobe would say later, and that was the only serious remark he would make about it in public. He was tired of defending himself. He wasn't going to do it anymore. He always said he could never be broken. He never anticipated that this resolve would be subjected to such repeated testing.

22

"YOU COULD BE THE GREATEST"

few days later the Lakers played the Sacramento Kings, who were in first place in the Pacific Division and leading the league in scoring with an average of 101.4 points a game.

Shaq woke that day with a headache that felt like a migraine. He'd been having headaches all week, a week in which he came close to a second career triple double, made 70 percent of his free throws, involved the other players, and heard Kobe applaud him from the bench. "Superman is still out there," he was saying, "and he's making his free throws too, so bring it on."

But against Sacramento, Shaq's shots weren't falling, and his teammates could see that he was a step slow, with his defense suffering as a result. Shaq knew it too. Generally speaking, the team went as Shaq went, which, against good teams, on occasions like this one, could be dangerous. "Stay strong," he told them. "Keep your focus. You guys are doing great. Just keep it close. I'm going to wake up, and I'll be with you."

For the first time in a long while, the Lakers became a defensive force. Horace Grant blocked 3 of Chris Webber's shots, sending Webber into a funk that he couldn't shake off. In the second half, Shaq's pace quickened. His shot was surer. He pulled down 15 rebounds. With the Lakers down 71–62 at the start of the fourth quarter, he stole a pass from Webber to Peja Stojakovic, dribbled the length of the court, and dunked. With 1:47 left, he made 2 free throws. The buzzer sounded on an 84–72 Lakers win. Charged up, adrenaline pumping, Shaq looked out at the crowd booing him in the Arco Arena and shouted, "Shut the fuck up!"

"San Antonio lost today," Rick Fox said in the locker room. This meant that the Lakers were two games out of first place in the Western Conference. How long had it been, Fox wondered, since he'd allowed himself such a hopeful thought? Imagine us getting there, he mused, and being number one after all the turmoil.

The next day the Lakers played the Phoenix Suns, arriving at the America West Arena with a sense of hope and anticipation. "If we don't take care of business tonight," Derek Fisher told the team, "the win yesterday means nothing."

Soon into the game, Jackson saw that they weren't playing with a full deck or full energy. Shaq was lumbering, he thought. As the Suns scored repeatedly, Horace Grant shook his head. Man, he thought, when you don't have one of your superstars and the other one isn't having a good game, you're talking about over half of your defense right there.

The offense was no better. One shot after another bounced off the rim. "Get ready to play," Jackson told them at halftime. But they dragged on. Whoa, thought Jackson, this is a painful night.

When the buzzer sounded, the Lakers had 83 points to the Suns' 104. Fisher had made 3 out of 9 shots. "I'm sorry, guys," he said when they all retreated to the locker room. "I just didn't have it tonight."

Rick Fox left the arena quickly, his jaw tight. It's ridiculous to get in the positions we've been in, he thought, and lay an egg every time. It seemed that whenever he wished for something good to happen, something bad happened instead. Wish for a win and you get a teammate being suspended; wish for a late push and someone gets injured. We help ourselves, Fox thought, then we kick ourselves in the ass.

There were eleven games left in the season. It was late in the day, too late maybe, to bring it to the table. And maybe that was why Jackson softened his tone when the team discussed the defeat the next morning. "Don't worry about it," he told them. "Whether we win or don't win, whether Kobe comes back or doesn't, we're going to be in the play-offs. We want to have home-court advantage, but there's no use thinking in those terms.

"You just go and play the game."

Then they were back at the Staples Center, playing Sacramento again for the last time in the regular season, looking to pull off a sweep of a very good team and grab the psychological boost that would come from that. Jerry West, who rarely attended games, made an appearance in the locker room. He was preternaturally tense and intense. "You guys gotta win tonight," he kept saying. Watching his progress through the room, Rick Fox thought, He's like an alcoholic returned to a bar.

The Kings pushed ahead early, leaving them behind by 10, then 15 points. When they trailed by 20, the crowd began chanting, "Kobe! Kobe! Kobe!" The chant spread through the arena until thousands had joined in.

Early in the third quarter, Fox hit a 3-pointer. Peja Stojakovic talked trash to him, needling him about his defending, making him so angry that he taunted Stojakovic all the way down the court and got rewarded with a technical. Stojakovic hit a free throw that set the Kings on a 20–2 run. As they pressed past 100 points, a reporter joked, "If the other team scores 110, do we still get the chalupa?"

The Lakers lost 108–84. This is sad, thought Brian Shaw, who'd gotten into early foul trouble and missed the one shot he took. We had a lot to play for in this game.

Jerry West watched the debacle from Jerry Buss's luxury box, his face expressionless. It was Jerry West's kind of luck that the first game he had attended in ages would be the game that saw the Lakers put together their first consecutive 20-point defeats since the dreary 1998–99 season.

A team is a community, which means that it can prevail only when its citizens settle on a common purpose and are ready to spend themselves in a common cause. For this to occur, each player had to place his own needs second to the team's welfare. That the Lakers were unwilling to do this so late in the game puzzled and troubled team-conscious players.

When you win a championship, thought Rick Fox, with all the joy and pleasure we received from that, you'd think we'd all be on the same page to do it again. You'd think it would be clear to everyone that together we create something bigger than any one of us. Why wouldn't that message be clear enough?

This question had become more pressing as the clock ran down on the season and the failure to pull together reached crisis proportions.

In the past, management of a team crisis had fallen on occasion to Jerry Buss, as it did after the 1980–81 season. Magic and Norm Nixon had feuded publicly during the play-offs, Nixon complaining that he wanted the ball more and Magic replying that if Norm wanted the ball, they'd give him one with his name on it. By way of steering them toward the requisite brotherhood, Buss took them to Las Vegas and sat them down during a break in the ensuing festivities. "I'm not going to trade either one of you," he told them, "so let's deal with this like men." The next season Nixon and Magic played amicably together, and the Lakers won the title.

But more often, handling crises fell to Jerry West. West had an impeccable sense of right and wrong. He had a moral authority that many young players had never encountered. West could reach these men. He understood them. It was West who said, upon hearing that Kobe had gone to the gym the morning after he sealed the Lakers' 1997 play-off loss with an air ball shot from 16 feet, "You can bet that he went right to that same spot and started shooting." It was West who was sent for when Shaq refused to practice for his new young coach, Kurt Rambis, West who cooled Shaq down when he was ready to punch out Dennis Rodman.

West had told Shaq repeatedly that he had to make allowances for Kobe's youth, that Kobe's evolving talents required extra patience. Now the feud between Shaq and Kobe was in its fifth year, and the play-offs were looming, and West was not inclined to tread lightly. "Shaq," he said, "you have to stop being a big baby."

A few nights later Kobe went to West's home for a spaghetti dinner, accompanied by Arn Tellem, his agent, and one of West's close friends. Kobe adored Jerry West. He loved him as a man and honored him as a myth. West didn't just play basketball, in Kobe's view; he *was* basketball. "He's the NBA logo," he always said. And perhaps he valued West even more now that his relationship with his own father was changing as he prepared to get married and his parents, with whom he had lived in Los Angeles until recently, returned to Philadelphia.

West and Kobe had strong similarities in their respective games: the brilliant shooting, the rabid defense, the focus, the will to win, and the need to adjust to a dominant center. After dinner West talked for a long time, and Kobe listened. He talked about the difficulties and rewards of playing with Elgin Baylor and Wilt Chamberlain, about the chemistry between Kareem and Magic. More than most people, West understood that talent is exception-making, that great talent is a burden to possess and often an affront to the less talented. Clearly it had been a long year for Kobe. He was, he had felt at times, on a team with people who hated him. "I'd hate you, too," said West, "if I were your teammate."

None of it mattered, West told him. What mattered was putting these problems aside, getting beyond them. His own years of losing had given West a reverence for the healing power of winning. "Shaq wants to win as much as you do," he said, "and if you work well together, the two of you could be the greatest team in NBA history."

23

READY AT LAST

The Lakers played the Knicks on Sunday, April 1. That morning Gary Vitti, the Lakers' trainer, worked on Kobe's ankle for three hours. By game time Kobe felt loose. When the team met in the locker room prior to the game he was psyched up and nodding emphatically as Jackson told them, "Your destiny is in your hand. You can run this thing out, and you can win the Pacific Division."

The Knicks' new forward Glen Rice would be playing his first game against the Lakers at the Staples Center since the Lakers traded him at the end of the championship season. The Lakers offered to hold a pregame ceremony to honor him, but he turned it down. "Glen's going to be dangerous," Derek Fisher said to the team. "I know he's going to stick it to us."

Kobe was excited to be playing, but the minutes that usually seemed so short to him seemed very long as the pain increased in the strained tendon of his ankle. He shot and missed. He tried to guard Latrell Sprewell but couldn't stay with him. He took three more shots and missed each one. Eleven minutes after he came onto the court, he limped off it. Jackson watched him disappear through the north tunnel, then turned back to the game, his expression bleak. This might be the end of our season, he thought. He may not be able to play again.

It was a low-scoring game. Rice didn't have his 3-point stroke going, and the Lakers missed ten attempts at 3-pointers. With six seconds left and the Lakers down by one, Rice got the ball and went for a 3-pointer that bounced off the rim. The Lakers called for a time-out. In the huddle, as they planned the next play, Shaq said, "Make sure I get it." The final countdown resumed, but the Knicks were expecting them to pass off to Shaq and sandwiched him between two defenders.

With 5.6 seconds left, Fisher got the ball 13 feet from the basket. In the locker room, Kobe's eyes were riveted to the television as he paced back and forth, oblivious to the pain in his ankle. How many times had he been in a position like this, one shot down, the ball in his hands? These were the moments he lived for.

It was a dream moment for Fisher, too. He had always wanted to make the winning shot. He looked at the basket. He didn't have the look he wanted, didn't feel his legs quite under him. To his left, Grant was wide open, but Fisher was too immersed in the moment to see him. He shot the ball. It spun through the air, swatting the left side of the rim, bouncing away as the buzzer sounded. It had happened too suddenly, too fast. I wish, he thought, that this game could go on forever.

Fisher's missed 3-pointer was balm to the spurned Glen Rice. "They keep pretending they don't need me," Rice remarked cheerily as he made his way from the arena.

That night Rick Fox went to sleep angry. The season was nearly over and they hadn't yet played as they wanted to play. He hadn't foreseen this situation, hadn't prepared for it. In his sleep he ground his teeth all night long. He woke up with his jaw nearly locked and in need of a root canal in the right side of his mouth.

After the game with the Knicks Shaq went home and called his mother. He was dejected, downcast. "You made 31 points," she said. "What happened?"

Shaq thought for a moment. "I don't have an explanation," he said.

That next day, seeking the explanation, he decided that it came down to the other guys not trusting him. "We just want to start launching up 3s," he told Jerome. "Why wouldn't they come to me every time? We always try to make the spectacular play. On this team we have guys who think they can do things they can't. We don't have no bona fide 3-point shooters. Except for Kobe, we don't have players on this team who can create a shot."

His hurt extended beyond the court. It was about not feeling needed. "Look at the Spurs," he told Jerome. "They know to throw it to Tim first. The Bulls knew to throw it to Michael."

Phil could say all he wanted about having the offense run through him, thought Shaq, but in the end whether the team did it or not was about them as players.

The Lakers boarded their chartered flight to Salt Lake City with the dull, sad sense that they had hit bottom. All season long they had figured they could always win the next time, the next week, the next encounter. They had run out of next. With no time left and everything to lose, they were learning the meaning of Samuel Johnson's dictum: "Nothing focuses the mind like the prospect of hanging."

"Let's show some heart," they told each other. "Let's quit fucking around."

Their first opponent, toughest of this road trip, was the Utah Jazz, with its one-two punch of Karl Malone and John Stockton, Hall of Fame players, two of the greatest in the game. Play-by-play announcers had uttered the phrase "Stockton to Malone" so frequently over the years that it had merged into a single word. Yet they had never won a championship, and their moment was slipping by. This made them easier to defeat on certain nights and harder to defeat on nights when they battled most effectively against sinking into NBA history as the bridesmaids of a sport whose brides were Michael Jordan and Scottie Pippen.

"Everyone has to step their game up," Shaq told the players. It was time to help each other through actions and words, to give each other the confidence that if they played their man a certain way somebody would back them up if they got in trouble.

With 2:40 left, the Lakers were ahead and tired. Karl Malone made 2 free throws that put the Jazz within 2 points. "Beat L.A.! Beat L.A.!" the crowd at the Delta Center chanted. It was the kind of pressure the Lakers had folded under in the recent past. They didn't fold.

They showed a defensive grit beyond any they had showed all season. Shaq overpowered Malone in the post and made 2 free throws for a 90–84 lead. Horry stole a Stockton pass and went for a dunk. Fisher stole a Malone pass. On the bench Ron Harper held his championship ring up to the camera as Devean George pointed to it and big smiles broke out across the bench. The win had everyone hyped except Robert Horry. "You know me," he said of his season-high 20 points. "I just try to take advantage of my opportunities."

Now if we could get a streak going . . . they said, not needing to complete the sentence. A streak took on its own momentum, its own energy. It carried you through another win and then another, and pretty soon you would be feeling invincible.

The Lakers hadn't lost to the Chicago Bulls since Michael Jordan left the team. But while the Lakers were becoming known for falling apart down the stretch, Chicago was becoming known for pulling games out in the last two minutes.

"They're a young team," Derek Fisher warned the players. "They don't have much to lose at this point. They're going to play loose basketball. And there will be some emotion in the building with Phil returning. We have to be prepared. It won't be an easy game."

As luck would have it, this was the tenth anniversary of the Bulls' first championship victory, occasioning the showing of a commemorative video that was a wallow into a distant past: Jackson with Jordan, Jordan with the team; a champagne-soaked Horace Grant. Jackson's hair was still dark; Grant's body had yet to fill out. It all seemed so long ago, thought Grant, as he and Jackson watched from their seats on the visitors' bench.

That night the Bulls went after Shaq, hacking him again and again. Shaq became furious, an emotion that he expressed in a series of angry dunks. You can't help but feed off that energy, thought Brian Shaw. And as it swept over the team, it bound them in a determination that led them to another victory.

Funny how it could all turn around, they thought. Funny how much there was to be said for this momentum that Phil always talked about.

And at some point along the way, as they traveled from Utah to Chicago to Boston, the men who play for the Los Angeles Lakers recognized that something had happened and that it was important and basic. Simply: they had endured. They had lived with doubt and defeat. And they had refused to cave in.

The World Champion Lakers came onto the floor to play the Boston Celtics and played three quarters of near-perfect basketball.

Only one player had a bad game, and that was Rider, who stalked off the court after Jackson put him into the game behind the younger, less experienced Penberthy and George, then took him out three minutes later when he made 2 turnovers. "I just want an equal opportunity," he told Jackson, "even if it's fifteen minutes. I can't play three minutes a half when we're blowing a team out and you put me in like I'm some scrub, which I'm not."

At halftime Jackson found him in the locker room. "You get your act together," he said, "and get back out there. I need men in the playoffs who can play roles even if it's just for one play. I have to be able to depend on you to deliver a full effort."

But Rider had been off track since his rookie days in Minnesota. Now perhaps it was too late, and perhaps he had sensed this all along. "I wish when I was in Minnesota," he had said at several points in the season, "that veterans would have taken me underneath their wing."

The Lakers headed into the fourth quarter against the Celtics with a 6-point lead. But the Celtics came back, pounding at them without letup. Point by point the Lakers' lead diminished along with their faith. How many times had they fallen apart in the fourth quarter, losing their sense of self, of one another? Too many times, they told each other, to let it happen again.

Heat refines impure things, Jackson had said months ago, when asked how the team might gain from its troubles. Now it was plain that this refining process had taken place. One by one the players glanced at each other: glances that bound them into a brotherhood, glances that were a pledge, a commitment to vigilance, a promise to stay alert, to rotate or slide over when a teammate needed it, to execute the offense in accordance with the triangle's precepts.

Brian Shaw pulled down 10 rebounds and got 9 assists. With the Celtics leading by a point, Fox got the ball to Grant along the right baseline. With Paul Pierce hovering over him, Grant threw the ball up, not certain where the basket was, but going for it anyway, and sinking a 16-foot turn-around jumper.

"That was a prayer," Brian Shaw said later. "That's why Horace keeps his Bible with him all the time."

"I had it all planned out," Grant joked. "I told Rick to throw it down by my feet so I could be the hero. It was a blessed shot for this team."

And it was, in ways that even Grant had not imagined, one of an increasing confluence of moments and events demonstrating to each of them a team's special power and the way that each man feeds the others and grows stronger in the giving. This was what Jackson had talked about. It's unselfish basketball, they told themselves and one another.

That night they left the arena with another win and a renewed sense of themselves. "In a forty-eight-minute game a team is like a jazz quintet," Jim Cleamons told them. "Everyone gets their solo, but it's all in the way they blend."

Kobe had come to understand this too. And it got to him.

On the team plane to Minneapolis, Kobe looked over at the guys playing cards across the aisle. Shaw cracked on Harper, and when he looked at Kobe he was surprised to see that Kobe wasn't pretending to sleep, that his eyes weren't fixed on his DVD player. He was looking at them, and he was grinning. "If you grin, you're in," Shaw said. Kobe nodded. At last, for the first time, he was in.

The Timberwolves were their last opponent of the road trip. Before the game the Lakers were so certain and carefree that they tuned the locker-room TV to the Masters golf tournament instead of to the game between Portland and Sacramento, teams they were certain to face in the play-offs.

Minneapolis was the hometown of one of their young players, Devean George, who had started to gain confidence now that Kobe was giving him playing tips and Jackson was giving him more minutes. In a recent game George had provided one of the season's agonizing moments when he got the ball, thundered down an open court, went for a layup, and missed. As the crowd gasped, he had thrown himself against the basket stanchion and held onto it like a child clutching his mother's legs, a moment illustrating that every opportunity to be a hero is equally an opportunity to fail in public.

Against the Timberwolves, George scored 10 points as the veterans cheered him on. It was a good sign, a sign of change and progress. This basketball team is coming together, thought Fisher, even if it's taken us all season long.

They were a good team, they realized, better than they or Kobe had thought. It was just that, while Kobe was playing, his talents and his opinion of them had daunted them so much that they weren't able to prove it.

The effect that Kobe's return might have on the team was a matter of anxious speculation, especially among players inclined to the general view "If it works, don't fix it." Without Kobe the Lakers had a four-game streak going. Shaq was NBA player of the week, scoring high, and satisfied now that the offense was running through him. "When I get these dog cookies," he said, "the dog will walk, sit, bite, run, fetch, do whatever you want him to do."

In the end, the degree of disruption Kobe caused would depend on Kobe. If he slides in seamlessly, thought Jackson, they can reincorporate him easily. But if he goes back to his own style of game and stops the offense from functioning, it's a problem.

With the play-offs only four games away, Jackson didn't want Kobe putting undue stress on his ankles. "Don't send him an alley-oop pass," he warned the players. In his first minutes of play against the

Phoenix Suns, Kobe headed downcourt. He felt OK, so he turned it up a little. When that felt OK, he turned it up a little more. Seeing Shaw on the wing, he pointed toward the rim. Shaw lobbed the ball up to the rim from 30 feet, and Kobe bounded upward, caught the ball, and threw down a dunk.

"You sure you're ready for that?" Jackson asked when he and Shaw returned to the bench. Kobe felt so alive, feeding on the cheers, the action, the adrenaline. "Yes!" he said.

But he was ready to pull off more than flashy moves for himself. He sent Fox a no-look pass for a dunk. He penetrated the defense, then kicked the ball out to Fox again for a 3-pointer. Whether other guys made their shots or not, he kept feeding them. This is extraordinary, thought Fox. He throws the ball to us and we miss, and he throws it again and we miss again. And he throws it again.

Kobe scored 20 points, a low figure for him, but he didn't mind. "It's not about scoring," he said later. "It's about stopping people."

That night the Lakers took their fifth game in a row, routing the Suns 106–80. "You got to give them credit," said the Suns' guard, Jason Kidd. "They're getting ready for the big dance."

Six days later they played the Timberwolves again. Kobe walked into the Staples Center with a diamond wedding band glinting on his left hand, a sign of his very private wedding ceremony on Dana Point the night before. He was buoyant, ready to play. In the first quarter he dished to Rick Fox for an open 3, then another. He threw him a perfect 75-foot pass for a dunk. Fox thought back to all the times he'd been on the wing, his defender covering Kobe because they had so little reason to think that Fox would shoot the ball. He thought back to the times Kobe said that he trusted himself more than he trusted his teammates. He thought of the times that Kobe spoke of his trust for them, but didn't show it. Every player on the team had needed to develop the confidence that Kobe had confidence in them. Now they had. "You know what, man," Fox told him, "you've really turned the corner. You're showing us by your actions, not just by talking."

Two quarters later, Kobe returned to his slashing, blinding offense. On his way to scoring 31 points, he kept passing the ball, and with each pass the team was uplifted. They played with more than skill. They played with emotion, so much emotion that it spilled from player to player. As they took their sixth consecutive win, the most they had put together all season, they were at last the team they were supposed to be.

They knew they were an even better team than they had been the year before. The defense was better because their starters were better. Fox defended better than Rice, Grant was better than Green, Fisher was better than Harper.

It was a team that had finally relaxed enough to reflect what was best in them, not only as players but as men: Shaw's grasp of human nature lent him the sense not just of where everyone was on the court but of where they would be seconds later; Horry's cool gave him the steadiness to play his best game when only his best would do; Fisher's heart gave him the push to fight to the end; Madsen's sense of brotherhood lent him the willingness to give the team everything; Fox's sense of purpose made him a ferocious defender, a player reborn into a game he had played long ago. As a product of the University of North Carolina, he had been coached by the mythic Dean Smith, who was coached by Phog Allen, who learned the game from basketball's inventor James Naismith. It was a lineage that imbued him with a sense the other players were coming to share: that they were upholders of the great tradition of team play, which Naismith had intended to be the most meaningful attribute of the game.

There were two games left in the regular season, and one was against the Trail Blazers, a team the Lakers had lost to twice since winning against them in their first game of the season. Their players had some fine, convoluted history between them: Harper and Pippen had won three championships together; Grant had once been Pippen's alter ego and best friend; as a kid in Philadelphia, Kobe had sat in the bleachers watching a great local high school player named Rasheed Wallace, and his father had played on the Sixers with the Blazers' coach Mike Dunleavy, who had coached the Lakers for two seasons.

Portland remained their nemesis. The two teams were one of basketball's feuding couples. They had met in the play-offs nine times. They knew each other's strengths and weaknesses, and they knew how to push each other's buttons. Few teams considered themselves better than the Lakers, but Portland did. And they *were* better when you went player for player, one to twelve. If they were the best team money could buy, they were also proof that there can be too many good players in a game where egos need feeding and there aren't enough minutes to go around. "Too many cats want the ball on the Blazers," Brian Shaw told the team before the game.

"But they're still dangerous," said Kobe. "We just have to come out and just kill them. If you want to be the best, you have to beat the best."

Both teams came on with play-off intensity. Portland would have only 5 turnovers, the fewest of any of their opponents all season. At halftime Portland led 54–53. By the time the Lakers had fought their way to a 99–99 tie, Portland was imploding. When Arvydas Sabonis unwittingly stuck a hand in Rasheed Wallace's face, Wallace responded by hitting him with a towel. In the third quarter Kobe went up for a shot. Sabonis hit him in the face. The referee called a flagrant foul. Shaq advanced on Sabonis. "You can do that to your teammate," he told him, "but you can't do it to mine." In that moment an old battle between Shaq and Kobe resolved itself as Shaq took on the task of protector and big brother, while Kobe, who had never before felt the need for a big brother, stood by silently, watching and listening as Shaq stood up for him.

Then the game resumed, and Shaq broke the tie with a 10-foot jumper. Moments later the Lakers had won, 105–100.

Then it was on to the final game of the regular season, against the Denver Nuggets, the team they had played when the troubles between Kobe, Shaq, and the team first erupted in mid-November. Back then Kobe wasn't passing to Shaq because he was getting hacked and missing his free throws. In this last game, Shaq made 13 of 13 free throws, while his coach Ed Palubinskas videotaped him from the courtside seat where he sat with the publicist he had recently hired.

When the game ended, the crowd went wild and the announcer intoned, "The Pacific Division Champions . . . your Lakers!!!!!"

And it seemed that, at their best and brightest, there was no team the Lakers couldn't beat now that their game was distilled into the flowing dance it was meant to be. So the season ended, with grit and generosity and eight straight wins. In the play-offs, it would come down to skill and hunger and heart, to dumb luck and team wellness and whether these attributes existed in sufficient measure.

"If you look at the whole year," Jackson told the players, "nothing's been easy. So I don't think we should expect an easy run to the top."

The next day, the Lakers' coaches met with Mitch Kupchak and Kurt Rambis to determine the play-off roster, choosing twelve players with the knowledge that no changes would subsequently be allowed. The hard choice was among Mike Penberthy, Tyronn Lue, and Isaiah Rider.

Rider was the obvious choice, but his unreliability was a flaw for which there could be no excuses this late in the game. The truth was, they placed more value on Penberthy's outside shooting and ability to run the offense. Then there was Lue, the outside choice, who had the advantage of being a speedy point guard in a series packed with other speedy point guards like Damon Stoudamire, Jason Williams, Steve Nash, and Allen Iverson. Ty was the team's little brother, Jim Cleamons noted. "Everyone likes him," he said. "It helps the chemistry to put in a player that all the other players are pulling for."

This had been a difficult season for Lue, but then all of his seasons had been difficult. In three years with the team, his role had never become clear, and injuries had left him playing in barely thirty games. Jackson tended to play him only when they were winning by 20 points and had five minutes left or, rumor had it, to let him be seen for a trade.

When Lue came to the Lakers in 1998 at the start of the lockout-shortened season, Del Harris had told him, "Push the ball as fast as you can." Lue was already amazingly quick, and he became one of the quickest players in the league. But then Jackson came in, bringing older guys, which meant that the Lakers were definitely not a running team. Lue had to slow his game down. This was important to do, he told himself, for the sake of the team. It happened to a lot of players, even to his favorite player, Damon Stoudamire. But Lue also knew that the slowing had taken a toll on Stoudamire's game.

For a player like Lue, the triangle offense was restrictive. It closed the court up, and Lue functioned best when you spread the court, put him in the middle, and let him be the man.

But now he was taking the last spot on the play-off roster. Rider was furious, in a mood so dark and angry that some of the guys worried he would do something foolish, while others joked that he would be seeking retaliation. Penberthy was stung. "Obviously they feel they're better off without me," he told the reporter Howard Beck, "so good luck."

The play-offs called for a level of focus you didn't often get when you were pacing yourself through the regular season. In the play-offs you win or you pack your bags and go home and feel bad all summer. There was no more *let's play the Nets so we can get to Boston; let's play the Kings so we can get to Denver tomorrow.*

There was no tomorrow. There was only now.

24

AIN'T NO TOMORROW

In the first round of the play-offs the Los Angeles Lakers faced the Portland Trail Blazers. It would be a best-of-five series against the team that could still taste the ashes of their loss last year to the Lakers in the seventh game of the Western Conference finals. Before heading onto the court to face them, the Lakers' huddle had the fervent quality of a tent revival.

"Strength and honor," said Brian Shaw.

"Let's go out there and be men," said Ron Harper.

They headed onto the court, one player, then another, jogging through the north tunnel. It was a moment they loved, that passage from the isolation of the locker room into the light of the court and the game at hand. You could feel your adrenaline pumping. You had a sense of charging into battle, of stepping into the arena literally and figuratively. This was when you felt touched by measures of nobility and valor, and you would break into a run and charge onto the court, where you were swept up in the lights, the thrill, the cheering. In those moments you felt bound into a brotherhood born of knowing what it feels like to make the big shot or to not make it, of the sense of oneness that comes when you signal your teammates with your eyes, of the excitement of diving for a loose ball, of blocking the potentially winning shot, of playing through hard times and good times and injury and pain.

They headed into the light of the court, united, moving forward, safe in the knowledge that they held in common a single goal: the shared imperatives to execute, to play hard, to play with intensity, with passion.

The Blazers would rise and fall with Rasheed Wallace, with his perfect fadeaways and jump shots and a talent and physicality for attacking any power forward in the league. Wallace's great strength was to play with an excess of fire, and this was also his great weakness. It seemed to Rick Fox that Wallace really preferred to play a little disturbed, that he was one of those emotional players who needed the game to be personal. As a result he had amassed 41 technical fouls this season and been ejected from seven games.

For the first three quarters the two teams jousted, each grabbing the lead, relinquishing it, then grabbing it again. Heading into the fourth quarter, the Lakers' 2-point lead put them in mind of the seventh game of the year before, when they emerged from a 15-point deficit to win the game. As they made their push, they saw a familiar look on the faces of Portland's players—a look of stunned disbelief— as the Lakers surged and Scottie Pippen battled to corral the Blazers' volatile mix of players.

Before game two, Pippen speculated that Kobe was faking his rib injury. "He wants to play injured in a play-off game," he told reporters, "so he can be like Mike."

It was a comment that only served to toughen Kobe's resolve. No matter what you say to bring me down, he thought, you have to see me in between these four lines. And between these four lines, that's my domain.

Pippen was a fearsome defender, and he went after Kobe, pulling out all the stops, talking trash to him, sticking him hard in the ribs with an elbow. Kobe could not be derailed. He drove the lane, shot from the perimeter, powered his way to the basket. The more he passed to the other guys, the more the game opened up for him offensively, and suddenly he found that because Portland had to respect the threat of his teammates he could drive the lane without getting closed off every time and get to the basket more easily.

Shaq was uncontainable, and efforts to make him otherwise landed the Blazers two ejections and five technical fouls. Jackson told Shaq to shoot the last technicals. As Shaq took his place at the free-throw line, Grant, Shaw, and Harper watched from the bench. Shaq sank the shot. As he dropped his hand over his wrist, the veterans on the bench dissolved in delighted laughter.

"Anytime you got Shaq stepping up shooting technical shots," said a saddened, weary Pippen, "you know it's pretty much over with."

Kobe's official reaction to Pippen's trash talk was the circumspect, quietly needling remark that it was disappointing, that he had looked up to Pippen when he was a kid. But privately he was angry, and the day of the third and potentially final game of the best-of-five series he walked into the locker room to see Pippen being interviewed on television. "You motherfucker," he said, as he glared at the screen, "this is your last day at the office."

The Lakers had grown stronger with each game, and this made the outcome of game three almost a given. Some said the Blazers lay down; others said they self-destructed. Either way, it was clear that in the end their enemy was themselves. "No towel in the NBA is safe," Larry Burnett of KLAC radio would say, "when the Blazers are angry."

And Scottie Pippen, one of the game's most brilliant competitors, would walk away saying, "This is the worst thing I've ever had to deal with."

The next series was against the Sacramento Kings, a team convinced that their time had come. "Anything happens now," their coach, Rick Adelman, told them, after they took the Phoenix Suns in the first round of the play-offs. This optimistic view of the Kings' prospects was shared by many observers, including the existing powers of *Sports Illustrated*, who had lately exposed the Kings to the infamous *SI* jinx by featuring them on its cover accompanied by the headline "The Greatest Show on Court . . . Basketball as It Ought to Be."

The Kings arrived at the Staples Center on a pleasant Sunday afternoon, each of the players disembarking from their chartered bus while conversing on his cell phone. "Talking to each other," Howard Beck said dryly.

The Kings, having beaten the Lakers by 24 points in the regular season, were unprepared for what the Lakers had become. The Kings had won that game without trouble, but the price of their victory was that it had fired the Lakers' determination.

Rick Fox played wicked defense in a grudge match against Stojakovic, shadowing him, stealing the ball, then dribbling down half the court for a ferocious dunk. Shaq was unstoppable, more aggressive now that he knew he could make his free throws. He was on a mission, so fed up with seeing Vlade Divac flop every time he defended him that he wanted to throw the ball down Vlade's throat. He traversed the court, dunking, blocking shots, reducing Chris Webber to a jump shooter, grabbing 44 points and 21 rebounds in the first game and 43 points and 20 boards in the second. These were numbers that left Rick Adelman telling his team what was entirely obvious: "We have to find a way to deal with Shaq." And they were numbers that made Shaq the first player in NBA history to post back-to-back 40-point/20-rebound games in the play-offs.

Then they were on to Sacramento. The key to the game, their coaches told them, would be riding the storm that would come early on. "The Kings and their fans will want to jump on us, try to rattle us," Jim Cleamons told them before the game. "You need to figure on an energy surge that lasts two quarters."

Before this, the third game, Shaq was uncharacteristically subdued. He had just learned that his cousin Lawrence, a firefighter in New Jersey, had died on the job. Shaq came from a long line of firemen and policemen, all of them tough and self-contained men for whom he had such respect that when he retired from the game he planned to be a sheriff. These men were emotional but not sentimental. Lawrence would want me to move on, Shaq told himself. He would want me to play the game.

As the Lakers came onto the court, boos echoed through the Arco Arena, where fans are famously rabid even on far less significant occasions. The Kings switched strategies, putting double teams on Shaq, which left Kobe free to take open jumpers and charge to the basket, scoring 36 points as the Lakers won 103–81.

Saturday was a day off, a day that Mark Madsen spent hanging out with Shaq and his stepfather. Madsen was thinking ahead to when Sacramento would be back in Los Angeles for the sixth game. "There's not gonna be a sixth game," Shaq told him. "This'll be over in four. Five at the most."

Before the fourth game Kobe was coiled and ready, telling the team, "Let's take the life out of them!"

By the end of the first quarter, the Lakers were ahead but hadn't gotten the ball to Kobe. It was clear to Rick Fox that Kobe was angry as he headed back to the bench. Fox went over to him, put an arm around him to settle him down. Kobe took a deep breath. He knew what to do and now he did it. "Good quarter," he told his teammates, "good quarter."

At the end of the third quarter, the Lakers trailed by 4. Kobe strode to the bench. His jaw was closed tight. His fists were clenched. "We're gonna win this fucking game," he called to his teammates. "Ain't no tomorrow."

He was ready to do whatever he had to do for a win. To get himself psyched he talked some trash to his opponents, and all of a sudden he was in the groove again. He was ready to push himself beyond exhaustion, to jump for every rebound and dive for every loose ball. He looks possessed, thought the Kings' coach, Rick Adelman. The Lakers saw that, too, and they primed themselves for a win.

Let's let the two big guys know we're gonna help them, thought Robert Horry. It's Christmastime for us now. We spent all year trying to be good boys. Time to open our presents.

Horry hit a critical 3-pointer, then Shaw followed with another. Fisher kept scoring, for a total of 20 points. Fox never let up in his defending. By the end, Kobe had scored 48 points, pushing them to a second sweep in the play-offs, on the way to what could now become the greatest postseason record in NBA history.

With less than two minutes left, the Kings sat on the bench, knowing they would be defeated. Their heads were covered with white towels, their expressions were chastened, like penitent monks. Harper hugged Kobe, who looked over to where Jackson sat on the bench. He met his gaze and sighed. Shaq wrapped his arms around him. "Way to have my back," he said. "You played awesome."

Just before the series began against the San Antonio Spurs, Allen Iverson was voted league MVP by the print and broadcast reporters who cover the league. Shaq was not pleased with this development. As many of those who cast ballots gathered at a Lakers' news conference, he told them, "It really doesn't bother me, 'cause most of you suits don't know what you're talking about anyway."

Most infuriating was that Tim Duncan had gotten eleven votes more than he had. The only thing that could have lit a fire under Shaq more effectively would be if he had come in third behind David Robinson.

The Lakers, the usually measured Robinson admitted, were not the Spurs' favorite team, and he recognized that the feeling was mutual.

The Spurs had embarrassed the Lakers when they swept them at the 1999 Western Conference finals. Shaq would never forget or forgive the way Robinson had shoved the victory in their faces, prancing and gloating right there in the Lakers' home arena. He was counting on the fact that none of his teammates had forgiven it either.

In game one, the combined force of Duncan and Robinson held Shaq back. Kobe took over, confounding the Spurs as he lost defenders to sink 3-pointers, slam dunks, and power jams, while his teammates rose from the bench and cheered. When the buzzer sounded, he had scored 45 points for a 104–90 Lakers victory, and Jackson was saying that Kobe was a more complete player than Jordan had been at his age. In the locker room, Shaq put a hand on Kobe's shoulder. "You know what?" he told him. "You're my idol." Kobe looked back at him, wondering for a fleeting instant if Shaq was kidding. But he wasn't. Kobe nodded, as gratified by the praise as he was stunned by it.

In the second game Tim Duncan took off on a mission. San Antonio played on top of their game, and the Lakers were outclassed for the first time in the play-offs. They faltered, losing their sense of purpose, their moorings. Then Jackson shouted at a referee and was ejected from the game. Not long ago Jackson had told them to thrive on adversity, and now they did, picking up their intensity, taking off on a 9–2 run, not stopping until the game was won 88–81, with Fisher hitting one 3-pointer, then another. OK, Fisher thought, this is what I've been waiting on.

The World Champion Los Angeles Lakers returned to the Staples Center to play their first home game in fifteen days. The San Antonio Spurs arrived at the arena the day before the game. Tim Duncan seemed tired, as if sensing that it was already too late. David Robinson was all smiles. Shaq's latest salvo in his ongoing vendetta against Robinson was to describe him as "a punk-ass" in his recent autobiography, *Shaq Talks Back*. Now at the Staples Center a reporter asked Robinson what it was that intimidated him most about Shaq. "His writing," said Robinson.

In this third game, the Lakers seemed unstoppable. Fisher sent Kobe an alley-oop pass that was just out of range, but Kobe retrieved it and slammed it into the basket. Shaq looked at Fox, sent the ball to Kobe with a no-look pass, then took two big steps toward the basket as Kobe sent the ball back to him for a right-handed dunk. When Shaq dribbled down the open court, Fox on one side of him, Kobe on the other, it became clear that a great change had taken place. Shaq had not dribbled all that way to have someone else shoot the ball, so he tossed it to Kobe instead of to Fox because he knew that Kobe would toss it back to him.

The Lakers won by 39 points. A rout like that, thought the Spurs' coach Gregg Popovich, could come only when a team lacks character or lacks belief, and his guys did not lack for character. So he had to conclude that somewhere along the way they had lost hope. "And it pisses me off," he said.

In the final game, the Lakers set out to seal what would become a 29-point win, sending Popovich's players to the bench dead-eyed and shamed and enervated. Popovich patted Tim Duncan's leg as Duncan sat beside him, head obscured by a towel. The Lakers had swept the Spurs for their fifteenth straight victory and a 15.5-point margin of victory in the play-offs, a margin greater than that of any championship team before them. "Custer had no idea," Popovich said when asked for a statement.

As the players made their way from the arena, frenzied admirers strained against the railings edging the north tunnel, reaching for them and beyond that, reaching for a connection with glamour, with history.

"Four more to go, man," Kobe said, as he entered the locker room, where he slapped hands with one exhausted player, then another.

Brian Shaw looked around the locker room and was relieved to see that everybody had their down-to-business face on, that no one was getting premature about it, that they had the sense not to be celebrating and acting like they'd won.

Shaq, remembering how Robinson had gloated over the Spurs' 1999 victory, took a devilish pleasure in refusing to do the same thing. "I'm a classy legend," he said with a grin. "It's not right to kick somebody when they're down."

As the quality of the victory sank in, Derek Fisher could hardly believe it. Teams that are good are good all year, he thought. It just doesn't make sense. If you had to pick a team that was going to fall apart, it was really us.

That week Shaq's agent, Leonard Armato, was driving down Sunset Boulevard when he stopped at a red light and noticed that the driver of the car next to his was Jerry West. "Those guys are having a love fest out there, aren't they?" said West. The light turned green. West hit the gas pedal of his Mercedes and roared away, looking more relaxed than Armato had ever seen him.

While the Milwaukee Bucks and the Philadelphia 76ers went to seven games in the Eastern Conference finals, the Lakers had ten days off. It was an unfortunate time to have to stop playing, to have to answer questions from reporters. When you're winning, you get a leave-it-alone mentality. You don't want to talk about it. You want to keep it fresh and not jinx it. They were all superstitious, determined not to alter anything associated with the wins: insisting that Chip Schaefer stretch them at the exact same time each day, that the equipment manager keep their shoes arranged as they were before—or in Rick Fox's case, not getting a haircut since the winning streak started, although, he said, all the goop he put on it was getting a little Gaylord Perry.

But the NBA required you to talk to reporters, so you did your best to answer questions about winning streaks and making history, about going to the finals and having a chance to defend your title. And you spent the whole ten days telling yourself that this disruption wouldn't disrupt you.

In the pause before the finals there was time for players to address their own situations. Robert Horry was considering whether he should opt out of his contract and join a team that would put him nearer to his wife, their son, and their daughter in Houston. He thought about this all the time, and at this time of year especially.

For Brian Shaw, the NBA finals came at the same time as a terrible anniversary: the day that his mother, father, and niece were killed in a car accident on their way to visit him. It had happened in June, soon after he entered the league. The memory never left him, and as June came around he thought about it more. He still felt they were watching over him, looking out for him, that no matter where he went they were part of it. He wished they could have seen him play these thirteen years, that they could have met his wife and their son, born two years ago, and the daughter who was about to be born. He had been able to enjoy his life. His family would have been proud, he thought, of what he'd been able to accomplish on the court and off it.

With the Sixers' victory over the Bucks, the Lakers' preparation for the coming contest grew both more methodical and more fevered. Jackson designated Tyronn Lue as the stand-in for Iverson during practice. For the first time in his NBA career, Lue had a clear role, and he got into it, putting his hair in cornrows, getting some stick-on tattoos, having Chip Schaefer cut up a white band for him to wear on his right arm.

When the Lakers next met with reporters, Robert Horry was asked if the Sixers' Tyrone Hill would be an opponent more his speed after

Wallace and Webber and Duncan. Horry started at the question. "Hey," he said, "don't jinx us, man."

Kobe was the one player on the team for whom playing in Philadelphia meant going home. It seemed strangely perfect to him; the year that had been the most difficult he ever experienced would come full circle and, at the end, bring him back to the city of his beginnings. But he kept this to himself. Now that he was feeling like part of the team, he did not want to mention anything that separated him from the brotherhood of players. This, he thought, was a sign of the way he had matured this season.

It seemed like ages since the season began with his feeling so full of expectations and excitement. Back then, his sense of romance about the game prompted him to find inspiration in a figure from a completely different world and time, Wolfgang Amadeus Mozart. "I really look up to him," he told Vanessa. "He was so young and when he started out as a kid he worked so hard, to the point where he'd do a whole composition in a day. I love that so much."

One of the goals he had set for himself was to be on the basketball court the kind of visionary that Mozart had been musically. "I want to be able to see things before they happen," he had thought. "I want to be able to play a whole game back in my mind." Those things had occurred this season, but they had paled in light of his other troubles. He had made a conscious effort to change, to involve his teammates. Now he steeled himself to get the job done, to stay strong, to be in the moment.

With his body sound again, it was time to set aside the hurts and troubles of the past. And if there was a single sign of his readiness to do this, it came during a scrimmage when he was sitting on the bench. "Hey Phil," he called out to Jackson, "put me in the game so I can sabotage it and win it in the end."

25

THE BIG DANCE

The Sixers were a united team. Every player had a specific role. They listened to each other and had one leader in Allen Iverson. They had won almost every individual award that season: in addition to Iverson's MVP, Larry Brown was Coach of the Year, Dikembe Mutombo was Defensive Player of the Year, Aaron McKie was Sixth Man. They also had a considerable number of injuries and only one player on their play-off roster, Eric Snow, who had ever been to the play-offs.

Their newest player, Raja Bell, had signed a ten-day contract in April, having served before then as second option on a YMCA league team whose first option was his father. Bell was eating at a Denny's in Sioux Falls, South Dakota, when he got the call inviting him to join the Sixers. He comported himself so well in the Eastern Conference play-offs that Jackson, in an interview with Marv Albert, commented that Bell "was the key to this series." Asked if he had heard Jackson's comment, Bell said, yes, he had, though he hadn't realized at first that the Phil Jackson who said this nice thing about him was "*that* Phil Jackson." The Sixers were green; the Lakers were not.

Larry Brown had yet to win a championship, though he had been to the play-offs nine times with four NBA teams. Brown was regarded by many as the finest coach in the NBA, the best teacher, with a gift for getting teams to play beyond their level of talent. He had been an exceptional player, even at the meager height of 5'9". His off-court style was low-key and pedestrian, befitting a man whose favorite adjective was "neat." But he had a burning passion for the game. It consumed him. He was always strategizing, sketching out plays, drawing little Xs and Os on napkins. He called his players "kids" and called Iverson "the little kid." In practices and on the court he was just this side of maniacal, shouting and gesturing and never giving up.

Twenty years ago, when Brown was coaching the New Jersey Nets, his path and Phil Jackson's had intersected when Jackson applied for the assistant coaching job and Brown turned him down. "Obviously, I was dumb," said Brown, adding that his decision had spared Jackson from becoming head coach of the Nets and having a terrible career. It was a telling statement, with its gentle implication that Jackson would not have fared well had he not gone to the Bulls where Jordan and Pippen were waiting.

It may be that Larry Brown's most remarkable achievement was to forge a line of communication to Allen Iverson, who had grown up in circumstances too hard to leave him with much respect for authority figures. It was this lack of respect that, after Iverson's fourth difficult year on the team, prompted the Sixers to arrange to trade him during the summer of 2000.

Later, when people noted that Iverson had almost been traded, Brown would make the point that in fact, he *was* traded, it was just that the trade was foiled when his teammate Matt Geiger refused to waive his 15 percent trade kicker.

But Iverson played a role in his own salvation. Not for nothing did the tattoos on his quadriceps read "Hold My Own" and "Only the Strong Survive." The spirit expressed in those words had powered him out of Newport News, Virginia, where people had tried to discourage him. "No one from here ever made it to the NBA," they would say. He always answered, "I'm gonna be that one."

From the time he joined the Sixers, declaring, "I'm gonna win championships with this team," he raised them from their standing as the weakest team in the league. He maintained that fighting spirit when the Sixers' president, Pat Croce, came to Newport News to inform him of his pending trade.

"If you're gonna fuckin' trade me," he told Croce, "then trade me for someone who's better and can help the team. But if you're gonna trade me because of the little things, comin' late, missing a shoot-around, I can change all of that."

"Do it," said Croce. "Walk the walk."

So they took him back, and he was made team captain, but in the early fall Croce was handed the lyric sheet to Iverson's first rap album. Croce had made his name and fortune as a motivator, and it was his way to look on the bright side of things. Iverson's lyrics lacked a bright side. They denigrated women, mothers, gays. Croce called Iverson to his office to tell him how disappointed he was, that the lyrics disgusted him.

"Because you don't know gangsta rap," said Iverson.

"I know I don't," Croce said, "but these do not look *positive*."

Days later, the venues of exhibition games the Sixers were playing were ringed with picketers: women, blacks, and gays. Iverson, ever defiant and not unaware of middle-class capitalist tools like advertising and promotion, got some free and useful publicity when news crews filmed him standing with legs apart and arms crossed in front of him, staring into the camera and saying, "If you're a hard-core hip-hop fan, this album's for you."

If Iverson had proved anything in his life, it was that he was not easily daunted. Later in the season he cut another rap album—scheduled for release, not incidentally, during the opening week of the NBA finals—and pulled it from release only when he was prevailed upon to do so by David Stern himself. By then, Iverson and Brown had journeyed from distrust to a certain familial fondness, which Iverson evinced when Brown was hospitalized with a hiatal hernia. "I could care less about the basketball part of it," he fretted. "I just hope he's all right."

Iverson was a distinctly American figure, emerging from circumstances that were a classic instance of the impact of poverty and the welfare state on large segments of the population, with a mother fourteen years older than he was, a stepfather who had done hard time, and his own record of arrests and jail time. His best friend on the team was Aaron McKie, another player who had grown up hard, his father dead, his mother abandoning him on the streets.

Phil Jackson dubbed Iverson "that little rascal," but few players had been more naturally inclined to observe Jackson's dictum to live in the moment. He was ready to give it all up, to prostrate himself, to expend every ounce of energy. Until lately, he had become furious when Brown took him out of games, so caught up that he could not entertain the radical notion that there would be other moments, other games. At a stated 6 feet tall and 165 pounds, he was the smallest man ever to be MVP, and was not only getting shots off but also leading the league in scoring.

He had played for no NBA team but the Sixers. He was their undisputed emotional leader, especially during the 2000–2001 season, which they finished with the best record in the league. "You've made the difference," Billy King, the Sixers' general manager, told him. "You decided to put us on your back. You decided to lead the team, and you get the credit." Now it was being written that he embodied all that was right about the new breed of players in the NBA. Just as he romanticized his struggles, he was easily romanticized by others, who described him variously as 165 pounds of scar tissue, a blur, this wisp, a tornado.

At his home court, the First Union Center, he would cup his hand over his ear as he paced the floor, as if saying to the crowd, "Let me hear ya!" The resulting roar testified to the fact that no player is more beloved in his community than the player who embodies its soul. Philadelphia was an eminently livable and beautiful city, with a lingering provinciality that was less a weakness than a strength. But its proximity to New York City had made it the butt of jokes since W. C. Fields's tombstone was emblazoned with the legend: "On the whole I'd rather be in Philadelphia."

Iverson was what Philadelphia was and wanted to be: the little guy you had to watch out for, the fighter it was easy to underestimate, the come-from-behind winner. The chip on his shoulder was a classically Philadelphia chip, the chip that comes from deep conviction that you deserve better.

"I'm glad everybody's predicting a sweep," he said in the days before the first game of the finals. "That's another challenge we've got to go through." As the finals drew near, he tapped his heart and told his teammates, "Championships are won here."

The contest between the Philadelphia 76ers and the World Champion Los Angeles Lakers was billed as the underdog against the undefeated, as David versus Goliath. "Didn't David win?" asked Larry Brown. "That's what my mom told me."

With the first game hours away, the Lakers were raising the stakes on themselves, voicing something they had been unwilling to voice all season: unless you go back to back, you are not a true champion.

In the Staples Center at game time, each team gathered in a huddle.

"We know what we have to do," said Harper. "Four more games. Take it one game at a time. We'll all get the job done."

"Let's get dirty," Iverson told the Sixers.

The Lakers' protracted layoff was of real concern to Phil Jackson. In league history, the only longer break was the eleven days the Lakers had off before taking the 1982 title. In 1996, the Bulls had an eight-day break, and it did not make Jackson more sanguine to recall that it took them half of the first game to get back into it.

The Lakers started fast and tough, Shaq dunking on the break, Fox hitting 3-pointers, the crowd chanting, "MVP! MVP!" as Shaq stepped up to the foul line. In the first eight minutes they pulled ahead 21–9.

"We got no movement," Brown told the Sixers. "We're not putting bodies on guys; we're too soft."

The Sixers went more aggressive, tightening their defense, yanking off Grant's goggles, knocking Fisher in the nose. At the same time, they amped up their offense. Iverson hit one fadeaway jumper after another. At halftime the Sixers led 56–50. It's a little shocking, thought Horace Grant, like we're in the twilight zone.

The Lakers' rust was only part of their problem. Their perimeter defense had slackened. They missed shots. Shaq missed free throws. Kobe struggled for his timing. "Keep it simple," Jackson told them. "When you throw to Shaq, throw high for example."

Guarding Iverson disrupted Fisher's shooting, taking it from the 60–120 he'd had in the play-offs to 0–4. Iverson was known for draining opponents. When you guarded him, you could never let down. He would shoot from anywhere, anytime, unmindful of his lowered percentage. I've never seen anything like it, thought Fisher. The guy is going to take 40 shots even if you're guarding him well and 50 if you don't.

The only thing keeping the Lakers in the game was Shaq. With one second to go in the first half, and the Sixers leading 56–48, he threw down a two-handed slam.

Midway through the third quarter, Iverson had 38 points. The Lakers were on the defensive, and the Sixers were on the attack. "We just fell apart," Jackson told his players, "and they got four layups in the process."

He put Tyronn Lue into the game, hoping that the one player smaller than Iverson could contain him. Lue made off with a steal. He floated to the basket for a layup. He sank a 3. With his own game faltering, Kobe marveled at his teammates, at how Fox and Horry and Lue hounded and pestered and wouldn't give up.

Later Iverson would complain that Lue held him. But he had to hand it to him, too, for playing so hard, for not being one of those guys who are too scared around the MVP to give it their all. As Lue chased Iverson around the court, Kobe allowed himself a quick grin. Those are two Ferraris out there, he thought, two speedsters.

Seven minutes into the fourth quarter, with the score tied, Larry Brown called a time-out. "Slow down," he told his team. "Take a deep breath. And understand we got five minutes to get one up on them, five minutes to get every rebound, every loose ball."

The Lakers pushed ahead. The Sixers answered every point.

Kobe shadowed Raja Bell. Figuring Bell would pass on a fast break, he didn't get back on transition defense and cleared the way for Bell to make a layup. Jackson called a time-out, storming toward Kobe, still yelling at him as he came toward the bench.

It was a disturbing and bitterly disappointing game for Kobe, one of those rare games in which he could not take charge of his playing. With eighteen seconds left and the score tied, he drove into a triple team and lost the ball. In the time-out, as he headed toward the bench, Shaq slung his arm around his shoulder. One by one, players who had regarded him as a showboat and a ball hog came to him as brothers. First Devean George, then Harper, then Shaw, Fox, and Grant. They patted him. They hugged him. It's all right, they said, don't worry.

"We're gonna do it," Shaq told him. "We're gonna be the champions."

Shaq scored in overtime, then Kobe came in with a vicious dunk. Shaq put them ahead by 5. Larry Brown called a time-out with 2:40 left. "Calm down, guys," he told his team. "It's all on them. They're supposed to win. We ain't even supposed to be here."

Then Raja Bell slipped past Kobe and Horry and sank a left-handed scoop. Iverson got an open 3, then another. He had taken 41 shots and scored 48 points. When Eric Snow hit a running 18-footer to put the Sixers ahead 107–103, Rick Fox slammed the ball against the floorboards, a rageful gesture acknowledging that the Lakers' winning streak was over.

"They can put the brooms away," said Iverson as he headed into the locker room. "We didn't do nothing yet," he added. "We got a long way to go."

Kobe left the arena with his jaw tight, eyes straight ahead, having just played his weakest game of the play-offs. His 7-for-22 shooting left the Sixers' Eric Snow saying, "I don't think Kobe Bryant had a Kobe Bryant kind of day."

Asked by a reporter which of the defenses against Iverson he liked best, Jackson replied, "When Larry Brown took him out in the first quarter."

The end of their streak was the end of their chance for a perfect record in the play-offs. It affected them all in different ways. As soon as the game ended, Horace Grant wanted to play another forty-eight-minute game. Robert Horry, who was never angry after games, went home angry and woke up angry the next morning. Derek Fisher was up at eight, heading to the Staples Center to practice his shooting until practice started.

"That was the best they can play," Shaq told the team. "They gave it a thousand; we gave it seventy-five."

The problem, they agreed, wasn't about any one player having a good game or not having one; it was about the team as a group and how the group could support each other. Weeks ago, these would have been empty words. With the team united, they were a game plan.

Before game two, the team gathered in a circle and each player put a hand in the middle. Jackson turned to Shaq. "Let's see if you can get a blocked shot tonight," he said. Shaq walked away, stung. The players waited for him to come back and give the count. But he was too angry. So Horace Grant said, "One-two-three," and they shouted, "Lakers!"

"We're the world champs," said Kobe. "Let's go out and play like them."

Kobe felt he had a lot to prove. He started proving it in the first minute, drilling a jumper from the top of the key. He had his rhythm. Relieved and buoyant, he went on to a succession of dunks and drives and pull-up jumpers, and he dished to his teammates.

"Hey, guys," Brown told the Sixers when he called a time-out, "I don't know what the hell's gonna happen in this game. But we got a series. We got to figure out how to play better." Brown was primed to crush the Lakers, for he knew that only two teams had lost the first two games of the finals and come back to win the series.

Now, the Sixers surged. Rick Fox watched intently from the Lakers' bench. "Don't worry about it," Kobe told him. "We'll figure something out. I'm gonna get it to you one way or another."

Both teams struggled for the lead as the clock ticked toward halftime. Kobe came through the top of the key and threw down a slam. With four seconds left, McKie passed out to Geiger, who sank an 18-footer to put the Sixers within 2 points.

In the second half, Shaq came back with a strength that would leave him with 8 blocked shots, tying the record set in the play-offs by Bill Walton and Hakeem Olajuwon. As he came 1 assist and 2 blocked shots from the first quadruple double in NBA finals history, he picked up 5 fouls that convinced Jackson to send him back to the bench. With five minutes left on the clock and the Lakers up by 2, he returned.

Shaw hit a 3. Jackson was rarely readable on the bench, but now his relief was apparent. Then Mutombo scored, shooting right over Shaq, giving the Sixers an 11–3 run since Shaq's fifth foul.

With 2:52 left, Jackson sent Ron Harper into the game. Harp had barely played since his arthroscopic surgery in March. But his special value to the team, at this point in his long career, had less to do with his playing than with his being what Jackson called the team's insurance policy. Harp was the guy, thought Kurt Rambis, who could jump on a bike careening down a hill and steady it. But this meant that when you played Harper, you announced to the opposition that you *needed* steadying, so you had to be very sure that once he got on the court the steadying would take place.

With the Sixers 3 points down, Shaq threw to Fisher, who sent the ball flying high into the basket for 3 points. Then Harper knocked one in for the first 2 of the 6 points he would post. Shaq drew a double team and kicked the ball out to Fisher, who sank another 3-pointer. Still the Sixers would not go away.

As Iverson scored 3 points, a dedicated Laker fan, Norman Pattiz, left his courtside seat and moved to the edge of the court. Pattiz was the owner of the Westwood One radio network and a fixture at games. "It's over." he shouted at Iverson. "You're done." Iverson, charged up and angry, turned to Kobe, talking trash to him with Kobe giving it back until Fisher gently but firmly pushed Kobe away and Raja Bell headed for Iverson.

As the clock ran down, Brown took Iverson out of the game. He left the court smiling, clapping his hands in tribute to the effort of his teammates. For the first time, thought Iverson, the Lakers felt they were in a war. With his team it was different. They'd been in a war every game, every series.

Iverson still believed the Sixers could win the championship. "It's everybody else," he said, "who don't think we can."

Nor was he about to concede anything.

"Are you fatigued?" a reporter asked.

"Fatigue is army clothes," said Iverson.

With Shaq shooting 14–32 at the free-throw line, Ed Palubinskas got on a plane for Philadelphia, a city that had not hosted a play-off series since 1983, the year the Sixers swept the Lakers in the finals, giving Dr. J his only NBA championship ring.

The Lakers were ready to win, fed up with hearing Iverson say that Philadelphia was the team with heart. "We've got heart, too," said Tyronn Lue. "We just don't go around boasting and bragging about it."

As the third game began, every man on the team knew that if one of them faltered, the others would pick it up. As Shaq controlled the game from the inside, Kobe came out and hit 7 of 7 shots. No matter what they did to stop them, the Sixers kept coming back.

By the third quarter the Lakers had a 10-point lead, but Kobe's jump shots weren't falling and were costing the Lakers, as rebounds from his misses went long and led to fast breaks. The whistle blew, and they retreated to the bench.

"Hey, let's pass it around," said Fisher.

Kobe nodded.

"Yeah, give it to me," said Shaq, "and I'll give it back."

They kept the lead going, but Iverson was on fire, reducing the Lakers' lead to 2 points. Shaq was on the defensive. Mutombo frustrated him, matching him rebound for rebound. Shaq was getting such an unaccustomed run for his money that when Mutombo returned to the bench at the end of the third quarter the crowd in the First Union Center came to its feet and gave him an ovation.

With just under nine minutes to go, Robert Horry nailed a right-handed slam. Horry was basketball's Reggie Jackson, the Mr. June to Jackson's Mr. October.

The Lakers took on a fearsome precision. "No gambling," Larry Brown told his players, "and if you can't grab a rebound, tip it."

With 3:14 left in the game, Shaq fouled out. Making his reluctant way to the bench, he turned to his teammates on the floor. "Win this one for me," he said. Moments later, Kobe hit a 3-pointer. The crowd chanted, "Kobe sucks!" "I don't care if they chant something, but they should chant something true," said Kobe. He was tired, legs aching, trying to save himself for the very last seconds, when he might be needed most.

With a minute left, the Lakers were up by 1. Shaw got the ball, looked at the basket, but then McKie charged toward him and he flipped the ball to Robert Horry, who was open in the left corner.

Horry sent an arching shot straight into the basket. Then he hit 4 free throws. The game ended 96–91 for the Lakers' second win. Again the team had stepped up when the premier guys couldn't. This, they thought, is what it means to be a team.

The Sixers walked out of the arena, their faces impassive. The only victory left to them that night was to not betray the depth and breadth of their disappointment.

The Sixers were down by one game going in, and no team had come back in the finals from a three-game deficit. "If you can't get going in this type of a game," Iverson told the Sixers, "there's a problem, man."

But his team was weary. The extraordinary energy they had put out to reach the finals had left the players with little reserve for getting through them. Eric Snow's foot was broken. Aaron McKie had spent the day in a hospital getting blood tests to check his electrolytes. Iverson was exhausted. As the Sixers took a day off, he said, "I don't know how rested you can get in a day, man, but I'm anxious to find out."

For all that, they came out for the fourth game with the fight they had always had, the fight that substantiated Iverson's claims about their heart. They hounded and badgered, rattling the Lakers enough to push them into 3 turnovers and 6 missed shots before they managed to score a point.

It was Shaq's game, and this meant not only that he posted huge numbers but that his presence on the court demanded so much attention that it left the others free to score. He was out for vengeance, out to get back at Dikembe Mutombo, who, he said, had forced him out of the last game with his "girly" flopping. Now he dunked over Mutombo, reducing the defensive player of the year to the merest hindrance, and leading the Lakers to a 22-point lead.

Iverson wouldn't go away. He reduced the lead by 10 points, charging through a 12–0 Sixer run. The Lakers fed off Shaq. And they fed off the 9 assists dished by Kobe. Shaw sank a 3-pointer. Then Lue. Then Horry. When the final buzzer sounded, they had taken the game 100–86, their largest margin of victory in the finals.

They were one game away from repeating. They had the Sixers' backs against the wall. But Jackson recalled that when they were one game away in last year's finals they had lost the potentially winning game by 30 points. On his way out of the locker room he turned back to the players. "Don't forget," he said, "that we were 3 up on Indiana."

Allen Iverson remained in the arena with some of his teammates for a long time. When they were ready to leave it was one in the morning and the oppressive June heat had been cooled by the damp night air. First Eric Snow walked into the players' parking lot, accompanied by his mother. Then came Aaron McKie with his fiancée and their twelve-year-old daughter. Finally Iverson emerged with his girlfriend and their two young children. They all settled into their respective cars. Then suddenly, McKie's daughter came rushing out of her father's Mercedes sedan and ran to the driver's side of Iverson's silver Bentley.

Iverson rolled down the window. He smiled, and chucked her under the chin, a slight gesture that managed to convey that she needed to be brave, and that being brave can be hard. "What's up, Kie?" he said.

She didn't answer. She hugged him. He hugged back. Then she ran to her father's car and Iverson drove off into the night, having demonstrated that there is more than one way to be a champion.

Outside the arena, on the morning of the fifth and possibly deciding game, Allen Iverson talked to reporters. In his hushed, affectless voice, he spoke about heart and effort. He was subdued, his resigned manner the opposite of his manner on the court, where he was looking ever more beleaguered, his chiseled features twisted in a pained frown. Still he had come back and back again. To win the championship would be a dream come true, he often said. Now he said it again, though he must have known that the dream was evaporating.

How would he feel, reporters asked, if the Lakers took the championship in Philly's arena? Iverson's smile was rueful. "If they win it here," he said, "or they win it in L.A. it means the same thing: they won it, and we couldn't get it done."

Inside the arena, the Lakers were on the court, joking and laughing and tossing around a couple of balls as several reporters looked on.

"Throw me back my ball," Harper called to Shaw.

"A ball's a ball," Shaw said.

"Place your bets," said Fox, as they formed a line to shoot layups.

Kobe threw the ball up. It wobbled on the rim. He jumped and tapped it in.

"It counts," he said.

"Fuckin-A doesn't count," said Harper.

"Fuckin-A does," said Kobe.

On the sidelines, one reporter spoke aloud to no one in particular. "They know it's over," he said.

In the year 2001, on the 15th of June, at seven o'clock on the night of the fifth game of the NBA finals, the Los Angeles Lakers filed off their chartered bus and entered the arena, one by one. Phil Jackson was first, followed by his assistant coaches. Then came each man on the team except for Isaiah Rider, who had missed the Lakers' bus for what would prove to be the last time ever.

As the arena filled with 20,500 men, women, and children, Shaq's bodyguard Jerome sat courtside, immersed in a newspaper article about the Lakers titled "Great Legacy Still Growing."

Seventeen minutes before game time, the players came onto the court. Derek Fisher shot baskets while mouthing the words to the rap song piped in over the loudspeakers. Ron Harper sat on the floor stretching, legs straight in front of him, hands holding his flexed feet.

This final contest of the season would be, in a sense, a coronation rite for the once and future kings, the game that would leave the Lakers with a 15–1 record in the play-offs—the best postseason of any NBA team ever. Shaq's extraordinary performance, with 13 rebounds and 5 blocked shots, would seal his claim to his second finals MVP, and his 29 points made him the third-highest scorer in play-off history, just behind Michael Jordan and Jerry West. Rick Fox posted 20 points. Derek Fisher converted 6 of his 8 attempted 3-pointers. Kobe came away with another 26 points and 6 assists.

In the course of the season, Jackson's enlightened coaching had uplifted each player until the team became greater than any of its members. Fisher had shown that he could be a scorer, inspire the team, and have fun doing it. Fox had been restored to the exceptional offensive player he had once been. Horry and Shaw and Harper had proved again that they could step up and do what needed to be done. Shaq was on his way to realizing his goal of being the biggest and baddest in Laker history. Kobe had become a player who made every other player better, while his own numbers repeatedly brought him close to triple doubles and evoked the memory of Magic Johnson, whose photographs papered the walls of the room he grew up in.

The final two minutes of the game began with the Lakers leading 100–89. Philadelphia made a run. The Sixers had brought the score to 100–93 when Derek Fisher hit a 3-pointer with 51 seconds left in the game. With that, the upbeat atmosphere in the arena changed with the swiftness of air pouring out of a balloon. One by one, the signs reading NO WAY L.A. and KOBE SUCKS were folded up and replaced by signs reading WIN OR LOSE, THANK YOU; THANKS FOR A GREAT SEASON; WE LOVE OUR SIXERS.

As the clock ran down, Brown took Allen Iverson out of the game. With the dream lost irrevocably, Iverson traversed the court's perimeter, applauding his teammates. Then, spent and sorrowing, he leaned on Matt Geiger's chest. Geiger held him. The young guys all wanted to be heroes, but eventually most of them understood why older players said they'd rather be a cog on a winning team than be the star of a team that doesn't win.

Moments after their victory, the World Champion Lakers were led out of the arena and into the visitors' locker room. They were greeted by frenzy and victory stogies and countless bottles of Dom Perignon. As Shaq opened a bottle, the cork slipped through his fingers, hitting one of the ball boys in the eye. More stunned than injured, he was ushered out into a back room. Players took turns sitting beside him as the celebration continued.

Only one player was absent from the festivities, and that was Kobe. While his teammates doused one another with champagne, he retreated to the bathroom and slumped against a shower wall. There was no further need to keep himself steeled, to remain in the moment. Finally, the toughest months of his life were over. With the victory won, he expelled the grief he had bottled up all season. Drained and spent, head buried in his hands, he sobbed. He did not seem to notice when a photographer wedged the heavy golden trophy under his left arm, then stepped back, readied his camera, and started shooting. Minutes passed. After a time, the onslaught of emotion subsided.

In the locker room, the players were still downing champagne when Shaq headed out to the press room. There, he approached the dais slowly, lowered himself into a folding chair, and said, "I'm drunk." Then he responded to a question about his legacy. "I don't really sit down and think about my legacy," he said. "I promised I wouldn't do that to myself. . . . I have two sons," he went on, "and when it's all said and done for me, then I can show them how nasty I was. I could open up the book and say, 'There was a guy named Mike. There was a guy named Magic. There was a guy named Charles. And here's your daddy, a guy named Shaq.'" While he spoke, Allen Iverson entered the room with his girlfriend and his own two children, prepared to honor the NBA's mandate that players speak to the press after games. Iverson's face was expressionless as Shaq spoke of this record-setting, history-making event, which had prompted him to give himself a new nickname: The Big History.

Then Shaq disappeared behind a curtain rigged up for the occasion. There, Kobe waited, ready to take his turn with the press. They embraced. "I told you we'd do it again," Shaq said.

Kobe moved toward the dais unaware that Iverson was also going toward it. As Kobe took a seat behind the bank of microphones, Iverson looked startled. Then, fed up and furious, he headed back to his family. "Let's get the fuck out of here," he said.

Kobe's mood was subdued. There was sadness in his face and eyes. "I have mixed emotions," he said, and this was painfully obvious. He had always thought that winning two championships would make him feel fulfilled. In the last half hour he had realized that this was not the case. Eventually he would recognize what he had gained from this season, as a player and as a man. But for now, he was aware only of the great price he had paid this season. And the shiny trophy on the table in front of him seemed a small thing to show for it.

An hour later, the World Champion Lakers left the arena. They filed back onto their chartered bus, taking their accustomed places, each man leaning back in his seat victorious and exhausted, talking to his family on his cell phone.

In the end, these men had become members of a community of players, and as such, they had placed the team's concerns above their own. In a sport fixated on dominance and all the rough-and-tumble machismo that implies, they had learned that winning comes only to those who honor the ethical system of selflessness found in civics books and Sunday sermons, men who merge their dreams and talents with the dreams and talents of other men.

Now they knew why winners do not speak of those elements of the game that can be measured in statistics and speak instead of communication and trust and unspoken bonds.

That summer, quiet came again to HealthSouth where the Lakers train. The court was empty. Had you looked down from the window in Jerry Buss's office, you would have seen a logo painted on the court's center, with the name of the facility written out in giant letters. These letters were grouped irregularly: HEAL THSOUTH.

Seen from that height and distance, the letters appeared to spell out the legend: HEAL THYSELF.

That's not what they said. But it's what happened.